Global Sourcing & Purchasing Post 9/11

New Logistics Compliance Requirements and Best Practices

Michael Assaf
Cynthia Bonincontro
Stephen Johnsen

J.ROSS PUBLISHING

Copyright ©2006 by J. Ross Publishing, Inc.

ISBN 1-932159-39-8

Printed and bound in the U.S.A. Printed on acid-free paper
10 9 8 7 6 5 4 3 2 1

Library of Congress Cataloging-in-Publication Data

Assaf, Michael, 1975–
  Global sourcing & purchasing—post 9/11 / by Michael Assaf, Cynthia
Bonincontro & Stephen Johnsen.
    p. cm.
  Includes index.
  ISBN 1-932159-39-8 (hardcover : alk. paper)
  1. Purchasing—United States. 2. Industrial procurement—United States.
3. Business logistics—United States. 4. Foreign trade regulation—United
States. I. Bonincontro, Cynthia, 1965– II. Johnsen, Stephen, 1973– III.
Title.
  HF5437.A87 2005
  658.7′2—dc22   2005011211

Phone: (954) 727-9333
Fax: (561) 892-0700
Web: www.jrosspub.com

TABLE OF CONTENTS

ACKNOWLEDGMENTS

This book would not have been possible if it were not for the support, insight, advice, and efforts of Charles C. Poirier, III. We want to sincerely thank Mr. Poirier for all his time, devotion, energy, guidance, and wealth of expert knowledge that he brought to every chapter of the book. We will be forever grateful.

We also want to thank others who touched this book with their talent and expertise: Donel Accorsi, E. Joseph Bento (President and CMO, EGL Eagle Global Logistics), Trudy Cole, Mark Dailey, Peggy Drazich, Kenneth Edds, Jack Hasnauer, Robert Hurley, Nathan Kelly, Diane Lewandowski, Darren Maynard (COO, NextLinx), Jean Mazet, Hallock Northcott (President and CEO, American Association of Exporters and Importers), Cheryl Poirier, Heather Rohaley, Robert Rudzki (President of Greybeard Advisors LLC), Marlene Russo, Michelle Stulberg (National Account Manager, Advance Relocation Services), Lisa Wallerstein (PIERS), Ken Wilson (for reading every word with a well-aimed red pen), and Marilyn Wilson. We appreciate your time and contribution to our project.

We thank our publisher, Drew Gierman, for taking a chance on three rookies. We truly appreciate his guidance and for learning our trade to make the book content even better.

Finally, to our families, Mary Beth, Alexander, Anthony, Casey, C.J., Jesse, Jordan, Traci, Isaac, and Lauryn. Thank you for supporting our crazy endeavor and for cheering us on.

ABOUT THE AUTHORS

 **Michael I. Assaf** is the Head of International Trade and Compliance and Import Operations for LANXESS Corporation (formerly Bayer Chemicals and parts of Bayer Polymers). His responsibilities include all international trade and compliance activities, as well as the daily operations for all LANXESS imports. Before taking this position, he was the Manager of International Business Promotion for Bayer Corporation, with major responsibilities in the areas of duty drawback, NAFTA, and other revenue-generating segments of international trade. Prior to joining Bayer, Michael was with Calgon Carbon Corporation, where he was responsible for managing the international supply chain function (sourcing, procurement, demand planning, import/export, transportation, and logistics) for Asia, Europe, Latin America, the United States, and Canada. He also had extensive experience with airline, freight forwarding, and stevedoring businesses in West Africa. Michael is an active participant in the American Association of Exporters and Importers' Duty Drawback Committee and is certified in Transportation and Logistics by both the American Society of Transportation and Logistics and the Chartered Institute of Logistics and Transportation. Additionally, he is a Certified International Trade Educator with the accredited International Import Export Institute and holds a master of business administration and bachelor of science in business administration from Duquesne University, Pittsburgh.

Cynthia A. Bonincontro is employed by Bayer HealthCare LLC and serves as the Import Control Officer for the Import Operations Department. She oversees the import activities for the four divisions within Bayer HealthCare, which include Animal Health, Biologicals, Consumer Care, and Diagnostic inbound supply chains. She has spent twenty years in the import and purchasing arena. She is an active member of various import associations such as the American Association of Exporters and Importers and the Central Atlantic States Association of Food and Drug Officials. Cindy also participated in the Certified Purchasing Manager Program. She is involved in government agency forums and seminars and provides insight back to the government agencies on importers' concerns and roadblocks. Cindy has experience with importing wide ranges of products (from medical device and pharmaceutical registered products to chemicals to spare parts) and the continual changes of products' intended uses that affect clearances. She has assisted the various company internal import supply chains with the streamlining of their import activities to gain cost controls and ensure security, compliance, and improved delivery turnaround. She works regularly with the foreign export entities.

Stephen R. Johnsen is Bayer Corporation's Manager of International Compliance and is responsible for the compliance of nearly $4 billion in annual international transactions. Steve administers the import and export procedures for Bayer's five operating companies. He is an appointed officer of Bayer's service company, Bayer Corporate and Business Services LLC, and is responsible for administration of its customs business activities. Steve serves on the Board of Directors of the American Association of Exporters and Importers (AAEI) and is an active member in AAEI's Chemicals and Bulk Commodities Committee, the American Chemistry Council's Subteam on Export Controls and the Chemical Weapons Convention, and the American Chemistry Society. He has extensive experience in creating corporate compliance organizations, crafting effective internal controls for international transactions, and developing auditing programs for import/export operations. Steve has a bachelor's degree in chemistry from Grove City College and is a licensed customs broker.

Web Added Value™

Free value-added materials available from
the Download Resource Center at www.jrosspub.com

At J. Ross Publishing we are committed to providing today's professional with practical, hands-on tools that enhance the learning experience and give readers an opportunity to apply what they have learned. That is why we offer free ancillary materials available for download on this book and all participating Web Added Value™ publications. These online resources may include interactive versions of material that appears in the book or supplemental templates, worksheets, models, plans, case studies, proposals, spreadsheets and assessment tools, among other things. Whenever you see the WAV™ symbol in any of our publications, it means bonus materials accompany the book and are available from the Web Added Value Download Resource Center at www.jrosspub.com.

Downloads available for *Global Sourcing & Purchasing Post 9/11: New Logistics Compliance Requirements and Best Practices* consist of slides that provide a high-level overview of the importance of an integrated logistics compliance system, a U.S. Customs 2005 Harmonized Tariff Schedule, and a list of helpful websites for regulatory product information and government forms required for U.S. clearance.

INTRODUCTION: WHAT'S BEEN HAPPENING?

The rain had finally subsided, but a sticky mist from the bay lightly sprayed across the dock. The stevedores continued their work in spite of the conditions as they feverishly loaded and unloaded containers onto or from massive vessels so large in size that one would take up an entire football field. These stevedores were growing tired from a long day's work in the chilling cold. They wanted to go home to their families (or to the local bar), but not just yet. From beyond the dock, a light flickered and the slow moan of a horn could be heard. The stevedores were far too familiar with the sound and evenly matched the moaning to their own exasperation.

"What do you think?" one asked of the other.

"Another delay," came the response.

"More paperwork, I guess," the third interjected.

"I don't know what's happening," the first said with a sigh. "Seems like nothing goes through like it used to. It always takes longer."

"Well," the second replied with a thin smile, "it keeps us busy."

"Yeah, more overtime," the third concluded. "I can use a little extra."

With a collective sigh, they opened their lunch pails to retrieve what might remain, as they waited for the signal to begin work again.

They would continue to stay a bit longer and wait for another ship to have its arrival approved. It could be a vessel carrying cargo intended to meet the needs of many people and companies. It could contain items that would provide food, sustenance, and clothing for some or equipment, chemicals, medicines, and machinery for others. The weight of the containers carrying the loads is tremendous, measured in tons. The stevedores are committed, and so they wait to unload the precious cargoes that have such deep meaning to the importers of the United States.

IMPORTING INTO THE UNITED STATES IS NOT WHAT IT USED TO BE

The wait takes time, and questions come to mind during the delay for those involved in the processing: What will take the most time and why does it? What are all these hidden costs that were not brought to my attention before? What is different? Who is doing what? And where is it being done? Those waiting for their goods have other queries: Why didn't my shipment get here sooner? Why did so many people need to be involved with just "my" shipment? Most of those who are waiting for the arrivals wanted it yesterday. They wait impatiently as well.

These questions represent common thoughts contemplated not just by those doing the physical handling, but also by exporters and importers every day, as they attempt to find answers to questions in an area they do not fully understand. The ins and outs of importing product into the U.S. cause these and more misgivings. Many individuals believe that imported products are delivered like the U.S. mail. Postage is simply applied to the packaging and it arrives at the designated doorstep. Doesn't it? There is no further government involvement, we assume, or rules or obligations once the mail-like delivery is started. Don't be ashamed if you are one of these individuals. How were you to know that there were multiple players involved and many new players whose appointments appear to be for the purpose of making your business life miserable?

You ask yourself what their real objective might be. Are they there to probe into your paperwork and the material you purchased. Are they asking what your product is derived from? Do they want to know what its intended use in the U.S. will be or how much you paid for it? And what takes place if you happen to be a food importer since 9/11 and you find that many more players are probing literally into every aspect of your business supply chain?

Like a great mystery novel, importing can be just as bewildering, often ending in adventures with unexpected and surprising twists coming before the climax. The field is by no means monotonous or unchallenging. The volume of product imported each year into the U.S. has increased substantially in the last five years, bypassing the number of exports dispatched from the U.S. With that increase, a bewildering array of new regulations, security complications,

Table I.1.   U.S. Trade in Goods, 1999–2003 (Census Basis, Domestic and Foreign Exports, F.A.S., General Imports, Customs, Billions of Dollars).

	Total Goods		
Year	Exports	Imports	Balance
1999	695.8	1,024.60	−328.8
2000	781.9	1,218.00	−436.1
2001	729.1	1,141.00	−411.9
2002	693.1	1,164.70	−471.6
2003	724	1,263.20	−539.2

Source: www.census.gov

and added fees and costs have appeared. It has become an entirely new business situation. Table I.1 reflects the volume change since 1999 to 2003. Table I.2 indicates the increase since 1996 to 2002.

Aspects of importing introduced as a result of the incidents of 9/11 have created a vast array of new conditions, without the commensurate appearance of people capable enough to cope with the new circumstances. Demand for top, knowledgeable individuals to work in the international trade arena has increased substantially in order for companies to stay on top of the new game and the new requirements. Working smarter is key to defying the unexpected that may come at any moment, ruining the timing and budget of your import plans. Determining if and how to procure product globally is a decision that must be examined carefully.

We, the authors, have experienced these challenges and survived. We have labored with the stevedores and others and have tried to cope with the new conditions. Indeed, our efforts have led to a better transformation into the new environment. We discovered that the importing adventure can be streamlined if you know what to expect and how best to react. The purpose of our book is to share this understanding and our first-hand knowledge in order to assist those who strive to procure product globally and import effortlessly into the

Table I.2.   U.S. Total Imports from Individual Countries 1996–2002 (Census Basis General Imports, Customs).

Country/	Millions of Dollars							Change	
								$	%
Region	1996	1997	1998	1999	2000	2001	2002	2-Jan	2-Jan
World	795,289	870,671	911,896	1,024,618	1,218,022	1,140,999	1,163,621	22,622	2.0

Source: www.census.gov

U.S. Our intention is to educate anyone involved in an import procurement transaction so that they may avoid unnecessary costs, delays, and noncompliance risks, while accomplishing the intended purposes in an optimal manner.

KEY IMPORTING QUESTIONS WILL BE ANSWERED

A typical question encountered in today's complex importing environment, beyond those already posed, is: How does one even begin to keep up with the continued changes and rising costs in the movement of freight from abroad? We have done the homework so that question can be answered and directions given. Importers, purchasing agents, foreign suppliers, brokers, forwarders, truckers, airlines, steamship lines, and railways, moreover, also have had their share of questions regarding the obstacles and challenges they now encounter. We will explain the types of issues involved in each of these areas and bring forward meaningful solutions. Our thesis is basic: New rules and regulations that are being instituted since the events of 9/11 have required significant changes to existing importing processes. These changes have introduced entirely new conditions to the import business, creating more questions than solid answers. A need has been introduced to present a simple and clarifying framework for operating successfully under the new circumstances. Our book will demystify these conditions and provide the required roadmap to a successful importing future and the "street-smart" education that can be carried throughout a supply chain operation.

1

IMPORTING AND INBOUND SUPPLY CHAIN PLANNING 101

Conducting business on a global basis has become an industrial norm. Businesses in virtually every industry find that they are now part of extended enterprises with trading partners around the world. Companies of all sizes can discover that some part of their supply chain contains a manufacturer in a distant land. In this new and ever-expanding environment, international procurement has become a major challenge, and success requires a number of skills that are not otherwise required for typical domestic procurement. Demand for top, knowledgeable, and experienced supply chain planning and import personnel is on the rise to meet these challenges.

NEW SOLUTIONS ARE REQUIRED FOR SUPPLY CHAIN AND PROCUREMENT NECESSITIES

As a company contemplates procuring product domestically or globally, many critical elements must be considered while analyzing cost, time, quality, service, and liability factors. With the growing emphasis being placed on supply chain management and the drive for optimization of process steps across an end-to-end value chain, purchasing strategically and globally has taken center stage and has become the popular means for obtaining product. If this is the chosen path taken for a corporation, the tragic events of 9/11 created a vast array of new and essential factors that must be considered, discussed, and instituted to procure foreign product effectively.

The volume of imports into the U.S. continues to be on the rise and has surpassed the number of exports out of the U.S. Among other factors, this condition brings huge, yearly increased revenues from duties, taxes, and fees for U.S. Customs. During recent years, the U.S. has steadily reduced duty rates, yet due to the rapidly increasing rise in imports, U.S. Customs is collecting more duties per year than ever before. It also entails serious requirements for the professionals involved in making certain that the needed goods and products are entered into the country properly and make their way to the required points of need without complications. The procurement specialist must learn the other cost factors that become entangled in the clearance and delivery process of product from beyond U.S. boundaries.

The field of inbound supply chain management encompasses successful operations management, which includes planning, accounting, procurement, regulatory compliance, forecasting, manufacturing, logistics, and distribution. It deals with new trends that are continually instituted and developed to better automate multiple business functions. In addition, new multilingual requirements and multicultural foreign markets increase this complexity. The key to the breakthrough in performance is found through a creative inbound supply chain view that breaks down the walls and borders between different internal departments, organizations, and cultures, all contributing to fulfilling the same customer and consumer needs.

The authors have experienced the trials and tribulations of working in this new environment and have first-hand experiences with an inbound supply chain operation — from imports of machinery and parts, to raw materials, to heavily regulated sample and drug products. You will also hear from other voices in the industry who will share their insights and recommendations for a successful and responsible global procurement process. This chapter and those following will provide training and will present valuable guidance to help corporations and their professional purchasing departments procure the needed products through the best systems and methods for their business requirements. We will introduce the fundamentals of importing and outline the major topics that need greater understanding in order to comprehend the reasons behind the logistics madness and the processes that have been foisted on the importing business.

START WITH THE BASICS

To begin, let us introduce the basics of importing, with the government requirements or "skeleton," and provide some exposure to the related procurement costs that make their way into your estimated expenditures. To add better understanding to what can be confusing information, we will provide various inbound supply chain planning scenarios to which practitioners will be able to relate. We have created a pseudocharacter, Chuck, who will take us through the general cradle-to-grave processes, based on his decision to acquire the needed products from a foreign source. The step-by-step story line will especially assist those struggling to become aware of all the elements involved with sourcing foreign products.

FOR SOME, COST IS NOT A FACTOR — GETTING PRODUCT IMMEDIATELY IS!

Businesses that are considering an import activity process or those that have one currently established within their corporation should realize that certain employees, on their own accord, order imported product. We will refer to these employees as "requesters" and they are not always concerned with costs. You will find these individuals within departments such as sales, distribution, marketing, research, product planning, etc. They exist outside the purchasing, procurement, regulatory, compliance, or logistics departments and are customarily involved with what they consider essential or emergency need. Those involved in just-in-time inventory fit this category, for example, for meeting a trade-show launch date or acquiring the last available research sample needed to complete a clinical trial study. While it is important to meet deadlines and/or complete study trials, compliance and cost control are important and must be reviewed, evaluated, and agreed upon for any imported product. These types of requesters must learn to involve the other elements of their internal inbound supply chain departments, such as imports, purchasing, compliance, regulatory, transportation, warehousing, etc.

With our first example, we present Chuck, who has hopes of launching a new developmental drug research program that could result in curing a particularly debilitating disease. Chuck has looked for help with his quest domestically, but has learned of a wonderful research lab located abroad that has the rare investigative samples available for just the kind of research work he intends to perform in house. Chuck has opted to explore what is involved to obtain the drug samples from the foreign supplier, placing him squarely in the middle of the new import experience. Costs at this time are not Chuck's main concern. However, he will soon learn that price negotiations should reside within his internal Purchasing and Logistics Department, and whatever Chuck agrees on, aside from the product price, will affect his research budget costs. Being advanced in the knowledge of procuring imported product and what to expect will position Chuck and his company favorably for future import purchase orders. Where does Chuck begin his endeavor? He starts by considering the options available in house.

Chuck works as Director of Pathology Research for a major pharmaceutical company that has annual sales over a billion dollars. He has overseen the development of many products that have not achieved the success needed to obtain approval from the Food and Drug Administration (FDA) for a clinical trial. Chuck, however, has a good feeling about the firm's latest research. He is now keenly interested in the current import requirements that have direct impact on a project that could dramatically reduce the number of people stricken by the disease, while increasing revenues for his company. Like Chuck, importers have the following basic import procurement options:

- Have the foreign suppliers make all arrangements to deliver it to your door.
- Have your firm make all arrangements to deliver it to your door.
- Have the foreign supplier take responsibility for delivery to the foreign port of export and you take ownership from there to your door.

Foreign suppliers can make arrangements for delivering product to one's door; however, many things can quickly become obstacles in that process. Offshore suppliers should not be expected to handle every aspect of the export to your final destination, even if the agreed terms include door delivery. There is a strong partnership between seller and buyer that is required to make successful imports. Regulations established since 9/11 have also evolved that require actions to be taken by parties aside from the foreign supplier, including the transportation companies involved. So we should begin our explanation by guiding Chuck and other requesters to the source of the regulations. Anyone who is requesting foreign product would greatly improve the chances of a successful import by researching first within their own company for an internal Import Department and then becoming knowledgeable in the involved import and procurement processes, steps, and procedures. For Chuck's needs, that would be the first piece of advice rendered.

INTERNAL ASSISTANCE ALREADY EXISTS

Due to the sample's delicate temperature requirements and limited supply, in conjunction with the urgency of his research, Chuck feels compelled to take control of bringing the samples to his lab. His expectations are to do it quickly and correctly the first time. There is no room for losing time and money or running compliance risks. Chuck wants to know all the processes, parties, rules, and regulations involved. These conditions are important for Chuck, the life span of his continuous import privileges, the company's bottom line, and for the security of the U.S.

Chuck does his research and becomes more familiar with his own company structure. He is aware of existing Import, Purchasing, Regulatory, Compliance, and Logistics Departments within his company that will help him in his endeavor. He will go to these groups as he seeks advice, but he will also assert reasonable care by learning as much as possible about the process, cost factors, and complications to be encountered. The best way to conduct this latter search is with an understanding of who's who in the government structure, as these players will have a place in Chuck's planning.

We will use the term "regulated" product(s) within this chapter and others to refer to products that are subject to U.S. clearance by other government agencies aside from just Customs. This may include the FDA or the Environmental Protection Agency (EPA). You will learn more about these agencies in Chapter 5. As with any "regulated" import product, such as a research sample, various government agencies may be involved and will determine your delivery turnaround and may add to your import costs if you do not plan properly.

Successful Import Product Procurement = Research and Preplanning

BEGINNING THE IMPORT PROCUREMENT PROCESS REQUIRES AN UNDERSTANDING OF THE LAW

Once inside the import function, Chuck finds that personnel of the U.S. Bureau of Customs and Border Protection (CBP) are the people who ultimately run the show. They are a group of decision makers who will clear or reject each import shipment that arrives into a U.S. port daily. For the purposes of our discussion, we will refer to this group as Customs (throughout this book, we will use CBP and Customs interchangeably). The people in this complex organization within the federal government have been running the import program for a very long time, over 200 years to be exact. Customs has been the guardian of America's trade laws and its purpose in today's world is less about collecting duties and more about protecting U.S. citizens and providing "homeland security." Customs exists to incorporate procedures that ensure the safety of the citizens of the U.S. So, the next time any requester has the urge to moan and groan that Customs is taking too much time to release his/her white powdery substance from Mexico, ever so innocent in nature, keep that in mind. Through our own struggles, we have found that Customs is genuinely trying its best to keep you and your loved ones safe from harm. September 11th prompted Customs to make a huge overhaul, and as more state and federal agencies get involved in regulating product, the amount of documentation required from importers increases. The U.S. permits anyone or any company to import goods into the country. Importing is not a right; it is a "privilege" that can be revoked, if abused.

We will discuss more about the new Customs overhaul in Chapter 9. For now, we can follow what Chuck learned about how Customs, along with the Treasury Department, instituted various acts that changed the course of how importers and brokers should import into the U.S.

Act I

As stated previously, all merchandise imported into the U.S. is required to be cleared through Customs and appropriate governing agencies, unless specifically excepted (such as a cadaver or funeral accessories). Chuck discovered that the Trade Act of 1930 was the first to be rolled out for changing the way this process was arranged. This act was the means of "informing" importers of the official import rules and regulations. Until 1930, Customs handled it all. For all merchandise entering the U.S., Customs determined (by manual means) the classification, value, duty rates, and entry type. Importers were at a cost disadvantage during these times as they were not directly involved or could not determine their import costs. As the volume of imported merchandise continued to rise, Customs' staffing became largely outnumbered.

Act II

After many years in place, Customs' staffing still remained limited and continued to experience the same repetitive problems when clearing imported product. They realized that their old system needed to be modernized. Customs decided to move from an "enforced" position, in which Customs identified importer's errors on entries prior to clearance, and shifted the legal responsibility from Customs to the importer, which resulted in the roll out of the "informed" position of the Customs Modernization Act ("Mod Act") in 1993. The Mod Act was published in Public Law 103-182, Dec. 8, 1993 (107 Stat. 2057). New updated computers and a new Automated Commercial System (ACS) were instituted to streamline and automate the Customs Service and improve compliance with trade laws, while providing safeguards and uniformity to importers. The ball was now in the importer's court. Some importers may have felt that this was added workload to their current responsibilities, but the smart procurement individual involved with importing saw this as an opportunity. In the following chapters, you will learn the areas in which decisions, once determined by Customs, can be made by you to save money.

The Mod Act officially introduced the controversial concepts of "informed compliance" and "reasonable care." The two concepts emerged to educate importers about ways to maximize voluntary compliance with Customs laws and regulations. Customs had to improve how they "informed" importers concerning the trade community's rights and responsibilities under Customs regulations and related laws. This concept is referred to as "informed compliance." The term "reasonable care," sometimes referred to as "shared responsibility," is used to describe the importer's responsibility to use reasonable care to enter, classify, and determine the value of imported merchandise.

In addition, the term is used to cover the provision of any other information necessary to enable Customs to properly assess duties, collect accurate statistics, and determine whether other applicable legal requirements have been met. Customs is then responsible for "fixing" the final classification and value of the merchandise. A Reasonable Care Checklist is available on the Customs website (www.cbp.gov). An importer's failure to exercise reasonable care could delay the release of its merchandise and, in some cases, possibly result in the imposition of penalties or, ultimately, cancellation of its import privilege. Good businesses make this a common practice within their import procedures and incorporate audits to gauge reasonable care performance. See Chapter 7 for further guidance on how this can be achieved.

Act III

As a result of 9/11, additional acts followed that have not been instituted solely by Customs. These new acts, which are discussed in Chapters 2 and 5, have been the most challenging to meet and can make importing a more costly endeavor if businesses do not work "smarter." Customs is obligated to communicate to the public what the laws are, and the public is expected to exert reasonable care in complying with those laws.

Chuck learns about Customs' Office of Regulations and Rulings (ORR), which has been given an expanded role of meeting the informed compliance responsibilities of Customs since 9/11. In order to provide information to the public, Customs has issued, on their website, a series of informed compliance publications on new or revised requirements, regulations, or procedures and a variety of classification and valuation issues. Customs also offers seminars, videos, and face-to-face meetings with importers.

WHO ELSE IS MINDING THE STORE?

"Does Customs work alone?" Chuck asks. The answer is no. There are over sixty other state and federal government agencies that report to or work alongside Customs that possess the same criteria to protect the U.S. from such things as illegal drugs, contraband, smugglers, weapons of mass destruction, etc. They get involved with regulating product and the documentation that would be required to import. A list of these agencies can be found on the Customs website (www.cbp.gov). When the term "regulate" is used, this indicates individuals within these various organizations who verify that any required or restrictive criteria set forth for a particular import product are upheld.

Many Agencies Bring Many Requirements to the Processing

As Chuck begins to get a feeling for how the system is structured and what takes place, he also finds that various government agencies have their own agendas and create their own rules, although certain agencies must adhere to Customs' vision and beliefs. These governing bodies can play a role with buying internationally. Expanded detail on each "other" government agency (OGA) is provided in Chapter 5. A key learning for Chuck is that it is important to maintain good record keeping in the event that any of these agencies decides to audit his documentation or procedures.

With further probing, Chuck finds that Customs maintains the standard rules and regulations for importing, entitled "Customs Regulations of the United States" 19 CFR 1-99 Customs Duties (Code of Federal Regulations). This grand-size manual contains every Customs regulation ever written. 19 CFR is a point of import requirement referrals, adherence, and understanding. It serves as a prealert to what is required in order to import. This manual greatly assists any procurement department's endeavor to understand the challenges and costs to procure products internationally. It plays a significant role in weighing the pros and cons of purchasing domestically or outsourcing. This should be one of the first points of referral for any inbound supply chain planning endeavor. There are essential factors for determining whether to purchase domestically or globally, as some restrictions may be in place that prevent flexibility with a product's manufacturing and distribution process.

To provide an example, if your marketed product involves bonded warehouse withdrawals to save on duty costs, specific steps are captured in the 19 CFR manual that must be adhered to in order to remain in compliance and continue such privilege under Customs laws. This type of cost reduction, as with the warehouse withdrawal privilege, may be restricted for certain products, and you will immediately learn that this is an obstacle for procuring globally. On

April 1, 2003, a new Code of Federal Regulations was issued to incorporate all changes to the import regulations post 9/11. Between editions, individuals can keep abreast of all proposed and final import regulations in the *Federal Register*, which is published daily by the Office of the Federal Register, National Archives and Records Administration. 19 CFR is available on the Customs website or can be purchased in hardcopy through the Superintendent of Documents, U.S. Government Printing Office, Washington, D.C.

DUTIABLE OR DUTY FREE, THAT IS THE QUESTION

The U.S. Congress also created yet another, equally large, manual entitled the "Harmonized Tariff Schedule of the United States" (HTSUS), the contents of which are interpreted and enforced by Customs. This manual is designed to coordinate an associated tariff classification and duty rate for any imported product from any foreign country. This manual should also be one of the early points of referral when determining whether to procure product globally as it provides the duty payment costs to Customs that will be involved. Every single item that enters a U.S. territory from a foreign entity must have a Harmonized Tariff Classification (HS Number) and coinciding duty rate determined for its entry. The duty rate is calculated against the value of the shipment to determine the duties and taxes that should be paid to Customs. A product's HS Number is similar to what a serial number would be to a certain product. Detailed information on product classification is provided in Chapter 7.

For those with inquiring minds who would like to know what happens to all those duties that Customs collects, this information can be found in Chapter 2, which will also offer general guidance on classifying, valuing, and identifying the proper country of origin and marking requirements among the multiple checkpoints required for importing. There are various declarations and/or OGA clearances that may be required for entry with a given commodity. A query of the HS Number by the broker will advise whether a certain declaration is required and which OGA applies. Customs' declarations are located on their website. This two-minute spot check will significantly save any corporation time and money if the following items have already been identified prior to U.S. arrival:

- Duty costs — *$$$*
- Product classification — *Time, $$$*
- Regulatory requirements — *Time, $$$, and Compliance*

These steps have often been taken *after the fact* and product then sits at the U.S. port waiting for these transactions to be completed. More than ever, "free time" at any U.S. port is running low, resulting in demurrage for storage costs for importers. Learn more about how to prevent unnecessary spending in Chapter 3.

PROCUREMENT PLANNING FOR THE INBOUND LANE INVOLVES PARTNERING WITH YOUR SUPPLIER

While still visiting with his internal Import Department, Chuck's knowledge continues to grow. He soon realizes that at the moment he places his order to the overseas supplier, a huge process begins that is commanded by strict rules and regulations dictated to the importers by Customs and OGAs. Chuck is told that these rules require action items to be completed "prior" to the shipment ever leaving the port of export.

Foreign suppliers, more than ever, need to be aware of and adhere to the latest U.S. rules and regulations. Since 9/11, the new rules and requirements are a must, and if not adhered to, shipments will not be dispatched from "any" port of export to the U.S. This first chapter centers on the general import process pre 9/11 to gain a fundamental understanding with some post 9/11 information. Reading further in this book, increased knowledge will be gained on the post 9/11 importing demands.

Throughout the book, Chuck will learn further how new action steps must be taken before his shipment(s) dispatches from overseas. Certain documentation must now be made readily available and needs to be issued by the "foreign supplier" and no longer by the importer. His risk of having his shipment thoroughly examined by any of the government agencies has greatly increased. Chuck may very well experience the heartbreak of having his shipment arrive, only to realize that unavailable required information will cause his shipment to be re-exported back to the foreign supplier. The good news is that any company can save time and money by simply meeting these new requirements and it does not require "rocket scientist" planning. The requirements are clear and need to be followed. The key is to create absolute supply pipeline visibility to all import requirements. Any inbound supply chain operation can implement a fully synchronized solution to meet new post 9/11 needs with impeccable levels of accuracy to eliminate barriers to information flowing through functional silos. Product can then always be cleared the first time with any government agency. It is critical to foster the needed changes for importers to meet customer deadlines.

Chuck listens intently to all of his instructions, but remains steadfast in his expectation to get the samples in without any glitches, while meeting all new and existing import requirements. Chuck's Procurement and Transportation Department is equally steadfast in wanting to keep costs down and out of the liability arena. Meeting these goals really depends on Chuck, his internal logistics staff, or any importer, and how proactive one is with the steps that are chosen and the plan created to meet the new requirements. This preparation makes a great difference in many aspects of the importing process. It will affect delivery turnaround time, costs to the bottom line, and compliance privileges. Chuck has just learned about the government structure. He now needs to learn about import ownership. An Importer of Record (IOR) Number identifies the importer to Customs. For a company, its IOR Number will be the same as its federal tax identification number or IRS Number. For an individual importer, your IOR Number will be like your Social Security Number.

FROM THE AGENCIES COMES THE REQUIREMENTS

Since 9/11, Customs audits the activities of a company's IRS Number more intently. A member of Chuck's import staff explains that an IRS Number to a company is what a Social Security Number is to an individual. At the time of entry, an IRS Number is required for transmission by the broker to Customs and OGAs (if applicable) and indicates who the IOR is for the clearance. Importers should never chance a bad decision that could tarnish their company's IRS Number in the eyes of Customs. Chapter 2 will better define the IOR.

Chuck and his foreign supplier will need to discuss who will have ownership for paying the duties and taxes due to Customs. He also now knows that a purchase order will need to be placed with his foreign supplier and the IOR will need to be indicated and documented, along with what was agreed to in the order. In conjunction with this agreement, Chuck and readers will learn about establishing terms of sale and trade (referred to as Incoterms [International Commercial Terms]) with the foreign supplier in Chapter 2. Incoterms are used in conjunction with a sales agreement or other methods of transacting the sale. These are major steps that need to be defined before the purchase order can be placed.

A FOCUSED ANALYSIS HELPS TO FACILITATE THE DECISION PROCESS

Given the various responsibilities and fees involved with the purchase order agreement, Chuck decides to run an analysis of what it would cost if he took ownership of the shipments or if the supplier provided delivery to his door. More on how this can be done is provided in Chapter 3. This analysis will help Chuck to make his final decision as to who should ultimately act as the IOR.

In the end, Chuck decides to take on the liability and cost to bring in the samples. This move gives him complete decision control and reduces his risk of being hurt financially. It also reduces the risk of damage or delays to the delivery and turnaround. As Chuck's preparation work moves further along, his foreign supplier, who works routinely with the same forwarder, makes a recommendation on a particular airline to utilize since they are more familiar with which carrier routinely enters ports in close proximity to their site. Chuck would benefit from having his shipment enter a U.S. port that is near his facility to reduce the inland transportation costs. Chuck's samples must be temperature controlled and this needs to be conveyed to the forwarder, broker, and trucker. More detail on arranging temperature maintenance and available options to ensure goods and save time and money can be found in Chapter 2.

THE ROLE OF AN EXPERIENCED BROKER CAN BE BENEFICIAL

Chuck's next job is to work with the internal import staff to choose a broker. Chuck reaps the benefits of having an internal Import Department as it will coordinate the clearance with the company's commonly used broker. It will also work toward reducing costs by working with the Transportation Department. Multiple cost factors and savings come into play when involving a broker. This is a must read and is discussed further in Chapters 2 and 3. An Import Department is a vehicle that helps requesters to maneuver through logistics options and requirements. The broker acts as a bridge between the Import Department and the government. Brokers are licensed to transmit government clearance information for importers and exporters, and they have a presence at the U.S. ports.

Chuck takes the time to make certain that the Import Department in his company has reviewed internal Customs compliance controls with the broker on his behalf. It is a good idea to advise the broker that *you* will be providing the information needed for clearance to *them*. A "broker instruction" letter is then prepared by the company's Import Department, which will be working closely on your behalf with the broker. This letter specifically outlines all the correct information that should be used for clearance, such as HS Number, regulatory information (such as a TSCA [Toxic Substance Control Act] statement), intended use of the product, inland shipping terms, delivery address, country of origin statement, etc.

There is one caveat to consider in this situation: Some brokers and couriers will make entry to Customs and the OGAs without input or broker's instructions from a company's Import Department. Some importers allow this arrangement without any postaudit work, but it is not an advisable procedure. This can be a very risky scenario as it puts the IRS Number and import privileges at risk of noncompliance should the broker make an error on information transmitted (for example, incorrectly classifying a product or providing the wrong regulatory information). It will also delay the shipment if the broker has no idea what regulatory information is required and needs to place the shipment on hold at the U.S. port while soliciting information from the importer.

Your company knows your products better than any broker does and is better suited to choose the correct tariff classification and regulatory information and advise its intended use to submit to Customs and the OGAs for clearance. You also know better who specifically manufactured the product. An import shipped from Norway does not necessarily mean the product was manufactured in that country. Country of origin identification is among the numerous items needed for entry submission. Requesters ordering foreign product may not always advise their internal Import Department about the order or how it will be shipped. As a result, if the courier was used on an import and does not forward its broker bill to the Import Department, an Import Representative trying to audit the information has no idea that the shipment exists. Couriers as well as brokers have been known to utilize a company's IRS Number without the company's consent for a particular entry.

The following documents are required for Customs clearance:

- Invoice, listing all the information required for clearance noted further below.
- Air waybill, truck bill, or ocean bill of lading.
- Packing lists with gross and net weights in kilograms.
- Purchase order.
- Material Safety Data Sheet.
- Permits (if applicable), such as from the U.S. Department of Agriculture (USDA), Centers for Disease Control and Prevention (CDC), etc.
- TSCA Certification (for chemicals), if not stamped on invoice.
- Declarations (if applicable), such as USDA Guidelines, End-User Letters, U.S. Goods Return, Repaired Articles, etc.
- North American Free Trade Agreement (NAFTA) certificates (if applicable).
- Debit or credit memos. An entry must be reconciled with Customs if the original purchase order had any value adjustments that affect the original duty payment to Customs.
- Visa for textiles or other quota goods.

The following information is required for Customs clearance and must be shown on the foreign shipper's invoice:

- The parties of the transaction and their addresses (seller/shipper, payee, consignee).
- Date of invoice.
- Currency reflected in U.S. dollars; however, if this is unattainable, foreign currency can be used for value, but must indicate currency for each line item.
- Country of origin (country of manufacture) for each and every line item.
- Complete and accurate description of each and every line item. If you truncate or abbreviate, a government entry review person may not understand what the product is. (This is routinely a common source of clearance delays.)
- Value of each and every line item, including free-of-charge items. (Ensure that the final total invoice value from each line item value has been calculated accurately.)
- Incoterms 2000 with named port and the U.S. port of destination (with itemization of freight and insurance charges if included in the price). This is discussed in Chapter 2.
- Proper packaging information.
- Values and descriptions for any "assists" (for example, dies, molds, tools, engineering work not included in the invoice price) must be item-ized on the invoice, as well as any royalty and licensing fees, any extra "special" packing costs incurred by the buyer, selling commissions, any proceeds of subsequent resale, interest payments, testing costs, or freight charges. Chapter 7 provides further discussion for this area.
- Net and gross weight in kilograms for each and every line item must be noted on the invoice. (Ensure that the packing list piece count and weights coincide with the invoice and bill of lading's piece count and weights.)
- Harmonized Tariff Classification for each and every line item.
- The Chemical Abstracts Service (CAS) Number for chemicals, if available.

If entry is not made within fifteen (15) *calendar* days from U.S. port of *arrival,* Customs has the right to seize the freight under what is called "General Order" and has the further right to auction off the shipment. No importer wants to run the risk of its competition gaining possession of its product. Working with all parties involved in your import shipment will eliminate this possibility. It is also costly to retrieve your shipment from General Order and it does not make your company appear as a competent importer to Customs. Ensure that your foreign supplier is preparing the correct and accurate documentation and information needed for U.S. clearance for each shipment.

PAYING UNCLE SAM

Continuing with the broker process, after an entry has been cleared and delivered, the broker will provide an entry packet. Most brokers will pay all your import costs when applicable and, in turn, pass that charge to you. This includes the duty payment due to Customs. The entry summary must be filed within ten (10) working days from the date of release. An entry packet should include the broker bill, which lists all the charges the broker paid on your behalf. For formal and informal entries, it should also include Customs Form 7501, which reflects the entry information and the duties and taxes paid. All Customs entry types and forms, great and small, are listed on the Customs website for your viewing pleasure. Any company's Import Department should audit these bills and associated backup forms to ensure that everything was paid and declared correctly. If the broker was neglectful in providing accurate information and duty payment to Customs, it will be a negative reflection on your company and not the broker.

The broker should have the entry packet submitted to the company immediately following the duty payment. This allows importers the time to audit the duty payment for any errors since it was processed under your company's name and registration. Customs allows ten (10) days from the date of entry to amend any errors by the broker. After that time, an official written request to rectify the entry and possibly the duty payment will need to be coordinated by the broker or internal Import Department. Eventually, Customs may do the auditing of your entries in the event they elect to audit your company's import operations. You can learn more about this in Chapter 7. Also, human error can cause incorrect charges to be assessed and paid to the trucker or airline, which could result in unnecessary overpayment.

Some brokers may not want to issue the broker entry packet until the shipment has been delivered to capture any pending charges, such as inland trucking costs, and then issue you only one billing. To avoid losing the ten-day window to correct mistakes, the broker should be instructed to send you a second billing for any additional costs. As well, broker bill bundling can unbalance a company's monthly budget expenditures. Upon receiving an armload of broker bills in one mailing from the broker, an Import Representative will process the bills collectively. The total monies calculated after payment processing of the broker bills is charged against a single or multiple project account(s), for possibly a considerable dollar amount.

AUDITING CAN PRODUCE DUTY REFUNDS, BUT IS ADDED WORK IF NOT DONE IN A TIMELY MANNER

By not auditing the duty information before the tenth day, additional work and unnecessary costs for your company could be encountered because a "Protest" or a "Supplemental Information Letter" (SIL) may need to be filed by an Import or Compliance Department to rectify any duty payment errors with Customs. This adds to everyone's workload as it entails collecting evidence and supporting information for Customs, justifying why the original entry was not processed correctly. An SIL can be used to correct errors prior to an entry's liquidation. A Protest must be prepared if the entry has liquidated. A Protest submission requires extended detail information if you are going to convince Customs to reimburse you. (Liquidations are mentioned further in this chapter.) Protests must be made within 180 days of the entry's liquidation or you are out of luck if you overpaid duty. Of course, Customs will accept voluntary tenders of underpaid duties at any time regardless of the entry's age of liquidation status. A company that repeatedly corrects entries via these avenues with Customs makes it stand out as an irresponsible importer, while causing extra time, expense, and unnecessary efforts.

Other reasons why an importer would revisit a duty rate that was not the result of any errors may surface during a postentry review. For example, a preferential duty program may have been identified for advantageous cost savings by your Compliance and/or Import Department that would qualify you for duty reimbursement for certain entries in which products were cleared under the previous, higher duty rate. Customs provides these procedures as methods for importers to recoup duty payment overages or to make additional duty payments for short remittance to Customs as a result of an incorrect duty payment. When the error is identified and what the error was will trigger whether a Protest, SIL, or a Prior Disclosure is required and your Import Representative can advise you accordingly as to which approach is necessary.

PURCHASING STANDARD PHRASES

All requirements should be thought through and captured in the "Purchasing Standard Phrases" (PSP) within the purchase order. The purchase order will clearly outline who is responsible for the entry, who pays the duties to Customs, and who assumes the liability for any loss or damage. (More about how to obtain duty-free status will be described in Chapters 3 and 8.) PSPs can also assist in capturing specific transportation requirements, set delivery schedules, communication chain contacts for delays, and status updates, as well as regulatory requirements needed. Once the purchase order is issued, a copy should be provided to the Import Department to serve as a prealert and to be used for auditing purposes. If a firm is utilizing a nonelectronic (manual) process to place import purchase orders, it may be time to automate the process. This will allow a system to provide prealerts, internal controls, screen for government requirements, and build product profiles for U.S. clearance, among the options available. (Read up on this in Chapter 11.) However, if budget constraints limit bifurcation or "branching" into existing logistics systems, then a software-based program such as Lotus Notes offers electronic import purchase order routing form capabilities. This is a nice feature to incorporate temporarily into a manually run import purchasing process linked to the departments involved and is discussed further in Chapters 4 and 6.

FINAL DETAILS SHOULD NOT BE OVERLOOKED

What else should Chuck do prior to placing his order with his foreign supplier? He should establish the product's clearance profile. As stated previously, the product will need to be classified with an appropriate HS Number. It also requires input from the Regulatory Affairs (RA) and/or Health and Environmental Safety (HES) Department to obtain the TSCA declaration statement (both described in Chapters 2 and 4 to be made on the invoice). In addition, the product requires review for potential regulatory clearance information for the various government agencies (FDA, CDC, or FCC [Federal Communications Commission], etc.). This should be an early point of referral for any inbound supply chain planning system, eminently for a regulated product.

Commonly, if the product that is being exported is basically anything other than an article, such as a chair or a spare part, the product most likely will require some type of regulatory information for clearance with a particular government agency. Any requester, such as Chuck, is obligated, *prior* to order placement, to screen the product with their RA and HES contacts and advise their foreign supplier and Import Department accordingly. We have seen many shipments, where much effort and cost was expended to bring material into the U.S., detained at the port because the FDA registration or a USDA permit was not coordinated prior to the shipment. Importer's shipments may have passed through in the past despite the lack of paperwork, however, since 9/11, these exceptions are no longer acceptable to Customs. As a reminder, Customs only allows fifteen (15) working days to make entry unless the Port Director grants an extension. It is worth the effort to make a quick phone call to the RA, HES, and Import Departments to verify if certain information is required for clearance with the government agencies. For example, this could be to verify if a USDA permit for a plant- or animal-derived product is needed or if a raw material requires any registration. Or perhaps, the product is radioactive and the inland Department of Transportation (DOT) information must be determined prior to dispatching to the trucker. If these steps are reviewed, this is one less item you need to handle after U.S. arrival.

If we check back on what our colleague Chuck is importing, his sample is noninfectious, but had it been, the CDC would need to be contacted by RA on behalf of Chuck to arrange for a required CDC permit. If applicable, this could take up to six (6) weeks to obtain, which serves to validate our point about having done the research prior to U.S. arrival. Following the same path as the OGAs, 9/11 has prompted the CDC to better scrutinize the import documentation and product.

Any information required for entry into the U.S. should be provided to the foreign supplier to be reflected on the invoice or be prepared on a separate document (depending on the information required). Chuck's import staff has already researched his sample and assigned an HS Number and TSCA declaration, which Chuck has forwarded to his foreign supplier to be referenced on the invoice. This step has improved his delivery turnaround and eliminated unnecessary storage, demurrage, or expedited Customs or brokerage service costs.

In the event a foreign supplier arranges shipment of its product to the U.S. on its own accord, at least the correct information has been built for the product and is made available to any broker/courier for entry. By the information appearing on the invoice, this precaution assists with reducing delays since the classification and TSCA determination step has been completed. With this information provided on the invoice, brokerage departments within couriers such as Federal Express or DHL also have the information to conduct the clearance with their own company IRS Number. Now, it should be made clear to any courier that you require a courtesy call from their courier's Brokerage Department when the courier's entry profile necessitates that "your" company's IRS Number be used for clearance. They should then solicit broker instructions from you to help them make the entry. Different courier services follow different parameters for when to use their own company's IRS Number or the importer's IRS Number. In a perfect world, a courtesy call by the courier will be granted for every shipment involving your IRS Number. Realistically, it does not always happen.

UNDERSTAND ENTRY NUMBERS AND FILER CODES FOR TRACKING AND AUDITING PURPOSES

Importers can do a Customs query to see which broker filer code has been used with their company IRS Number. An Entry Filer Code is a unique three-character code assigned to Customs brokers, importers, and others who conduct business with Customs through the Automated Broker Interface (ABI), a system used by brokers to transmit clearance information to Customs and the OGAs. (A broker filer code listing of names and companies is located on the Customs website.) Chuck has learned about entry filer codes and is further educated by his internal Import Department on the associated entry numbers. An Entry Number is the reference number for the entry clearance file. Customs and the FDA use this number as a point of reference when contacted, however, the USDA utilizes the bill of lading number to distinguish which shipment is being examined and/or cleared. The entry numbering scheme used for the transaction number is at the discretion of the entry filer provided Customs' required format is used. An entry filer who handles transactions, such as an importer or broker at several districts/ports, but prepares entries at a centralized location, may wish to number all entries in sequential transaction number order or assign blocks of numbers for each district/port. Entry numbers must not be duplicated. Duplication of an entry number results in rejection of the entry documentation. This rejection is considered fatal and repeated occurrences disqualify a user from operational status. Learn more in Chapter 11 on how to tap directly into Customs' ACE (Automated Commercial Environment) Portal System to view any entry made under your IRS Number, query clearance information, and create various statistical reports.

As Chuck is now aware, all brokers, importers, and others who prepare and file entry documentation with Customs on a regular basis are assigned a unique, three-position national entry filer code and then a nine-position data field for the entry number to a specific shipment. When the entry filer codes are assigned and established in the system, each is identified as a broker, importer, carrier, Customs port, or other filer along with the districts/ports where they are authorized to file entries.

WRAPPING UP IMPORT PROCUREMENT PREPARATION

Chuck moves along with his knowledge and completes his purchase order homework and has submitted it to the foreign supplier. He has agreed on Incoterms and the selected forwarder, broker, and inland trucker that will be involved. Chuck does not wish for his shipment to import via a courier service, even if this may reduce his cost since the sample size is small. Occasionally, cutting costs may cause more nuisances in the end. Courier services work well for importing, however, if you have a commodity that is subject to OGA clearance or requires special shipping needs, it is better to ship via a commercial airline. You do not have as much control with a shipment's clearance, temperature maintenance, or delivery when using a courier service. For example, a delivery address change or a requested expedited clearance cannot be made once the courier has picked it up. With a commercial airline, such changes can be made right before it ships or after it lands. Utilizing a commercial airline with the same service provider that can act as his forwarder, broker, and trucker gives Chuck the flexibility and control in the event of any unexpected need, such as arranging refrigeration space at the U.S. port.

Chuck's supplier is made aware of the Advance Manifest Ruling (new post 9/11 requirement, Chapter 9) and will act accordingly. The samples will not be used in a food application, so their import does not necessitate a Prior Notice entry under the Bioterrorism Act (BTA) (also a new post 9/11 requirement, Chapter 5). This means that the entry will not need to be registered and cleared prior to dispatching from overseas to the U.S. Having the broker do a quick check on the HS Number will alert whether or not the ABI system will require BTA information.

COMMUNICATION IS KEY TO MAINTAINING COMMITTED CUSTOMER ESTIMATED TIMES OF ARRIVAL

The supplier has quoted Chuck an estimated time of arrival (ETA) to the U.S. port and agreed to provide prenotification paperwork to Chuck and his Import Department. The foreign supplier has also committed to advising Chuck of any delays on his side and if they will affect the initial ETA first provided. This is an essential step, as Chuck may need to requote his original delivery date to his customers, such as the scientists who have booked flights to the U.S. to assist with Chuck's research once the samples reach his company. This situation can occur. Scientists arrive before the samples and end up waiting unnecessarily for the shipment. In the event both the scientist and the samples are traveling together, a hand-carryon shipment can be arranged, but this is not a recommended route by any means. Importers run the risk of having the wrong information or comments relayed to Customs by the individuals who are hand carrying the products. For those who desire to pursue this route, we recommend that you involve your company Import Department to arrange for a broker to preclear your shipment prior to boarding your flight. They will provide you with the preclearance paperwork and assistance you will need for foreign Customs at the airport abroad.

For Chuck's shipment, his foreign supplier has advised that he will ship via a commercial airline early in the week and ensure that the flight runs during working hours to enable the clearance process to begin once the samples are confirmed on board. This is referred to by Customs as a "wheels-up" entry. Customs will permit importers to preclear air shipments prior to U.S. arrival if they are of a perishable nature, medical emergency, or involve a plant shutdown (workers losing pay). The broker to Customs may also request a "walk-through" entry for an air shipment as well. This requests that Customs make this entry a priority above other importers' entries for clearance "after" it has arrived into the U.S. port. Customs will charge the importer an expedited service fee. A hardcopy of the air waybill document must be available to perform either one of these Customs expedites. Providing just the air waybill number is not sufficient for entry. Companies are advised not to abuse this privilege. Customs will catch on and grow tired of hearing your IRS Number and start to think someone is "crying wolf." For ocean shipments, entry can be made five (5) days prior to the ETA into the port of arrival.

Chuck's product will be packed with fresh dry ice at the time it leaves the foreign supplier's facility. It will be repacked a second time prior to loading due to the two-day commute from the foreign supplier's door to the port of export. Aircrafts do not have temperature-controlled cargo areas. The temperature in the cargo area depends on the climate. If needed, the broker will arrange for a third repack after clearance in the U.S. port. Customs will not permit any shipment to be repacked prior to clearance as they consider this to be a manipulation of the shipment. If absolutely necessary, a broker can obtain repack approval prior to clearance from a customs agent. This agent will need to witness the repack. It is very important to have a packing list prepared and readily available to know which box requires a repack in the event of a large shipment. Most brokers will pay any repacking charges on an importer's behalf and add the cost onto their broker bill. More temperature-controlling options and cost savings are noted in Chapter 3.

FOLLOW-UP IS ESSENTIAL TO ASSURE PROPER PROCESSING

A week has passed and Chuck obtains a copy of the invoice, air waybill, USDA and FDA End-User letters, packing list, and purchase order from his foreign suppliers in advance as promised. Chuck checks with his Import Department to ensure that they have received the paperwork as well, which they have. The Import Department audits the import documentation prepared by the foreign supplier to ensure that all requirements have been met for preparing the invoice and consigning the shipment appropriately.

Importers can educate their foreign suppliers on U.S. import requirements by providing a one-page instruction sheet that can be utilized as personal guidance for preparing the invoice and consigning the shipment to help avoid any delays after the shipment arrives in the U.S. If a country of origin statement, for example, is missing from the invoice, the invoice will need to be amended by the foreign supplier. The importer cannot manipulate the foreign supplier's invoice. Foreign suppliers will also need to certify any amended invoice adjustments to Customs from the original that was first submitted.

Chuck's shipment is due to arrive at the U.S. port within forty-eight hours. Although Chuck has an Import Department, as a first-time importer and someone running solo on a one-time import shipment, he soon realizes that he does not know how to issue brokers' instructions to the broker and should feel compelled to do so. (Recall that we advised against brokers clearing on their own accord.) It is important to keep the compliance control in your firm's court. Chuck's internal Import Department's responsibility is to issue broker instructions to the brokers for entry. They will prepare and issue the broker instructions for Chuck's shipment.

In the absence of an in-house Import Department, a good broker can provide guidance for importing, but you must work with him or her. Do not let the broker make compliance decisions on tariff classifications or regulatory submissions. If you have plans to continue to import, it would be a great idea to establish a knowledgeable import staffing department and compliance reporting structure within the organization. The building of such an organization will be discussed in Chapter 7.

If an in-house Import Department is available, like Chuck's, they will prepare the broker's instructions. An import staff is trained on tariff classifications, Incoterminology, regulatory information, and transportation requirements, among other topics. A good Import Department should offer the following services:

- Provide instruction sheets to foreign suppliers to use as guidance for preparing the invoice used for Customs clearance as well as with consigning the shipment. By the Import Department helping the suppliers, they also prealert them to the shipments that will be forthcoming, thereby ensuring that the foreign supplier knows to provide the import documents prior to export.

- Properly identify which company IRS Number to utilize for clearance.
- Harmonized Tariff Classification.
- TSCA Declaration.
- DOT Hazmat.
- Invoice requirement clarification.
- Consigning guidance.
- Suggested ports of arrivals.
- Import coordination.
- RA coordination.
- Logistics and brokerage coordination and expedites.
- New rules and regulations information as a result of 9/11.

ENTRY SELECTION PROCESSING 101

The next step is to move into the preparation and distribution of broker's instructions prior to Chuck's shipment reaching the port. Chuck's Import Department is determining an entry type to be utilized for clearance and will dictate this request to the broker. The different types of entries and when they apply depend on the type of business in which the importer is involved. The most common entry types are:

- **Consumption entry** — Formal entry.
- **Informal** — Similar to a formal entry; however, value must be less than $2,000.
- **Section 321** — Entry made if value is less than $250. We recommend this type of entry be utilized only if no regulatory information is required for entry.
- **Other entry types, such as foreign trade zones and in-bond entries** — Postpone Customs entry formalities such as duty payment and processing fees. Avenues that can be taken to assist with saving on costs via these entry types are discussed in Chapter 8.

Please note that for any importers that are shipping regulated product, which means there is need for clearance by another government agency aside from Customs, certain entry types are not advisable. For example, a Section 321 should not be utilized because regulatory information is not required for entry transmission, but should be included since it applies to the product. Meaning, if your product requires clearance with the FDA and requires an FDA code to be entered by the broker, a Section 321 should not be utilized since the FDA code is not required for transmission under this entry type. Written consent should be made available to the broker from the importer when a Section 321 entry would be permitted. Informal entries provide for cost savings for importers as the merchandise processing fee (MPF) range is reduced. This fee and others are discussed further in Chapter 2.

The documentation that must be filed by the broker includes:

- Customs Form 3461
- The invoice
- A bond
- Evidence of the right to make entry (for example, the bill of lading)

Making entry for consumption is a two-part process consisting of:

1. Filing the documents necessary to determine whether merchandise may be released from Customs' custody
2. Filing the documents that contain information for duty assessment and statistical purposes

BOND (ENTRY BOND)

The entry must be accompanied by evidence that an appropriate bond is posted with Customs to cover any potential duties, taxes, and charges that may accrue. Bonds may be secured through a resident U.S. surety company, but may be posted in the form of U.S. money or certain U.S. government obligations. In the event that a Customs broker is employed for the purpose of making entry, the broker may permit the use of his bond to provide the required coverage.

The following lists the Customs bonds available:

- **Single Transaction Bond** — This bond is designed to cover only one importing transaction at one port of entry. The bond amounts required by U.S. Customs are illustrated in Table 1.1.
- **Continuous Bond** — This covers virtually all types of importing transactions (excluding antidumping and countervailing duty entries) and is placed automatically on file with U.S. Customs at all U.S. ports of entry for one (1) year. The amount of a Continuous Bond is usually 10 percent (10%) of the annual estimated duties for the next calendar year and is rounded up to the next $10,000. The amount is rounded up to the nearest $100,000 if the annual estimated duties exceed $100,000. A Continuous Bond will never be less than $50,000.

Table 1.1.   U.S. Customs Bond Amounts.

Bond Type	Bond Amount
Basic single entry (general goods)	Invoice value + duty
Quota or visa entries	3 times invoice value
Automobiles (nonconfirming)	3 times invoice value
Entries requiring other	3 times invoice value
Federal regulatory compliance	3 times invoice value
Temporary importations	2 times estimated duty
Goods unconditionally free of duties	10 percent of invoice value
Antidumping and countervailing duties	Determined by Customs

Entry summary documentation is filed and estimated duties are deposited within ten (10) working days of the entry of the merchandise at a designated customhouse. Entry summary documentation consists of:

- The entry package returned to the importer, broker, or authorized agent after merchandise is permitted release.
- Entry summary (Customs Form 7501).
- Other invoices and documents necessary for the assessment of duties, collection of statistics, or the determination that all import requirements have been satisfied. This paper documentation can be reduced or eliminated when utilizing features of the ABI.

The entry process can begin when a shipment is confirmed on board the carrier (aircraft or vessel) or when it reaches the U.S. port or border. We cannot stress enough that it is best to begin the entry process as early as permitted. The IOR, in this case Chuck's Import Department, will arrange via a broker to file the entry documents for the goods with the Port Director at the named port of entry. This can be done via a manual or automated system, such as ABI. We will describe more about Customs' automated system and what is new on the horizon in Chapters 11 and 12. For Chuck's shipment, the broker utilizes the ABI system, which is used to transmit to Customs and the OGAs. Certain brokers utilize their own systems to link into the ABI system. This is important to know in the event of entry transmission system error problems. Brokers may receive entry rejects and assume the error is due to a glitch in Customs' ABI system when, in fact, it is a glitch in their own system.

There are limitations here. Certain OGAs have different clearance processes, some of which are manual. The USDA, for example, is still using a manual process. The USDA routinely clears freight via the bill of lading manifest information from the Automated Manifest System (AMS) that describes to the

USDA what products are moving with each bill of lading. If the manifest information is too generic, such as shippers using the term "chemicals, not otherwise informed (NOI)," it is going on hold. The USDA will then review hardcopy paperwork from the shipment, update the ABI system, and advise back in hardcopy form to the broker assigned to the shipment for the importer if the shipment is released or held. More USDA information and OGA backgrounds and how they can affect your time and money are found in Chapter 5. In addition in Chapter 5, a generalized description of the flow of a regulated import clearance is provided to assist in understanding the steps involved for better time line planning.

As standard "rule of thumb," average delivery turnaround is two to four working days for air freight shipments and seven to ten days for ocean shipments from port of export to your door. (Suggestions for delivery improvements are captured in Chapter 3.) The bulk of turnaround time depends on how flawless or less than flawless the entry submission is and whether or not a direct port-to-port movement of the freight was secured. An import entry is complete when Customs and the OGAs have authorized the shipment, the releases are clearly reflected in the ABI system, and all duties have been paid.

IT IS NOT ALWAYS CLEAR SAILING

We are going to do a check-in with Chuck at this point. Chuck's Import Department has provided all the necessary information needed for clearance while in flight to the broker. Within twenty-four (24) hours, Chuck's shipment arrived and was cleared by Customs and the USDA, however, not the FDA. The broker has advised Chuck's Import Department that the ABI system reflects an "FDA Exam." It is unclear as to why the system is still reflecting this term as the broker had already provided the FDA with the entry hardcopies. Chuck has been working steadily with the Import Representative, Bob, in the Import Department. Bob advises Chuck that he will contact the FDA directly to obtain further information. Bob contacts the port FDA Compliance Officer, who advises that the samples need to be inspected physically and will adjust the system to reflect "FDA Intensive Exam." (More on the exam process in Chapter 2.) Bob immediately contacts Chuck about the delay and then makes a quick call to the broker. The broker has some interesting news for Bob. Somehow, the shipment had already been delivered to Chuck's facility late yesterday afternoon. There was a mix-up in the ABI system that caused the broker to believe it was ready for dispatch to the trucker. Bob quickly passes this information on to Chuck. Chuck hurriedly hangs up with Bob and contacts his company warehouse to confirm the products did arrive and seeks guidance on how to get the samples back to the port for FDA inspection. The Warehouse Manager, Peggy, did not contact Chuck regarding the samples due to the lack of a contact name on the delivery address. They were unsure as to whose shipment it was. Chuck is dumbfounded as to how his tight and secured shipment is totally unraveling right in front of his eyes.

Chuck takes a deep breath and then inquires whether or not the samples were placed in the warehouse freezer storage. Peggy advises, "No." Company policy is not to place any dry ice into refrigeration/freezer facilities due to the toxic fumes that could be generated. Chuck completely forgot to check on this one. He knew the samples would be repacked, but felt that a third repack on arrival would not be required as the product would go straight into the warehouse freezer on delivery. He did not want to risk a delay.

"Now what?" Chuck declares. The samples are probably useless, but would need to be reviewed by the Quality Assurance Department (QA) before destroying them. Should Chuck send them there first and if they are found to be of no value to his research due to the temperature damage, just toss them? Chuck appraises his Import Representative, Bob, of the situation that has occurred. Bob informs Chuck that whether or not the samples are of any value at this point to his research, the shipment has not cleared the FDA and must be returned. Since the broker made the error with dispatching the shipment prematurely, they will absorb all trucking expenses. Bob and the broker's job are to work with the FDA on getting them what they need for inspection. The broker will arrange to move the freight, once obtained, to the examination site. The FDA will arrange an inspection for the samples in the next day or so. The broker contacts one of the local trucking services that the brokerage firm utilizes to dispatch a truck immediately to Chuck's facility to retrieve the shipment. Chuck does not have time to get an evaluation on the condition of the samples from his QA Department, so he decides to have the samples repacked with fresh dry ice. Peggy can make this arrangement in the warehouse. Forty-six (46) hours had passed since last repack.

Inspections by any of the government agencies can be random or can be for a specific reason, such as the importer has outdated registration information on file with the government agency. In Chapter 4, you will find regulatory registration information that may apply to certain products. These registrations are what the OGAs require for clearance. They are an important time element with inbound supply chain planning of regulated products. If an importer's shipment is not properly prepared for entry into the U.S., there are fines and penalties that may be placed on that importer. Since the passage of the Customs Mod Act, importers to the U.S. now assume key responsibilities that were originally managed by Customs. This reassignment of responsibility is important because the Act also includes new U.S. Customs Service "enforcement tools" in the form of more severe fines and penalties for companies that fail to comply with the new regulations.

Chuck's samples are picked up from his warehouse and delivered to the Centralized Examination Site (CES) facility for inspection. Within twenty-four (24) hours, the FDA Inspector examines the content of the shipment and is satisfied. The ABI system is updated by the FDA Compliance Officer to reflect an FDA "May Proceed." The broker, who has been monitoring the release status hourly, notes the release and ensures that a copy of this ABI transmittal reflecting the "FDA May Proceed" term is supplied to Bob in the Import Department for his files. Bob places a copy of the FDA "may proceed" ABI screen print in the entry folder to close out their file. Finally, the samples are redelivered back to Chuck's warehouse where Peggy immediately contacts Chuck of its arrival.

IS ALL LOST?

As Chuck and the research scientists stand over the samples in the lab, they contemplate if all the efforts to import them were futile. They should soon find out. They proceed with the testing. To their amazement, the samples are found to have a seventy-two-hour defrosting window that still permits the samples to remain useful. Chuck is elated and proceeds with his research. Read more in Chapter 4 on how Chuck and his research team can learn about registration time lines for drug and device products. For Chuck, a registration code will need to be secured before importing any drug sample for human clinical trials and could take up to several weeks or months. Shipments will be detained at U.S. ports if imported prematurely otherwise. Learn also about FDA end-user declaration letters that need to be generated by the foreign supplier in Chapter 5. Information contained in the letter must be accurate for the imported sample's intentions and can assist with improving clearance turnaround.

THE ENTRY REACHES CONCLUSION

Meanwhile, as Chuck's research progresses along, the entry is still unfolding. The process does not stop once the shipment is delivered. Duties need to be paid. Audit checks need to be conducted. Paperwork needs to be filed and Customs has roughly 314 days to finally close the entry. This is called liquidation of the entry and is the final computation of duty. It gives both the importer and Customs the time to audit entries for errors. After an entry is filed,

Customs will review the information submitted. "Date of Entry" is the date Customs releases the goods. Customs will liquidate the entry with no changes. Customs posts a bulletin notice in the customhouse at the port of entry, a notice of liquidation, and provides (by mail) a small 5 × 7 carbon form (Customs Form CF 4333, titled "Courtesy Notice of Liquidation") to the address on file for the IOR. The term "liquidation" means that Customs is finished with the entry; however, the importer still has 180 days after the date of liquidation to take a further look and then finally be completely finished. The form will reflect what the entry liquidated at a certain value amount. If the entry liquidated correctly or if there were any problems with it, it will be noted in the form as a suspension or extension and Customs will then mail a 5 × 7 carbon form of a different color to the IOR. Something as simple as a typographical error on the entry, which was not caught at the time of audit, may have been the culprit to your entry not liquidating correctly. For instance, the broker may have typed an incorrect dollar value, which caused the duty payment to Customs to be lower as a result. An increase or decrease in duty payment may need to be arranged by the broker on your company's behalf. Liquidated entries, unless protested within 180 days from date of liquidation, represent final calculation. Importers can also protest the tariff classification of the appraised value on which duty was assessed.

Importers should also note that Customs or the FDA can request that your shipment be sent back. It is possible that Customs may release merchandise and later demand that it be returned. They have that power. This condition could happen for various reasons including improper marking or, if it is determined to be restricted or prohibited merchandise, the FDA may feel they released it prematurely. If Customs demands return of the merchandise, the importer may not have to file an entry summary or duties as long as it is returned and an application to destroy or export the goods is filed within ten days of entry. A brief diagram of the time line entry process is provided in Figure 1.1.

MAINTAINING GOOD RECORDS PAYS OFF DURING A GOVERNMENT AUDIT

Finally, there is the need to maintain a tight record retention policy within an internal Import Department. Chuck is not obligated to maintain anything from his import sample shipment. His internal Import Department will do this for him. The U.S. Customs Service Office of Strategic Trade Regulatory Audit Division created a "Record Keeping Compliance Handbook," published in June 1998. The handbook was written to assist importers in developing and maintaining a Customs record keeping compliance program for entry information

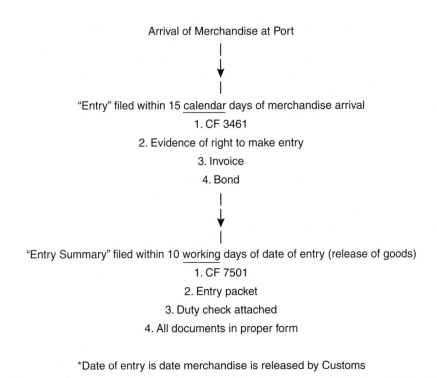

Arrival of Merchandise at Port

"Entry" filed within 15 <u>calendar</u> days of merchandise arrival

1. CF 3461

2. Evidence of right to make entry

3. Invoice

4. Bond

"Entry Summary" filed within 10 <u>working</u> days of date of entry (release of goods)

1. CF 7501

2. Entry packet

3. Duty check attached

4. All documents in proper form

*Date of entry is date merchandise is released by Customs

Figure 1.1.   An entry process diagram time line.

and documents: The "(a)(1)(A)" list of records. The handbook and list are available on the Customs website (www.cbp.gov).

A compliant Import Department will adhere to the requirements set forth in the (a)(1)(A) list. In the event of an official audit by Customs, the importer's record retention will be evaluated thoroughly. Not every item noted in the (a)(1)(A) list will be required to be physically in an import file, however, the information, forms, etc. must officially reside somewhere within the company. For example, the Power of Attorney agreement (discussed in Chapter 2) or bond information should be made available if requested by Customs. This information may not necessarily reside in an Import Department, but perhaps the Legal or Compliance Department of an organization. Customs may review the file for specific documents, such as the invoice document or bill of lading. Importers should set a precedent of what is to be readily available in an import file, the certain order to maintain, and what other government and regulatory information is to be maintained external to an Import Department.

CONCLUSION

Chuck has really stretched his knowledge of the import flow and we hope readers have achieved this as well. We have familiarized you with the basics. Chapter 2 will take the import and procurement process to another level of detail. An awareness will be gained to roadblock poor planning and redundant mistakes, which have been the source of many noncompliance issues and added costs to importers. Chapters 2 and 3 will provide the insight into the most common errors with importing. Educating the requisitioners and the foreign suppliers is key to achieving paperless releases from Customs and the OGAs.

2

OPERATIONS AND PROCUREMENT

Whether you are reorganizing your existing supply chain processes or developing new ones, there are multiple ways available to determine whether or not to venture into a global procurement process. Purchasing domestically has its set of requirements, costs, and time lines. Purchasing globally has an entirely different set of prescribed requirements that involve meeting and adhering to rules and regulations, post 9/11 security measures, and additional challenges and costs. However, the cost to procure product from foreign suppliers may still have an advantage over the domestic cost. In this chapter, we will strive to provide a level of detail for inbound supply chain planning that is lacking from global business literature. For example, we will consider: What are the "actual" costs and why do they exist? What are the "specific" obstacles? What do you "really" need to know for your business planning and who should be included? Why should you even consider importing products from a foreign vendor? We can provide answers to these types of questions and the opportunity to learn from others in the industry who have offered to share their expert knowledge and experiences.

Robert Rudzki, President of Greybeard Advisors LLC (www.greybeard advisors.com) and former Senior Vice President at Bayer Corporation, assists with the educational path. A leading figure in North American procurement, Rudzki founded Greybeard to provide strategic and focused advice to new businesses striving to achieve and sustain success and to help established businesses improve their bottom-line performance substantially. Rudzki also holds board positions with numerous companies and has first-hand working experience with the various scopes of global procurement projects. His insights are useful for any firm interested in doing a complete job with overseas sourcing and delivery.

Rudzki advises, "Whether it's global, national, or local procurement activities, there are certain fundamental procurement business processes that must be in place. Strategic sourcing and negotiations management, for example, are two foundation business processes that are relevant regardless of geographic scope. Nevertheless, offshore procurement can be more involved than in-country procurement due to such factors as language differences, cultural differences, legal and regulatory issues, security concerns, and unusual cost and time line factors. A key to success, therefore, is to have a strong foundation in modern procurement practices, supplemented by a comprehensive understanding of the unique factors and costs and benefits of doing business with a chosen offshore supplier."

Rudzki continues by remarking, "It is important in global procurement to carefully select team members for each project. The team represents the global needs for the entire organization, not just the local needs of the division they are drawn from." Furthermore, he draws particular attention to the procurement acronym "LCCS." "With Low Cost Country Sourcing (LCCS)," Rudzki suggests, "the basic idea is to search out the lowest-cost-producing nations around the world for different commodities and services. Whether raw materials, hardgoods, or IT services, consider finding and awarding business to qualified suppliers in those countries. This technique has proven to be a significant opportunity in the last few years. Furthermore, as new democracies are born around the world in developing countries, companies and entrepreneurs emerge and can become — with a little help from a mentoring customer — globally qualified suppliers. This is a dynamic area. The potential pitfall with Low Cost Country Sourcing is to assume that today's low-cost country for a given commodity will remain the right choice for the foreseeable future. With changing world currency relationships and economic pressures in different countries, today's low-cost country for one commodity could be replaced by a new low-cost country in some other part of the world. The challenge for the procurement organization is to constantly monitor the marketplace and identify and quickly act on the latest market intelligence regarding low-cost suppliers."

BASIC PROCUREMENT 101

Working with first-hand knowledge and not hearsay, and with an understanding of the fundamentals, you will be assisted in your decision to procure product domestically or globally, and how to do it effectively. We will provide various processes through which certain companies involved in inbound supply chain operations have optimized their output to customers. Additional fixed and variable import costs that are not involved with domestic purchasing will be discussed so they can be understood. Each of these important aspects will be detailed throughout the book, as we elaborate on the solutions and answers to the questions we hear being asked.

Let us begin with the basics. Jack Hasnauer, Head of Technical and Services Procurement for an east coast–based chemical company, has experience working on capital projects as well as in the maintenance, repair, and operating supply (MRO) area. Hasnauer provides insight with the basics for procuring products domestically compared with internationally. He describes the following experience, "When a requisitioner has a need for an item, he/she would more than likely have an idea of who to purchase the item from in the U.S. and would provide the name(s) of the supplier(s) to the Purchasing Department. Purchasing would then identify other suppliers that could provide the same item and depending upon the amount of the spend, would issue a Request for Proposal (RFP) to obtain the necessary pricing, terms, and delivery information." "Domestically or internationally," Hasnauer continues, "suppliers can be found by word of mouth, through memberships in professional organizations such as the Institute of Supply Management (ISM), Internet searches, and reference tools such as 'The Thomas Register.'"

Hasnauer proceeds with the basics, "When buying commodities, it is best to use the competitive bidding process to obtain your best overall deal. If you have a repetitive requirement, try not to buy one at a time. Take your total volume out for competitive bid and put it in written agreement form for an extended period, i.e., a year or more. This can be done via a local, regional, national, or global agreement. Such agreements will enable you to obtain increased savings through greater committed volume to a given supplier."

"Whether you are buying commodities, equipment, or service, this process can work equally well and deliver significant benefit to your bottom line," recommends Hasnauer. He shares the following scenario, "Let's assume you are buying a piece of engineered equipment. You will need to have a detailed specification from the Engineering Department or from whichever group within the firm requires the equipment. Assume further that a tight performance specification is involved. You could rely on the commercial portion of the RFP to capture these specifics; however, the best and cleanest way to ensure accuracy is to attach a detailed specification that has been drafted by the Engineering Department or the 'end-user' to the RFP and reference it accordingly. This reduces the likelihood that a critical piece of information will not be provided to all of the bidders. When an RFP is issued, if it does not sufficiently describe the item to be purchased, the proposals that are received will not be consistent, i.e., 'apples to apples.' You won't be able to make an accurate evaluation of them without a significant investment of 'clarification' time and, thus, you will not be able to make an informed decision."

"Another step," Hasnauer describes, "that can be taken to ensure that you are receiving the best deal is to conduct 'bid clarification' meetings upon completion of the bidding process with the several lowest bidders that meet specification. The purpose of these meetings is to review each bidder's proposal in detail to ensure that your expectations are going to be met and that there will be no surprises at the eleventh hour. It is advisable to meet with at least the two lowest bidders that meet specification as you cannot assume that the lowest bidder can meet all of your requirements until their bid is thoroughly evaluated. While evaluating bidders in parallel may require more effort, it may prevent schedule slippage if the lowest bidder does not meet specification; therefore, the second or third bidder must be awarded the order."

"Ultimately, if the relationship with the selected supplier proves beneficial to both parties, you may want to develop an 'Alliance' and share proprietary or confidential information to take further cost out of the process, improve delivery, and to enable each party to take advantage of the relationship to the fullest extent possible," Hasnauer offers. "A critical step in this process is to develop and institute metrics to measure such critical requirements as lead time, quality, etc. Collectively, these metrics are known as Key Performance Indicators (KPIs), upon which each Alliance partner's performance will be measured. Through these measurements, it can be determined if the Alliance partner is performing at the agreed upon level of service."

Hasnauer wraps up his comments with a thought on delivery and shipping. He states, "While the vast majority of shipments occur without an incident, invariably a shipping problem will occasionally occur. In most cases, sufficient pressure can be brought to bear on the supplier by the Purchasing Agent to resolve the problem in a satisfactory and timely manner. If a critical shipment experiences significant delays or shipping problems, however, it is recommended that you immediately contact the appropriate member(s) of the Logistics Department and ask that they intervene. Acting in concert, the Purchasing Agent and Import Representative can usually resolve any shipping problems/disputes that arise. Naturally, depending upon the criticality and severity of the problem, the end result may be an escalation of the issue within each organization's chain of command," Hasnauer concludes.

WITH U.S. IMPORT RULES AND REGULATIONS CHANGING, PRE AND POST 9/11, WHY CONSIDER FOREIGN SUPPLIERS?

A quick reference to history books will show that the 1930 Smoot-Hawley Tariff Act provided the initial legal structure for international trading, which continues its purposes to this day. The term "tariff" has the same meaning as "duty," which refers to a listing of products that can be imported into a country and their applicable duties. The duty is a tax imposed by the government on products imported into the country and is a percentage of the value of the goods. Tariffs are collected by the Customs Department as a source of income for the government. A few years later, the Reciprocal Trade Agreements Act of 1934 initiated the U.S. trend toward lower tariffs and freer trade, a trend that also continues to this day. These reductions or elimination of certain tariff/duty rates assist the U.S. in importing at less expense. In addition, the U.S. has not adopted a Value Added Tax (VAT) for U.S. clearance as other countries have done. A VAT can be 16 percent of the value of your shipment. If someone in Canada is purchasing from another country, other than the U.S., this tax would be in addition to any duties and taxes one would pay. So why not stretch a corporation's legs and venture more into securing product from outside the U.S. borders? Chapter 8 discusses further how to take advantage of lower tariffs. For now, let us start by listing reasons why one should be motivated to consider global procurement:

1. **To take advantage of the U.S. minimal duty rates** — As stated above, the U.S. has dramatically reduced its tariff rates. The U.S. is the cheapest country for obtaining goods from another country.

2. **Lower duty and tax costs via understanding "entered" value** — Entered value means using the product price value on the invoice and then subtracting any eligible deductions approved by Customs such as freight and insurance depending on the Incoterm. You then have a lower value on which to calculate the duties and taxes (merchandise processing fee [MPF], harbor maintenance fee [HMF], etc.). The rule of thumb is if the foreign supplier is paying the freight and insurance and they are incidental to the import of your product into the U.S., then you may deduct these costs before calculating the duty owed.

3. **To obtain lower exchange rates for the purchase order** — Exchange rates can work to your advantage at a particular time. The rate enforced on the day the documents are presented to Customs is used for calculating the duty against the entered value. If the exchange rate is down in a particular foreign country, this may be a prime time to purchase from them and possibly lock into a short- or long-term price agreement.

4. **To take advantage of lower labor costs that make for lower product prices** — One of the main reasons that businesses decide to import goods is lower labor costs in many overseas countries. Foreign manufacturers are often producing products in much greater quantity than in the U.S. due to the larger markets in their location. They can, therefore, be more competitive on price than a smaller, domestic producer.

5. **To determine what is new in the other neighborhood (new products and fresh ideas)** — For those business owners who like to be market leaders, importing new and innovative products can provide a competitive edge.

6. **To investigate the import statistics for advantageous trends** — Perusing the current statistics can help you to analyze pricing and volumes and assess the market share as well as uncover intriguing sources of goods. These can be found on the U.S. Department of Labor, Bureau of Labor Statistics website (www.bls.gov).

7. **To discover an alternative to a domestic supplier** — Even if you do not intend to procure product globally in your immediate future, it can still be useful to know what is "out there" and how much it would cost. This analysis can provide a valuable guide for negotiations with domestic suppliers so you do not end up paying too much or buying a product that is not exactly what you need.

8. **To protect a known brand in a way that can influence the sale** — For some businesses that deal in the top end of the market, having unique prestige products and labels can be their competitive advantage. In this instance, importing the products yourself may be the only way to protect this uniqueness.

9. **To discover particular cultural skills and products that may also influence the sale** — A product such as an oriental rug produced in the U.S. simply does not have the same value in the eyes of the educated customer as one produced in Asia. Therefore, when considering products that have an ethnic background or are manufactured using traditional offshore skills, importing is the only alternative.

ADDITIONAL TALENTS AND EFFORTS MAY BE REQUIRED

"The world is your oyster" cliché is not so understated for procurement considerations. The U.S. has its share of supply and demand, while offering a wide variety of marketed products to U.S. citizens. Now, let us consider the size of the U.S. and compare it to the rest of the world, then step outside the U.S. border window. What do you see? There are many more suppliers to consider. Chuck found a foreign supplier that could meet his needs after exploring domestic possibilities. How did he do this when it is more difficult to pinpoint a global supplier of a particular product due to the vast number of places to look and the enormous number of options? Chuck had an advantage; he already knew what he needed. What about the businesses who are looking to find the "next hottest thing" to market? How would one even begin to find a foreign supplier and commence a business transaction with them? It would be like looking for a needle in a haystack. Let us provide you with some specific methods to assist with your endeavor.

1. **Get out there and network** — Network with individuals in the field in which you are pursuing options. Learn from their processes and best practices. Get their business cards. There are always seminars or training forums provided to many procurement personnel. Take advantage of one within your area.
2. **Surfing the web can provide an inexpensive way to research** — This option is a good starting point, as it will only take time and tends to be inexpensive. The Internet is full of new ideas and contacts. Use search engines to locate products or services using a variety of keywords to broaden your scope.
3. **Join business-related industry groups and associations** — As you become involved in associations within your field, you gain valuable knowledge and contacts through the tasks you conduct to support your organization's cause. You generally find that many of your new associates are effectively using offshore sources of supply.
4. **If the budget permits, try some focused traveling** — If you are a veteran who has traveled to other countries, you are already aware of the cultural differences between the U.S. and many foreign destinations. These differences need to be taken into account when considering how you would work with these companies. Look out for unique products or services that the people and businesses use in their own country. Visit trade shows and businesses in the same industry as your own. For example, if you own a light fixture shop, then visit some light fixture stores overseas to observe materials, styles, display ideas, and business systems that are used.
5. **Read and research** — Books, trade journals, magazines, newspapers, etc. — read them all. Subscribe to certain publications, exchange with colleagues, or make use of your local library. Remember to add research while browsing a bookstore.
6. **Visit or contact local embassies and consular representatives** — Make contact with the local embassies of the countries from which you want to import. They should have a trade section with information about products and services.
7. **Join your local Chambers of Commerce** — These volunteer assemblies of delegates provide products and services to promote commerce

in over 130 countries. These organizations host overseas trade delega-
tions, which provide an avenue for establishing contacts with possible
suppliers.

8. **Contact the U.S. Council for International Business (USCIB)** —
The USCIB serves the trade community through its affiliations with
various organizations such as the International Chamber of Commerce
(ICC), the Business and Industry Advisory Committee (BIAC) to the
Organization for Economic Development (OECD), and the International Organization of Employers (IOE). Now if that is not enough
acronyms for you, let us also advise that the USCIB works with and
advises the World Customs Organization (WCO), World Trade Organization (WTO), and the office of the U.S. Trade Representative (USTR).
All of these associations and their purposes can be found on the Internet.
Meeting with the USCIB may give you ideas concerning your global
procurement needs.

9. **Take time to attend location or foreign trade shows** — Most industries will hold trade shows in various countries. Attending these is a
great way to collect information and expand your network.

10. **Get to know your foreign supplier** — There are both good and bad
foreign suppliers. You need to protect yourself by getting to know as
much as you can about your foreign suppliers before committing to a
permanent supply agreement. This may necessitate visiting their business and facilities as well as conducting conference calls. They should
be able to supply you with references so that you can make inquiries
with other businesses using their product or service. Check their annual
reports, if available. Request a trial shipment to check the quality of
the product, service, packing, and efficiency of the business. Have them
explain their repair process, for example, in the event their product has
equipment failure.

11. **Consider the cultural and language differences** — There are a few
tricky protocols when setting up deals with foreign suppliers, especially
when you encounter new cultural and language difficulties. You should
make an effort to learn the culture of the country, its people, language,
and in many cases, its religions. Try contacting your local Chamber of
Commerce for information or seminars on working with overseas
countries and cultures.

WHAT ARE THE "ACTUAL" CONSIDERATIONS?

We learned from Chuck and his import experience in Chapter 1 that when you
think you have covered every checkpoint in your planning, there may be that

one forgotten link to tie up. In Chuck's case, he failed to alert his warehousing staff of his expected shipment. He did not confirm his own company refrigeration guidelines and restrictions and he did not check that his foreign supplier put a delivery contact name on the paperwork. Sometimes importers need to learn by trial and error, but we would rather know all the possible mishaps that can surface ahead of time so as to avoid a similar fate. This is where you involve the right people from the start and then if budgets permit, do a test-run import to work out the possible complications.

Even if you are procuring product on a bigger scale than Chuck, you need to follow the same curriculum and involve the same departments. When a company has received an approved capital expenditure project, what do they do? They organize a meeting with the "starter team" to celebrate and begin linking the involved processes with their vision. These are individuals who, during a group meeting, have a thunderclap thought on an idea on how to improve a process. They quickly move to identify and involve the key players. A product line's departmental "family," for example, usually involves several key functions in a supply chain:

- Manufacturing
- Engineering
- Purchasing
- Accounting
- Marketing
- Sales
- Distribution
- Warehousing

But where are the other in-house players or "family members" that need to be incorporated into a global supply chain planning session?

- Importing/Exporting
- Regulatory Affairs (RA)
- Compliance
- Legal
- Transportation
- Security/Risk Management
- Health and Environmental Safety (HES)

These departments should have been consulted prior to calculating the final figure and company commitments on that capital expenditure project. These departments can also save you money and time. They can provide an understanding of basic import timing, associated costs, liability, transportation options, and the potential barriers that should be considered. If a light fixture company ventured into an imported clothing line market, new rules and regulations such as quota and textile declarations would have to be considered. Do you want to get your global supply chain upper management's attention? If so, you advise them that by strategically placing these department individuals in the planning, the supply chain program can achieve immediate cost reductions of an additional 2 to 4 percent. By reading on in this book, you will continue to learn how this can be achieved and how post 9/11 requirements must be checked in various aspects of the process for the acquisition of foreign product.

WHAT OTHER "PLAYERS" SHOULD BE INVOLVED?

Those firms that are importing merchandise, either for their own use or for commercial transactions, particularly when they find importing procedures complicated, are wise to hire a Customs broker. Customs brokers are private businesses that can handle the clearance of your merchandise on your behalf. A list of brokers licensed to conduct Customs business in a specific port, by state and ports, can be found on the Customs home page (www.cbp.gov). There is also an "Informed Compliance Publication" about Customs brokers that appears under the "legal" tab within the listing. Remember, even when using a broker, the Importer of Record (IOR) is ultimately responsible for the correctness of the entry documentation presented to Customs and all applicable duties, taxes, and fees. Since 9/11, we have found it very valuable to establish a close working relationship with our brokers to help keep our import knowledge abreast of changes being made to the clearance and transportation of goods process.

POWER OF ATTORNEY FOR BROKERS

In order to utilize a broker for inbound procurement, importers need to inquire whether their company has an active Power of Attorney (POA) established for any broker they will use for the movement of the goods from abroad. In Chuck's situation, his Import Department handled this matter on his behalf. A POA is a legal instrument that is used to delegate legal authority to another party. The person who signs (executes) a POA is called the Principal. The POA gives legal authority to another person (called an Agent or Attorney-in-Fact) to make property, financial, and other legal decisions for the Principal.

It is important to research whether or not the broker has a brokerage business existing for the selected U.S. port through which the shipment will be destined to arrive or pass through. Certain brokers do not always have an established brokerage presence in every U.S. port. For example, broker "JCB Brokerage House" has over 100 U.S. port offices in which they can conduct clearances. However, if a shipment crosses through Laredo, Texas, JCB does not have an existing port office to conduct the clearance. JCB must then acquire a subsidiary to perform such a function on its behalf. In an effort to circumvent this limitation, some firms try to transfer a POA to subsidiaries of a particular broker. That move may only create extra work for everyone involved. The only factor that would prompt us to recommend this procedure would be if an importer already has an established relationship with the broker who possesses a good, solid reputation for conducting accurate and timely border clearances. If a company does not have the benefits of in-house import operations, a POA can be accomplished by reviewing the POA forms with the Legal Department.

Importers are well advised not to sign any broker's POA form. Rather, they should consult their Legal Department to establish a POA form for the broker from the company. Not just anyone in a company should sign off on a POA, as some brokers will simply fax a POA form for signature. Do not succumb to this effort if your foreign supplier selected the broker for you, no matter how urgent your shipment is. You will see this type of maneuver with express couriers, who are known for faxing POAs to anyone in a corporation to gain immediately the rights needed to get your shipment cleared using "your" IRS Number. The General Counsel or designated officer in your company should sign and approve any POA.

In Chapter 1, we indicated that you should get the compliance ball in your court, especially when it involves clearances. Miscellaneous, nonregulated samples or small-quantity shipments are less risky to ship via a courier and can be a cost savings as the air freight and inland delivery charges are reduced. It should be made clear, however, to any "courier" service provider such as Federal Express, UPS, or DHL, that you require a courtesy call from their courier's Brokerage Department when the courier's entry profile necessitates that "your" company's IRS Number be used for clearance. Different courier services follow different parameters when they use their own IRS Number or when they should use the importer's IRS Number. For example, if the product requires FDA clearance or if the value is too high, the courier will use your IRS Number.

HOW MUCH, PLEASE? BROKER AND CUSTOMS COSTS

Depending on the size and complexity of your business, and at a particular stage in the importing process, you could be at an advantageous or disadvantageous stage with your broker. Brokerage competition is good, as it keeps brokers on their toes when they know there are other brokers with which you are interacting. Reverting back to Chuck and his area of the pharmaceutical business, let us consider that Chuck moves into the clinical trial stage with his product and will have repeating imports, two every week. The shipments will move via a commercial airline, need temperature requirements, and have a short delivery turnaround range. An advantage for Chuck and his Import Department is to meet with a capable broker and discuss his needs.

What will Chuck's ongoing costs be? Who will expedite his shipments? Who will care enough to see that nothing goes wrong? Let us first consider brokerage costs. Not all brokers charge importers a standard fee for a particular transaction. Broker service fees must be negotiated and agreed in writing. These fees should be provided to your Accounting Department, or any outsource payment company, to ensure adherence to the fee amounts. There must be some safety net within a corporation to ensure that at the time of broker payment, if a fee amount is over or under the agreed amount or any added accessorial charges were placed on your broker bill, they will be caught. Some brokers will either abbreviate or assign a numerical coding next to each fee on their itemized bills to represent the description of the charge. If they cannot fully describe the fee, you should ask for a fee agreement that lists the cross-referenced coding to each fee and its meaning.

Do not always assume that each charge on the broker bill is a brokerage fee. The broker should be providing you with sufficient backup to each charge they paid on your behalf. With new post 9/11 security fees being charged by the airlines, for example, you may find them all separately itemized on the broker bill or bundled and incorporated into a flat airline rate. These fees are usually referred to as War Risk Surcharge or International Security Surcharge (ISS) as well as Security Fee (Sec.). Listed below are the fees that were incurred to import Chuck's pharmaceutical sample shipment. These are erroneous, fictional fees and have no basis for applicability.

- Broker fee: $80 — Broker fee for making entry
- Duty: $100 — Customs fee for duties
- Other taxes: $25 — Customs fee for merchandise processing fee (MPF)
- OGA fee: $15 — Other government agency (OGA) fee for FDA entry
- Wheels-up: $50 — Customs fee to preclear while in flight
- Special runner fee: $20 — Broker fee
- Expedited fee: $25 — Broker fee
- ISC fee: $15 — Airline fee for international service costs
- Sec. fee: $20 — Airline fee for security costs
- Transportation expedited service fee: $500 — Trucker fee

Routine broker fees can vary from $60 to $150 per transaction, depending on import volume, port location, product requirement demands, and how much logistics business is based with the broker. These are all negotiable fees. Broker bills should always be audited for human error or bogus fees such as an "effort surcharge" of 15 percent. Do not hesitate to challenge the broker on any fee that was not negotiated previously. Hidden fees are the most problematic for any importer to truly get their hands around. Therefore, a procedure must be in place to ensure that each and every fee is broken down, described clearly, and includes backup documentation supporting the fee payment (for example, a copy of the trucker bill). Airlines and steamship lines will "lump" accessorial fees together, so it is not always a case of the broker intentionally not breaking down particular fees.

A second fee consideration involves Customs, as they charge various fees depending on the particular entry, how long your shipment has been sitting at the port, urgency of the shipment, if it needed inspection, etc. For a formal and informal entry, routine charges made by Customs include:

- **Duty** — Duty rate multiplied by your entered value. An entered value is the value minus allowable deductions by Customs, which include insurance and freight, depending on your agreed Incoterms. *For example: Chuck's sample cost $2,000. It was a dutiable product of 5.0 percent: $2,000 × 5.0 percent = $100 (duty payment).* No deductions applied, since Incoterms were Delivery Duty Unpaid (DDU). (Depending on Incoterm, insurance and freight can be deducted from the total invoice value.)

- **Merchandise Processing Fee (MPF)** — 0.21 percent times the entered value. Under a "formal entry," importers pay no less than $25 and pay no more than $485 regardless of entered value. Under an "informal entry," importers pay no less than $2 and pay no more than $25 regardless of entered value amount. *Chuck's sample value was $2,000 × 0.21 percent = $4.20 = $25 min.*

- **Harbor Maintenance Fee (HMF)** — 0.125 percent times entered value. If the routing makes good business sense, shipments may move via the Montreal, Canada port and then be railed to the U.S. port. If this route is taken, the HMF is waived since it applies to U.S. seaports only. This fee did not apply to Chuck's shipment since it arrived via air.

CUSTOMS AS A SOURCE OF REVENUE

Customs' revenue, collected for fiscal year 2004, was $25 billion more than in fiscal year 2003, which was $24.7 billion, and in 2002, Customs collected $23.8 billion. This difference reflects the increase in the amount of imports coming into the country. For the last five years, 68 percent of all imports value was duty free. The value of imports into the U.S. for fiscal year 2004 totaled $1.36 trillion, while 2003 totaled $1.2 trillion, a significant increase over 2002 when imports into the U.S. were valued at $1.1 trillion. This increase was also reflected in the number of trade entries processed and in the total volume of international traffic processed by Customs.

What are these fees for and where do they apply?

- **Of the revenues Customs collects, the proceeds are divided** — Some of the money is returned to the Treasury to fund other federal agency programs. Other money is returned to the Governments of Puerto Rico and the U.S. Virgin Islands, while other funds are put aside to refund importers for drawback payments for trade activity. A portion is then also retained to offset various program costs allowed by law.

- **MPF** — This item is an added Customs "duty-type" fee that is used to put funding into Customs systems and pay salaries of inspectors and other employees of Customs who are involved in inspections. Depending on type of entry, an importer would not pay more than $485 max. on this fee per import.

- **HMF** — This fee has been the subject of many discussions, as it has no cap. The Water Resource Act of 1986 created this fee and is an *ad valorem* fee assessed on port use associated with imports, admissions into foreign trades zones, domestic shipments, and passenger transportation. The fee is assessed only at ports that benefit from the expenditure of funds by the Army Corps of Engineers for maintaining and improving the port trade zones (that is, U.S. ports). The fee is paid quarterly, except for imports, which are paid at the time of entry. Customs deposits the HMF collections into the Harbor Maintenance Trust Fund. The funds are made available, subject to appropriation, to the Army Corps of Engineers for the improvement and maintenance of U.S. ports and harbors.

- **Antidumping duty** — In addition to your Customs duty, an antidumping duty may apply to your product. The duty rate varies and can be very high as it is imposed to offset the difference between the price at which a foreign producer sells product in the U.S. and its home market, generally. Antidumping duty costs were instituted to protect endangered domestic industries against unfair trade, such as price discrimination or below-cost sales, since the foreign cost of production cannot be easily known by domestic courts.

- **Countervailing duty** — Countervailing duty is imposed to offset the effects of impermissible government subsidization of an imported product. Examples of countervailable subsidies are tax rebates on exports, lower freight rates on exports, low-interest loans, and income deductions for overseas expenses.

Since antidumping and countervailing duties can affect the landed cost of merchandise and delay the liquidation of entries, a set procedure is recommended to be followed for importers to ensure compliance with Customs. To offset antidumping and countervailing duties, and to gain commercial advantage, some foreign sellers offer to reimburse U.S. importers for all or part of these special duties. As a result, Customs requires that an appropriate statement be filed to comply with Section 353.26 of the Commerce Department Regulations. In the event no reimbursement is agreed, it is very important for an importer to verify to Customs that it is not being reimbursed in any way for antidumping or countervailing duties via Customs' Non-Reimbursement Certificate. This declaration form can be found on the Customs website. Generally, if the foreign producer pays the duties for the importer, the duties are doubled.

Today, Customs is still a growing, major source of revenue for the federal government, returning over $16 to the taxpayer for every dollar appropriated by Congress. In the early days, Customs officers administered military pensions (Department of Veterans Affairs), collected import and export statistics (Bureau of Census), and supervised revenue cutters (U.S. Coast Guard). Customs also collected hospital dues to help sick and disabled seamen (Public Health Service) and established standard weights and measures (National Bureau of Standards).

CUSTOMS ENTRY CLEARANCE OPTIONS CAN SAVE MONEY

Supply chain planners should consider various options for clearing their shipment to increase company savings. We discussed the most common Customs type entries; however, there are alternate clearance procedures that can be explored for cost savings and time enhancements. An immediate release of a shipment may be accomplished in some cases by making application for a special permit for immediate delivery on a specific Customs form (3461) prior to arrival of the merchandise. This is an area in which one of the new post 9/11 security requirement programs improves the turnaround time.

Carriers participating in the Automated Manifest System (AMS) (Chapter 9) can receive conditional release authorizations after leaving the foreign country and up to five (5) days before landing in the U.S. If the application is approved, the shipment is released expeditiously following arrival. An entry summary must be filed in proper form, either on paper or electronically, and estimated duties deposited within ten (10) working days of release. Immediate-delivery release using Customs Form 3461 is limited, so you need to check with your broker on the types of merchandise. Refer to Chapter 9 for the new post 9/11 security requirement, Advance Manifest Ruling, that utilizes the existing AMS System to transmit specific information to Customs prior to a shipment's dispatch to the U.S.

If it is desired to postpone release of the goods, they may be placed in a Customs bonded warehouse, under a warehouse entry agreement. The goods remain in the bonded warehouse for up to five years from the date of importation. At any time during that period, warehoused goods may be re-exported without the payment of duty or they may be withdrawn for consumption on the payment of duty at the rate of duty in effect on the date of withdrawal. If the goods are destroyed under Customs supervision, "**no**" duty is required to be paid. While the goods are in the bonded warehouse, they may, under Customs supervision, be manipulated for cleaning, sorting, repacking, or otherwise changing their condition by processes that do not amount to manufacturing. After manipulation and within the warehousing period, the goods may be exported without the payment of duty or they may be withdrawn for consumption on payment of duty at the rate applicable to the goods in their manipulated condition at the time of withdrawal. Certain goods may not be placed in a bonded warehouse and you should consult your Import Representative, broker, or Customs Agent for applicability.

Importers do not pay any duty or import fees until after clearance has been made. As stated before, some brokers will pay all Customs duties, taxes, and any associated import costs on behalf of the importer. If they do not, a company can pay duties to the broker or directly to Customs. A company check can be issued by the importer's Accounting Department or an importer can be set up via an automated clearing house (ACH) account or via the Automated Commercial Environment (ACE) Secure Portal to pay Customs directly (Chapter 11).

SPECIAL REQUIREMENTS

Here is where we get into the bits and pieces of importing requirements and added checkpoints while meeting requirements in the planning process. Along with entries, there are various Customs declarations that may be required for entry associated with a given commodity. Certain declarations can save money in two ways.

1. If a declaration is required for clearance and is made readily available to Customs, this reduces your risk of delivery delays.

2. Customs permits certain products, depending on their intended use in the U.S., to be entered duty free as long as the appropriate declaration has been prepared. A query of the HS Number (Harmonized Tariff Classification) by Customs or a broker will advise whether a certain declaration is required or can be used — a declaration form completed either by the foreign supplier or importer "declaring" what needs to be declared. For example, certain textile products require a textile declaration. Also, a research sample may qualify for duty-free treatment under a special Prototype provision and a declaration from the end user may provide you with the necessary backup to make this claim. This information is available on the Customs website along with the various declaration forms. Import Departments should have these declarations made available to importers within their organization so as to maintain uniformity of the forms to Customs.

MORE BITS AND PIECES: QUOTAS

In addition to declarations, certain products have quotas assessed to them, such as textiles along with the textile declaration. Quotas may be eliminated altogether in the near future. For now, you should research general quota information and quota requirements for certain commodities prior to importing into the U.S. Import quotas control the amount or volume of various commodities that can be imported into the U.S. during a specified period of time. U.S. import quotas may be divided into two types: absolute and tariff rate.

1. Absolute quotas limit the quantity of goods that may enter the commerce of the U.S. in a specific period.

2. Tariff-rate quotas permit a specified quantity of imported merchandise to be entered at a reduced rate of duty during the quota period.

Once a specific quota has been reached in a particular category, goods may still be entered, but at a considerably higher rate of duty. Quota information is available on the Customs website. Select the "import" tab and then the link "Textiles and Quotas." This section contains links to information on subjects like Textile Status Report for Absolute Quotas, Visa and Exempt Certification Requirements for Textiles, Commodity Status Report for Tariff Rate, and the publications box of the related links column provides general information and the link "Import Quotas."

TOXIC SUBSTANCE CONTROL ACT

The TSCA is a popular topic misunderstood by many. When entered merchandise falls under the importation requirements of another government agency, additional forms and certifications are often required, such as the TSCA. Again, Chuck had the advantage of having an internal Regulatory Department to help determine the appropriate TSCA statement to be placed on the invoice for his sample. Under the statutory mandate of the TSCA, the Secretary of the Treasury shall refuse entry into U.S. Customs territory to any chemical substance, mixture, or article that fails to comply with any rule, order, or civil action in effect under the TSCA. Importers of chemical substances in bulk or mixtures are required to certify that the shipment either complies with all applicable rules and orders thereunder or is not subject to the TSCA. Chemicals listed on the TSCA inventory list receive a "positive" TSCA statement (declaration) on the invoice.

Regulated products governed by the FDA or CDC, for example, usually have a negative TSCA declaration, meaning "otherwise regulated" by another agency and not the TSCA. Articles such as packaging, a chair, or a spare part are not applicable to a TSCA declaration at all. Suppliers can reflect the appropriate TSCA declaration on the invoice, which will be provided by the requester or the Import Department This procedure assists with courier shipments as it eliminates the guessing game on the part of the courier company for clearance. Importers can arrange for TSCA stamps that indicate a responsible party's signature for stamping the invoices appropriately. Following are the TSCA declarations:

1. **TSCA + positive certification** for shipments subject to TSCA. I certify that the chemical substance on this invoice line complies with all applicable rules or orders under TSCA and that I am not offering a chemical substance for entry in violation of TSCA or any applicable rule or order thereunder.
2. **TSCA − negative certification** for shipments not subject to TSCA. I certify that the chemical substance on this invoice line is not subject to TSCA.
3. **No TSCA** applies.

Customs and the EPA have committed to work together in the electronic environment. The EPA and Customs continue to monitor imports of chemical shipments to determine if shipments and their documentation comply with the certification requirements and substantive mandates of the TSCA. Customs will refuse entry to any shipment until certification is submitted properly.

Failure to comply with the requirements may result in a violation of the TSCA. These fines and penalties can be very steep and have the ability to cause a huge loss of revenue for a company for just one incident. TSCA determination can be tricky and it is another checkpoint that should be researched prior to importing any product that is, or contains, a chemical. For example, products such as ink pens or glue can be problematic to import as the chemical composition of the ink or glue may not be clearly documented on a Material Safety Data Sheet for a "positive TSCA" determination. Your RA or HES Department can assist you on TSCA determination for your imported product and its intended use.

Some companies have implemented an import form within their systems, in which routes from the requester to the RA or HES Department for TSCA (and regulatory, if applies) determination are detailed. The form then routes electronically to the Import Department to prepare the product profile for clearance. Finally, the form directs itself back to the requesters after the HES, RA, and Import Departments have reviewed it. The requester can then place his/her order. More on this technology is covered in Chapter 11.

DETERMINE DUTY RATES

The Harmonized Tariff Schedule (HTS) provides duty rates for virtually every item that exists. As discussed in Chapter 1, the HTS is a reference manual that is the size of an unabridged dictionary. Experts spend years learning how to classify an item properly in order to determine its correct duty rate. For instance, you might want to know the rate of duty of a wool suit. A classification specialist will need to know certain specifics. Does it have darts? Did the wool come from Israel or another country that qualifies for duty-free treatment for certain of its products? Where was the suit assembled and does it have any synthetic fibers in the lining, etc.? The U.S. International Trade Commission Tariff Database link within the Customs website will take you to an interactive database that will enable you to get an approximate idea of the duty rate for a particular product. You must be aware that the duty rate you request is only as good as the information you provide. The actual duty rate of the item you import may not be what you think it should be.

The importer decides on the initial HS Number to be used for clearance; however, Customs makes the final determination of what the correct rate of duty is at the time of postauditing, not the importer. For very specific duty information on a particular item, you may request a "binding ruling." You may also receive guidance by calling your local Customs port. Classification is further discussed in Chapter 7.

Binding Rulings

To help facilitate the import process, so there is no misunderstanding of which HS Number applies and the correct duty rate is applied to a particular product, a binding ruling can be arranged with Customs. Importers can request a written ruling from Customs for the proper HS Number classification and rate of duty for their merchandise. For information on Customs ruling letters, select the "legal" tab on the Customs home page, then select the link "Rulings," and finally the link, "What are Ruling Letters." When requesting a binding ruling, importers should follow the procedures outlined in Part 177 of the Customs Regulations (19 CFR 177). The Customs Regulations may also be accessed via the "legal" tab. You may research the results of previous ruling requests by using the Customs Rulings Online Search System (CROSS). Customs may have already issued rulings on products similar to yours that you can use for guidance. To access CROSS, select the "legal" button on the home page and then select the "CROSS" link. Binding rulings are further discussed in Chapter 7.

RIGHT TO MAKE ENTRY

If you have decided to import, but you and your foreign supplier are unclear as to who is going to be responsible for the import, then several issues need to be resolved. Even if you decide to accept responsibility, how do you capture it correctly on the import documentation? This chapter further clarifies the definition of "Importer of Record" (IOR) and the impact of importing consigned merchandise. The IOR is defined as the owner or purchaser of the imported goods, or when designated by the owner, purchaser, or consignee, a licensed customhouse broker. The IOR assumes the most responsibility for compliance with the Customs regulations for a given import and is liable for legal and regulatory noncompliance related to an import entry. Customs Directive Number 3530-02 is found on the Customs website. It expands on the codified definition and explains that the "owner" or "purchaser" would be any party with a financial interest in a transaction or who ultimately gains from the sales transaction. This includes but is not limited to:

- The actual owner of the goods
- The actual purchaser of the goods
- A buying or selling agent
- A person or firm importing on consignment
- A person or firm importing under loan or lease
- A person or firm importing goods for repair or alteration or further fabrication

The invoice and air waybill/bill of lading needs to state the consignee as Company A or Company B.

In Chuck's company, the Import Department has designated that the Import Control Officer (ICO) will investigate any shipment where Chuck's company is not the purchaser of the goods; for example, if his sample ships to a U.S. lab and not his company. If the IOR is not self-evident, the ICO will determine whether Chuck's company has a financial interest in any imported merchandise. The general rule of thumb to follow for determining that your IRS Number should not be utilized for an imported shipment entry would be a transaction in which your company has no financial interest. In which case, the ICO or Import Representative of your company is to instruct the broker and/or shipper that your company is not the IOR and the appropriate importer must be identified.

There may be circumstances where more than one U.S. company share a financial interest in a given import transaction; for example, if one company has separate operating companies. The IOR would ideally be the company that would ultimately benefit the most from the shipment, but can really be negotiated to some extent between the companies who share a financial interest in the imported merchandise. In such cases, appropriate personnel from each company should consult with their main Compliance Department and, if necessary, the Legal Department to determine which company is properly the IOR. It may be in your company's best interest to advocate/negotiate either for or against being the IOR in a given transaction.

INCOTERMS ARE AN ESSENTIAL NEGOTIATION COMPONENT

When locking into a global procurement agreement, Incoterms are a significant tool to be understood and used wisely to define the "who's responsible for what?" and "at what point?" Incoterms are not used in "domestic" sales contracts. Chuck believed that he had his pricing secured when he placed his purchase order with his foreign supplier, but was he aware of negotiating Incoterms in his favor? Did he divide costs, risk, and responsibilities between his company and his supplier? Incoterms facilitate the conduct of international trade and have been the source of many confusing conversations. Published by the International Chamber of Commerce (ICC) in 1936, the terms are not law or all inclusive. They are intended to assist in defining the respective roles of the buyer and seller in the arrangement of transportation and other responsibilities, and to clarify when the ownership of the merchandise takes place. They are used in conjunction with a sales agreement or other methods of transacting the sale and must be specified in order to apply. Abbreviated by three-letter

English language acronyms, they provide a quick reference of responsibilities by naming the Incoterm acronym and the named place of destination. The port of export and the U.S. port of destination must be named with the itemization of freight and insurance charges (if included in the pricing). A list of Incoterms 2000 is available on the Customs website (www.export.gov/incoterms.html). Incoterms are usually updated every ten years, take three years to make a change, and have been translated into as many as thirty-four languages.

Chuck learns that his company's Purchasing and Import Departments can assist importers in understanding the costs and liability they are agreeing to under certain Incoterms. Any importer should "always" be educated in this area when negotiating rates and fees. If the company decides on terms "Ex Works," it must realize that the company has been made responsible for the export compliance requirements in the named foreign port of export. We would generally advise any company to disagree with this Incoterm written in any purchasing contract. "Ex Works" is routinely misunderstood and misused by many foreign shippers. The shipper is required to act as the Exporter of Record. Even if your supplier refuses agreement to any other Incoterm and prepares the contract stating "Ex Works," this does not capture a factual depiction of this Incoterm transaction. The forwarder involved with pickup and delivery to the foreign port is using the supplier/shipper's name on the export paperwork as being the responsible party and not the importer's. An alternate Incoterm similar to "Ex Works" would be "FCA" (Free Carrier) and can be used for any mode of transportation. FCA entails that title and risk pass to the buyer including transportation and insurance cost when the seller delivers goods cleared for export to the carrier. The seller is obligated to load the goods onto the buyer's collecting vehicle; it is the buyer's obligation to receive the seller's arriving vehicle. Any transportation costs incurred to the seller from its door to the foreign port of export could be separately billed to the buyer. However, if all else fails, a "bastardized" Incoterm of "Ex Works, cleared for export," may be used in your purchasing contract.

Another example involves "DDP" (Delivered Duty Paid). In this situation, the foreign supplier has agreed to pay all costs and should act as the IOR. DDP also holds the supplier liable to risk of damage/loss for this shipment. If anything would be lost or damaged, the foreign supplier is responsible for reimbursing the company and filing the insurance claim.

INSURANCE IS ANOTHER AREA OF NEGOTIATIONS

There are generally two types of insurance associated with international transactions: marine and nonpayment, described as follows:

1. **International shipping (marine insurance)** — Insurance obtained prior to the international shipment of merchandise. This value is not dutiable and will not have a duty rate calculated against its value. It does not require declaration on the invoice.
2. **Nonpayment premiums** — Insurance premiums incurred by a foreign supplier to ensure against nonpayment by the buyer and passed on to the importer as part of the invoice price. This value must be indicated on the supplier's invoice as it is a dutiable value, meaning that the duty rate will be multiplied against this value to produce a duty payment to Customs.

Purchasing insurance enables the party, usually the buyer who has the risk of loss, to recover the entire costs associated with the importation of merchandise in the event merchandise is lost, destroyed, or otherwise unusable. Additionally, the owners of any cargo on board a vessel that is damaged must share pro rata in "general average" to repair any damage done to the vessel. Failure to obtain insurance will result in direct liability to the owner in the event of damage to the vessel. Responsibility for procuring marine insurance depends on the terms of sale of each individual transaction. For example, a shipment sold as "CIF" (Cost, Insurance, and Freight) would require the shipper to obtain the insurance; whereas, a shipment sold as "FAS" (Free Along Side) would require the buyer to obtain the insurance. Regardless of who purchases the insurance, the amount is not dutiable. Customs will permit the insurance to be deducted from your invoice value depending on the Incoterm to achieve a lower value to calculate your duty rate against. Rule of thumb would be if you, the buyer, have paid for the insurance (and freight) so it is not part of the price you will pay for the merchandise; you cannot deduct it from your invoice value to achieve a reduced duty payment. If the seller is paying for the insurance (and freight), you may deduct the amount from your invoice value since you are absorbing these costs into your unit pricing.

GOVERNMENT AGENCIES HAVE THE RIGHT TO INSPECT WHATEVER/WHENEVER

When it comes to filing an insurance claim, no claim can be made against the government at any time. For example, Customs can tag a shipment for examination at any given time. If anything should happen to the shipment, the loss is yours. It also should not be taken personally if your brochures are pulled from the shipment to be examined and not your import associate's white powdery substance. Even though Customs has developed more complex targeting cri-

Figure 2.1. Advance applied X-ray technology allows Customs officers to see inside entire seaport containers. (X-ray container exam compliments of www.cbp.gov photo gallery.)

teria since 9/11, it is still a somewhat random process and nothing personal is involved, unless the company has a poor "track record" or the entry was questionable.

Under Title 19 of Customs Regulations, Section 1467, of the U.S. Code (19 USC 1467), Customs has the right to examine any shipment imported into the U.S. and it is important to know that the importers must bear the cost of such cargo exams. It is also the responsibility of the importer to make the goods available for examination. A broker can arrange for an importer's shipment to be moved to the Centralized Examination Site (CES), which is a privately operated facility, not in the charge of a Customs officer. This site allows the merchandise to be made available to Customs officers for physical examination (see Figure 2.1).

The CES facility will unload (devan) your shipment from its shipping container and will reload it after the exam. The CES will bill you for its services. There are also costs associated with moving the cargo to and from the exam site and with storage. Rates will vary across the country and a complete devan may cost several hundred dollars.

The CES concept fulfills the needs of both Customs and the importer by providing an efficient means to conduct exams in a timely manner. A broker can keep an importer abreast of the exam status. The Automated Brokerage Interface (ABI) System provides various messages that keep the broker updated. A hold by Customs, the USDA, or the FDA will be indicated in the ABI System by the governing agency with the terminology of "FDA Hold" or "Customs Hold" or "PQ Hold."

If the government agency decides that it wants to simply review the hardcopy paperwork, the system will be updated with the term "FDA, Customs or PQ Exam" by the government inspector. There is no need to move the shipment to CES and the broker will send a "runner" to the government agency with the hardcopy documentation. Now, if the government agency wants to have the freight examined physically, it will reflect "FDA, Customs or PQ Intensive" and will then be required to be moved to CES. This is helpful to understand, because when you contact your broker for an update (a good broker will keep you abreast without you having to contact him/her first) and when he/she reads off what the ABI System states, you will have a better understanding. Many brokers offer a tracking on-line system where importers can log into the Internet to obtain their clearance and delivery information. However, these tracking systems tend not to generate "live" information and may run routinely twelve to twenty-four hours behind. Shipments are released after a delay or exam provided no legal or regulatory violations have occurred.

An importer may contact the appropriate agency that is detaining your shipment to obtain further details of the delay (for example, the FDA) so indicated to you by your broker. However, if a regulated product is involved, the importer's internal RA Department may need to be involved. RA should be contacted after it has been determined that it is not an innocent typographical error or missing paperwork that is causing the problem. RA would be appreciative of this human error prescreening before contacting them. In the event the clearance rejection was a result of the FDA not understanding a product's registration information, RA may need to review the regulatory information that was presented for clearance by their department.

In Chuck's case, his Import Department would be notified by the broker of any such FDA detainments and would work with its internal RA contacts to rectify the rejected release. It is a good idea to keep a roster of your RA contacts for each product line as well as a list of contacts with Customs, OGAs, airlines, brokers, forwarders, and truckers. If the shipment accrued storage, demurrage, and examination costs as a result of an examination or any delay by Customs or any OGA, the importer must cover the additional charges. In addition, the importer suffers the consequences of any theft or financial impact that the delay had on the company. There have been situations in which a company's shipment was tampered with or stolen while residing at a CES site and was perceived to pose a security risk.

MAINTAINING YOUR "COOL"

Physical government inspections and exam delays can be more problematic for temperature-sensitive products. If an imported product requires maintenance within a certain temperature range, a uniform process can be established to ensure protection of the product within a particular port. Generally, major ports have larger refrigeration facilities available, so for any product that requires temperature control during transit, transportation companies and U.S. ports should be researched for temperature-control size capabilities and indicate such requirements on the bills of lading.

It is best to ensure, when importing a rather large-size perishable product, that any involved airline is going to have room for your product on arrival. No product is temperature controlled while in flight unless placed in a rented temperature-control unit. There are various temperature-controlling devices to rent from an airline — Enviro containers and LD-3 units offer larger-size controlling units; MYX containers are a more commonly used container as they can accommodate a smaller, dimensional shipment; reefer containers can be used for ocean shipments.

It is best to check with the selected airlines to determine availability and cost. A temperature-recording device or a Pareto chart can be placed in the container for quality assurance purposes to track the temperature ranges throughout the transport of the product. These recording devices must be listed separately on the invoice with a fair market value as well as indicated on your bill of lading so as not to have any product piece count discrepancy with Customs. A commonly asked question from requesters is: What is the temperature in the aircraft or in the warehouse? The answer is: The temperature is equivalent to the local weather temperature. Some requesters are baffled that their perishable sample, which imported into the port of Miami in August and did not indicate that it needed to be placed in refrigeration, was completely melted on receipt. This is, again, where planning and tracking of a shipment is essential. It is also a huge advantage to prealert your Import Department to your global procurement plans. Allow the other players in the supply chain process, such as your Import Department, to assist in making arrangements for your product to be safely maintained to your door.

If Chuck had chosen to utilize a rented container for his perishable samples, he would have needed to ensure that the forwarder had indicated on the air waybill that the LD-3 unit remains with the product until final destination. Chuck's warehouse would have arranged for the return of the unit to the airlines. It is very important for this information to be on the air waybill, as some airlines will mistakenly remove product from an LD-3 unit at the U.S. port to use for an export shipment. They will take your product out of the unit and place it (hopefully) in refrigeration, but have been known to simply put it in their warehouse…to thaw.

It is equally important to research refrigeration capabilities as not all airlines provide such services and if they do, they may not have a large-enough capacity to accommodate the shipment size or another importer may have already booked the refrigeration/freezer space. Chuck's broker and Import Representative would be an avenue for him to further explore these options of renting units from an airline for his future imports.

Chuck used his purchase order as an additional opportunity to advise his supplier of refrigeration requirements and to provide the import documents to his Import Department prior to exporting overseas. He captured this verbiage in the Purchasing Standard Phrases within his purchase order. This should be a fundamental best practice for every purchase order. As a side note, the Import Department needs a copy of the purchase order to verify that the pricing on the invoice being used for Customs clearance matches the pricing on the purchase order. Any price fluctuations, credits, and debits should be reported to the Import Department as they may affect the accurate duty payment due to Customs. The Import Department should have access to all company systems that store purchasing, accounting, and receiving import information to verify pricing, what price was paid on the actual invoice, and what was actually received. Any noted discrepancies should be reported immediately to the Import Department. Departments within any inbound supply chain, especially the Accounting and Receiving Departments, should be provided information concerning these requirements via some type of awareness training. They should also be expected to work with their Import Department to arrange an audit process for capturing overages/shortages, such as a routing spreadsheet, listing receiving/imported shipments. An example spreadsheet to communicate such information is provided in Chapter 4, Table 4.1.

BILLS OF LADING AND LIABILITY

Bills of lading, air waybills, and waybills all can be used to note any special requirements aside from temperature maintenance. Bills of lading for the various modes of transportation are one of the most important, yet least understood, documents involved in the international carriage of goods. They provide information as to whom the consignee is, who has all rights of action, and who is subject to all liabilities in respect to those goods. It is as if the contract contained in the bill of lading had been made with themselves. This does give the consignee the ability to have pertinent information captured on the bill of lading. This assists ships' officers, operators, and managers to understand fully the legal implications of the bill of lading agreement in the event of problems and issues that may surface with the movement of the freight.

The forwarder is the responsible party for preparing the bill of lading based on information provided by the foreign supplier. It is important for your foreign supplier to provide the forwarder with correct information. If the bill of lading is consigned incorrectly, it is most likely due to a supplier error and not the forwarder and should be addressed immediately. Otherwise, the incorrect information will continue to be reflected on the bill of lading for future shipments.

FORCE MAJEURE

Documents such as bills of lading include a force majeure statement, which means "greater force." These clauses excuse a party from liability if some unforeseen event, beyond the control of that party, prevents it from performing its obligations under the contract. Typically, force majeure clauses cover natural disasters or other "Acts of God," war, or the failure of third parties (such as suppliers and subcontractors) to perform their obligations to the contracting party. It is important to remember that force majeure clauses are intended to excuse a party only if the failure to perform could not be avoided by the exercise of due care by that party.

When negotiating force majeure clauses, ensure that the purchasing agreement contains this clause, which applies equally to all parties to the agreement. It is also helpful if the clause sets forth some specific examples of acts that will excuse performance under the clause, such as wars, natural disasters, and other major events that are clearly outside a party's control. Inclusion of examples will help to make clear the parties' intent that such clauses are not intended to apply to excuse failures to perform for reasons within the control of the parties. Steamship lines are covered under force majeure in the event a vessel travels through unexpected horrific weather conditions, which literally cause containers to drop into the ocean.

CONCLUSION

This chapter's intent was to take the reader to another level of detail regarding global procurement decision making. With so many process areas of which to be conscious, it is important to know the resources that are available because procuring product globally requires more than just knowing where to look for a supplier. We have provided these essential levels of information. We captured how in-house entities are a source of knowledge and savings for corporations. Use them and use them wisely.

Moving to the next chapter, we will provide further insight into the other players involved who also serve in equally important roles. In some corporations, these players and additional elements remain a missing link in global supply chain planning. Also learn the key to master the creation of your own personal third-party logistics analyst, with no added costs, and how "bundling" services and shipments can optimize your supply chain operation. We will put on our transportation hat and discover the players in the physical movement of product from beyond the U.S. boundaries.

3

TRANSPORTATION IN THE POST 9/11 GLOBAL PROCUREMENT ENVIRONMENT

Since 9/11, the public and business sectors have become more educated regarding the new security rules and requirements that affect multiple aspects of conducting global business, but much remains to be learned. Mr. Hallock Northcott, President of the American Association of Exporters and Importers (AAEI) (discussed in Chapter 6) sums up the new post 9/11 security situation for U.S. importers who have procured product globally, by stating, "In pre 9/11, 'security' meant: Don't steal my stuff! Then what happened after 9/11? All of a sudden, the post 9/11 security priority has been redefined as being the top priority for the country!" Mr. Northcott is accurate with his statement. Placing the "risk" in the container en route to the U.S., while still on foreign soil, is now part of the main focus Customs uses to ensure that another horrific incident cannot happen.

Transportation has not been excluded and serves as the most critical point at which a security breach may occur. The ability to load a bomb or weapons of mass destruction must be nonexistent. This condition places the transportation service providers at the center of physically ensuring that such events do not happen. Individuals and corporations that procure product globally must now share the responsibility of ensuring safety and monitoring their supply chains, including oversight of the employees of truckers, steamship lines, airlines, and railways — the individuals who are in contact with loading freight. These people are present when the containers are loaded and sealed and must comply with the new regulations.

The service providers, moreover, are expected to adjust to the new processes and systems introduced through the post 9/11 requirements executed by U.S. Customs, while still meeting delivery dates. Chapter 9 will discuss the latest regulations from Customs under the Department of Homeland Security (DHS) in greater depth. In this chapter, we will venture into areas where cost and delivery time can be reduced, while still meeting new security measurements under the post 9/11 environment.

It is still possible to achieve just-in-time inventory for imported merchandise, even when the government ultimately controls your delivery outcome. By establishing reasonable rules, requirements, and expectations for your clearances and deliveries, the new challenges of moving product through the new post 9/11 environment can be met while adhering to original estimated costs and time lines. We will break down the various areas that seem to be the most critical to consider and are of the most interest in today's import industry. Finally, we will provide insight and guidance to conquer and prevail with a strong, dynamic, international logistics operation.

SELECTING THE RIGHT "PARTNER" IN THE GLOBAL INBOUND PROCUREMENT ROUTE

When a supply chain management team researches the pros and cons of purchasing domestically versus globally, the options and saving factors typically favor procuring some products globally. Let us assume this is the chosen path for the product you desire to market and distribute throughout the U.S. You have identified your internal key departments as well as external entities that will work with you to move further into transporting product from your selected foreign suppliers. Transportation procurement by domestic means involves trucks, railways, and airlines. Global procurement expands transportation to involve ocean shipping as well as new payment methods, exchange rate considerations, and document preparation. Additional controlling factors must be considered to ensure the most reliable transportation formula to meet your needs. New strategic arrangements, as a best practice, can be developed every day from growing partnerships with brokers, forwarders, and truckers. Companies do not have to venture into the global arena alone. A partnership can be formed, giving you the advantages of discounts and options on logistics, clearance, record keeping, and automation. This is essential for companies that are developing new activities, products, and sources. We begin by understanding how the selection of the right "partner" (carriers and forwarders) can have a direct impact to your bottom line.

When a company's internal logistics, transportation, and supply chain management services are combined and made to work together, the results can be remarkable. When expanded to involve external transportation or logistic providers, the outcome is a cutting-edge best practice for a transportation logistics system to support international commerce. The partnering between internal and external resources will then provide supply chain management and an inventory control system with global tracking and positioning, order fulfillment, asset transfer, and security component services.

A top-performing Logistics Department is another good partner to have as they will negotiate the best rates for transportation freight by any means. If you have an internal Logistics Department, you should include it in your planning process. Knowing the "going rates" with a particular trucker or steamship line will assist you in evaluating your overall transportation costs. Another equally important resource to contact is your broker. (Remember to research your options both internally and externally.) A brokerage company that offers expanded services is also a good partner to acquire. This may be key to further reducing rates that your own Logistics Department has negotiated for the company. This is an achieved benefit from brokers who are bundling services with other importers.

With the system in place, the discussion moves to bundling of transportation. Bundling equals more volume. More volume equals reduced rates. You have freight that needs to be moved from the foreign supplier's door to the port of export. If water separates you from your supplier, it will then need to move by other means from the port of export to the U.S. port. From there, U.S. inland transportation must be arranged. In addition, somewhere in between, rail freight may be required for reaching a final destination. It is important to determine if there is a service provider bundling somewhere that would allow you to piggyback onto their rates. Some brokerage companies offer, in addition to clearance and record retention services, a wide range of forwarder and trucking options.

To illustrate, let us revert to Chuck, who has set up a blanket purchase order for monthly imports of research samples. Chuck may now want to consider a door-to-door service. What was once referred to as "one-stop shopping" is now referred to as "total ownership programs." This condition leads to a sensible best practice when re-engineering the transportation under your business lanes. Total ownership takes one-stop shopping to the next level. While "one stop" was more for one point of contact, "total ownership" offers one point of contact, bundling services for gained savings, improved delivery time, tracking, and a partner who understands your business and will continue to evaluate your business lane for continued improvements.

This technique entails utilizing the same forwarder, broker, and trucking service to forward, clear, and deliver the product. Chuck will have someone who will grow with his changing business needs. He will not need to stress over finding a trucking service to meet his requirements and then have to negotiate additional rates with the various truckers. Bundling his transportation requirements with one service provider enables better preparation for special trucking requirements with the trucker accommodating the load. For instance, if Chuck would require an air ride truck, a flat bed, or an expedited truck, the broker would ensure that this would be lined up and readied on freight availability. There are multiple brokers who offer total ownership programs. If you are involved in export activities as well, consider bundling your import/export business to gain superior service control and fee rates with a broker.

Many companies are moving into bundling services with the same service provider that already accommodated their processes to meet the criteria of new post 9/11 requirements. Such a move gives you total control of your shipment and can also reduce transportation rates. The following are recommendations to consider when selecting the best "partner" to fit your transportation requirements before signing a contract.

- Do they offer forwarding, brokerage, and trucking services?
- Can they supply you with free warehousing?
- Are they Customs-Trade Partnership Against Terrorism (C-TPAT) members? (As part of a comprehensive plan to confront the terrorist threat to the U.S., the Customs service has established C-TPAT. This subject is discussed in Chapter 9.)
- Are they Automated Commercial Environment (ACE) participants (see Chapter 11)?
- How well equipped are their systems to meet new post 9/11 transportation requirements to the U.S., such as Advance Manifest Ruling transmission and Prior Notice (Chapters 5 and 9)?
- What is the size and flexibility of the service provider?
- Are they involved in all modes of transportation?
- Who are their other customers? References are great.
- Forwarders can get better rates with steamship lines and airlines because they have more tonnage than you. Ask what type of rates they can secure.

Table 3.1. Example of a Status Shipping Report.

	CTB Sailing Schedule	
	Invoice No. 103062	**Invoice No. 051765**
Load date	10-May-04	24-May-04
Size	40′	40′
Gross weight	62.787 kg	879 kg
Container no.	CCPIV438846	CCPIRP06328
Vessel	Jordan Spirit	CTB Montreal
B/L no.	WALDLKF0989	ESGCAP07432
Sailed	15-May-04	29-May-04
ETA Montreal	29-May-04	12-Jun-04
ETA Chicago	7-Jun-04	22-Jun-04
Actual	TBA	19 days
Days in transit	23 days	24 days

- Do they offer satellite security tracking devices for trucks and containers; as well, do they offer satellite tracking containers, a.k.a. smart boxes?
- Do they offer refrigerated containers and/or warehousing?
- Do they offer electronic status information on sailing information or clearances? See Table 3.1 for an example information chart.
- Request their financials and run a credit check.
- Insist that they define their rates in written form.
- Obtain a copy of their insurance certificates.
- Do they offer an automated environment for handling and processing your shipments — product inventory profile, on-line tracking, reporting capabilities, government releases, dispatch information, etc.?
- Inquire whether they utilize electronic bill payment with their customers (electronic database interchange [EDI]) to obtain a larger discount, since they will not need to wait for manual payment.
- Will you be looking to automate with this service provider? If so, what types of automation systems can they offer?
- What best practices have they implemented into their processes that could be a benefit to you?

There will also be a list of what the service provider will need to know about you:

- Your type of business
- Your expectations of a lead time from your carriers

- Territory and lanes you will be utilizing (if known)
- Late shipment penalty causes
- Agreed Incoterms, place, and geographic locations
- Frequency and size of volume in lanes
- Special requirements — temperature-sensitive product, air ride trucks, thermal blankets
- The U.S. ports you currently ship to
- The countries from which you will be procuring product
- If you are looking for total ownership
- Packing specifications

A face-to-face meeting should be arranged with the various service providers to ensure clear communication of the business needs and what the provider has to offer. A written request for bid should be drawn up to capture rates, terms, modes, fleet, volume, geographic areas where freight will be transporting, special services, warehousing services, compliance requirements, etc. If you are "interviewing" several service providers, a request for bid should capture information for "each" provider. Create a spreadsheet listing all providers' information to get a side-by-side snapshot of which firm offers what and at what rate. This side-by-side snapshot will also assist if you elect to acquire more than just one service provider, to quickly assist with auditing for accuracy of the broker billing packet. You may use one service provider for your border-crossing routes and another for all your ocean import routes.

A BROKER AUDIT CAN REVEAL UNNECESSARY COSTS

Conducting a broker audit of any service providers that have been awarded business is another best practice to institute. It is essential for you to keep track of their performance. Collect data on various areas throughout the months and capture this specific information, by port and by broker entry writer, on a spreadsheet. This will ensure that you do not forget any specific information that is important for you to review with your broker. Agree to have face-to-face meetings quarterly, or as often as necessary, with your new partner (broker) to review performance and address any key issues of concern for immediate correction. A broker audit may be conducted by a company's internal Import and/or Compliance Department, but you should participate.

Chuck ensures that his Import Department meets with his broker to review his needs as well as his company's compliance requirements. His Import Department has established a good working relationship, so as to understand clearly each other's processes and requirements. Chuck's Import Department reviews each bill the broker paid on the company's behalf, as well as the clearance entry document (entry summaries, Customs Form 7501) prepared by the broker. Following are some suggested areas to review:

- Did the broker use the information correctly as provided to them by Chuck's company?
- Were the right duties paid?
- Did the broker mark in Box 36 of the Customs entry summary Form 7501 that they are the agent and not the owner of the shipment?
- Does the broker list your company's correct IRS Number and address information on the 7501?
- How many broker error reports had to be generated as a result of the Import Department finding errors on the broker's billing packet? For example, did the broker charge an FDA fee when the shipment did not need FDA clearance?
- How many suspicious fees were indicated on the broker bills that you needed to have clarified?
- How do you feel about their compliance performance? Are they displaying traits of noncompliance risks?
- Did the broker incorrectly claim a North American Free Trade Agreement (NAFTA) preferential duty rate? If so, where did the broker obtain the NAFTA certificates to move forward with clearance (or didn't they)?
- If under a total ownership program, what has the turnaround on clearance and deliveries been averaging? Is there room for improvements?
- Did the broker outlay excessive payments on your behalf without seeking approval first, such as demurrage charges?

Chuck's Import Department takes the initiative to solicit feedback from the broker on Chuck's own Import Department's performance. Remember, you are in a "partnership" and feedback should be given by both parties involved. A broker may provide feedback on:

- What can be done better to improve your company's efficiencies and keep costs down?
- Is the Import Department providing timely broker instructions in order to obtain Customs releases in a short time frame?
- Does the broker understand the information being provided for clearance and dispatch?

- Does the broker clearly understand your expectations?
- Is Chuck's company providing enough lead time for the forwarder/ broker to arrange for pickup, or to move forward with clearance on all required documentation?
- Will template reports need to be established to capture information for future evaluation of delivery time lines?
- Will transportation and clearance information and updates need to be provided to key individuals within the company?

Various companies choose not to keep "all their eggs in one basket." As already mentioned, companies may choose a selected few "partners" under a total ownership program or they may choose multiple partners for specific business lanes. Working with multiple service providers (brokers, forwarders, truckers, steamship lines, etc.) may require constant juggling of business lanes and maintaining a streamlined compliance process. Be careful about committing to more than three or four service providers. You want to do enough to witness the drive generated among these service providers to gain and maintain a company's business. These various service providers will go beyond supplying broker clearance services. They will offer business strategies that can further improve your supply chain. They know what works and what does not.

Let us take railing for an example. Are you aware of the problems when railing product, as most forwarders and brokers are? They can track the congestion at the Montreal railhead and provide alternative solutions. If your service provider is not constantly working to improve your business vision, then it is time to look elsewhere. Do not let the relationship get stagnant.

BASIC OPTIONS

- **Broker A** — Handles 10 percent of your business. *Advantage:* The broker can center on one area and become very efficient at it. *Disadvantage:* The broker does not have an opportunity to share additional tonnage cost savings to you as a result of their relationships with other logistics partners. They also cannot truly show what they are made of if they are just handling one type of business lane (for example, border trucking).
- **Broker B** — Handles 90 percent of your business. *Advantage:* They can really show what they can do and have come to know your business well. They are familiar with your needs and can offer suggestions for improvements as a result of their interactions with other importers. *Disadvantage:* You have placed most of your eggs in one basket. There

is no opportunity to see how other brokers conduct business. Fee costs may tend to get higher as the broker may not feel it needs to buck for offered discounts. The broker may get too comfortable.

WHERE CAN I SPECIFICALLY SAVE TIME, MONEY, AND AGGRAVATION USING A CUSTOMHOUSE BROKER?

Many companies can conduct the "transportation" aspect of their supply chain in house; it becomes very challenging, and often costly, to try to stay on top of the game. Many companies choose to outsource this aspect of the supply chain business to the service providers who arrange for pickup, movement, and delivery. Moving and delivering an import purchase order has become such a complex function that it is becoming difficult for an individual to handle it alone. One would need to be constantly abreast of transportation availability and requirements, timing of clearance statuses, government agency delays, examinations, new automated processes, etc. A good forwarder/broker can do this for you and has the ability to adapt to his/her customer's changing environment. They also can help monitor new and changed activity to ensure transportation compliance with the new complex Customs regulations since 9/11. Some of the more important new or proposed rules and requirements, post 9/11, to counterattack any risk to security weak points are listed below. The requirements must be complied with before your shipment even leaves the port of export. Some are further detailed in Chapters 5 and 9.

Advance Manifest Ruling

This was one of the first new rules to kick off a series of post 9/11 requirements. The ruling calls for service providers to file a cargo manifest hours in advance of leaving the port of export to the U.S. The ruling applies to all modes of transportation and each mode has its own set of time lines that must be adhered to. The Advance Manifest requirements were rolled out in various stages, starting with the ocean imports. In the first week alone, when compliance with the ocean ruling became mandatory, Customs rejected many shipments that were in violation of new cargo-description requirements. The "24-hour rule" required ocean carriers to submit detailed cargo manifests electronically to U.S. Customs at least twenty-four hours prior to loading containers on board a vessel bound for the U.S. It also prohibits vague descriptions such as "Freight All Kinds (FAK)," "Said to Contain," and "General Merchandise," although these descriptions are still permitted on bills of lading, but not manifest transmissions.

Shipments that did not meet the deadline, or that had insufficient information, were not permitted to be loaded on board. Of 142,000 bills of lading that were reviewed that first week, thirteen containers headed for U.S. ports were held up for having inadequate descriptions or violating rules covering timeliness of reporting and consignee disclosure.

When Customs implemented the Advance Manifest rules for all modes of transportation, they looked to the already existing Automated Manifest System (AMS). This would be an easy, transitional avenue for service providers to transmit the additional required information. Under the new twenty-four-hour rulings, the time required for information to be transmitted to Customs was pushed up. The old way allowed carriers to provide alert information to U.S. Customs usually forty-eight hours or more before U.S. arrival (depending on mode of transportation). The new way requires the carriers to provide some added information to U.S. Customs "X" amount of hours in advance, depending on the mode of transportation, prior to exporting or even loading from the foreign location. Importers should challenge "new" "AMS fees" added to their carrier and/or broker costs that their service providers "claim" they must now charge. Is it a genuinely justifiable new fee for which the new AMS process has added many man-hours to your carrier's responsibilities?

U.S. Customs Service Commissioner Robert Bonner advised industry executives that Customs' computer system could handle the new requirements. Customs was prepared to cope with the large influx of data through its AMS. "The system exists; it is fully operational. We are not asking for anything we can't effectively use," Bonner was noted as stating. He stressed that the rules serve good purpose so that terrorists will not use the supply chain as a conveyance for another attack against the U.S. "Time is our enemy," Bonner said.

The Maritime Transportation Security Act of 2002

The goal of the Maritime Transportation Security Act (MTSA) is to prevent a maritime transportation security incident, such as loss of life, environmental damage, transportation system disruption, or an economic disruption to a particular area. The MTSA is a significant piece of legislation that reinforces the national and global importance of security for the maritime transportation system within our communities, ports, and waterways. MTSA responsibilities lie with the Coast Guard and involve a series of "family of plans" concepts to increase MTSA awareness so as to coordinate information and to deal with potential threats. Vessels and facilities that load/carry certain dangerous cargoes (such as flammable, potentially explosive, caustic, or environmentally hazardous) must have individual security plans that address security measures such as access controls, communications, restricted areas, cargo handling and monitoring, training, and incident reporting. In addition to the "family of plans," there is a "port plan" called the Area Maritime Security Plan (AMS, not to be confused with Automated Manifest System), which covers facilities and waterway venues such as parks or public piers that are not required to have individual security plans. The Coast Guard has operational plans for 2005 to deploy resources and established protocols for working with other agencies that add an additional layer to the "family of plans."

The Proposed Maritime Security Act (S. 2279)

Although this proposed trade bill has not been approved, we mention it to raise awareness on how trade bills can affect how a global supply chain can conduct business. The S. 2279 trade bill strives to set up fines for cargo remaining dormant at the U.S. port. It was introduced in the 108th Congress in 2004, containing a provision calling for a fine of $5,000 per bill of lading for cargo left on the pier more than five (5) days. Such a provision is, of course, at odds with the Customs regulations regarding a General Order, which permits fifteen (15) calendar days at the U.S. port. To avoid the penalty, the bill allows cargo movement to a public store or General Order warehouse for inspection, which is clearly contrary to the requirement placed on importers to file an entry before moving cargo. The bill did not progress in 2004 from the House Committee on Transportation and Infrastructure. In order for it to be considered by the 109th Congress, it will have to be reintroduced. Affected parties can petition Congress protesting the execution of such a bill.

Container Security Initiative

The Advance Manifest rule is necessary to ensure success of the Container Security Initiative (CSI), another program that started in January 2002. It calls on foreign ports and authorities to work with Customs officials, based at their ports, to prescreen containers before they leave for the U.S. Customs targeted the enlistment of the top-twenty mega-ports of the world. At the time of publication, nearly forty ports from various countries have joined CSI. The top-twenty mega-ports handle about six million containers annually shipped to U.S. seaports. U.S. Customs launched the CSI to prevent global, containerized cargo from being exploited by terrorists. Approximately sixteen million cargo containers are shipped into the U.S. each year via ship, truck, or rail. Globally, forty-eight million, full, cargo containers move between major seaports of the world annually. The initiative is designed to enhance security of the sea cargo container, a vital link in global trade. One of the core elements of CSI involves placing U.S. Customs inspectors at major foreign seaports to prescreen cargo containers before they are shipped to America. U.S. Customs officials, working with their foreign counterparts, for example, would be in a position to detect potential weapons of mass destruction in U.S.-bound containers at these foreign ports.

Electronic Gizmos

The Customs ACE offers a single, consolidated window for processing trade transactions, trade enforcement and compliance, and multiagency mission information. (ACE is also covered in Chapters 11 and 12.) The ACE system's electronic communication devices will incorporate various electronic communication devices (such as transponders, radio frequency identification [RFID] tags, state-of-the-art security devices, smart cards, and biometrics) to help inspectors focus on sensing and responding to threats. Test-run containers have been put out to test these gizmos. The tracking is working.

Transportation Security Administration

The DHS Transportation Security Administration (TSA) issued security directives that require random inspection of air cargo and passenger aircrafts that carry cargo and require that foreign all-cargo air carriers comply with the same cargo security procedures that domestic air carriers must follow. This procedure may contribute to import delays.

DUTY-FREE OPPORTUNITIES SHOULD BE EXPLORED

Another way that brokers can be effective tools is to have them explore duty-free opportunities for your particular business lanes. Certain dutiable products may enter the U.S. duty free depending on their intended use and length of stay. Listed below are two areas that may be utilized for cost savings in various commodity business arrangements where a temporary importation is required. (Duty-free opportunities are explained further in Chapter 8.)

■ **Carnets** — You can achieve duty-free status via a Carnet. There are three types of Carnets that you may find on the Customs website (www.cbp.gov). The most widely utilized is the ATA Carnet. "ATA" stands for the combined French and English words "Admission Temporaire – Temporary Admission." It is an international Customs document that a traveler may use temporarily to import certain goods into a country without having to engage in the Customs formalities usually required for the importation of goods, and without having to pay duty or value-added taxes on the goods. Not all countries participate in the ATA Carnet process. The U.S. does allow for the temporary importation of commercial samples, professional equipment, and certain advertising materials by a nonresident individual. Carnets are a security that participating countries accept as a guarantee against the payment of Customs duties that may become due on goods temporarily imported under a Carnet and then not exported as required. The Council for International Business can be contacted to determine if the country to which you are traveling accepts Carnets. The U.S. acceded to the ATA Convention on December 3, 1968 and began issuing ATA Carnets in late 1969.

■ **Temporary Importation under Bond** — Another duty-free option for reverse logistics (page 84) is a Temporary Importation under Bond (TIB). A TIB is similar to a Carnet, but without having to keep track of an "original" document (the Carnet). You must, however, monitor the TIB trail because a product can route from country to country under the same TIB. TIB is also a procedure whereby, under certain conditions, merchandise may be entered, for a limited time, into U.S. Customs' territory duty free. Instead of duty, the importer posts a bond for twice the amount of duty, taxes, etc. that would otherwise be owed on the importation. Under this procedure, the importer agrees to export or destroy the merchandise within a specified time. Not all items can be entered under a TIB and circumstances should be reviewed with your broker or Customs. All piece counts of a TIB entry must be accounted for and recorded. Customs may need to witness any destruction of product entered under a TIB. TIBs may route between foreign countries as well and must be tracked accordingly until their final termination. A TIB must be closed out prior to re-exportation from the U.S.

Table 3.2 illustrates the pros and cons of the two types of Customs entries. They both work well for trade show events, for example, that would need to route from country to country or even simply once to the U.S. If a U.S. company wants to evaluate a piece of the latest machinery from a potential new foreign supplier, it may be able to utilize either one of these scenarios for clearance to avoid duties costs. Although these are alternatives for reverse logistics to avoid duty payments within the various countries, the downfall of both scenarios is the cost to post the necessary bonds.

For the item you are having returned, repaired, etc., we recommend that it should be classified first to obtain the appropriate HS Number and duty rate. If the product(s) are entitled to a duty-free rate under their original HS Number,

Table 3.2. Carnets Versus TIB Entries.

	Pros	Cons
Carnet	No forms, other than the Carnet, need to be filed for goods entered (that is, no invoice).	With both types of entries, failure to prove exportation on a Carnet (or TIB) subjects the importer to liquidated damages equal to 110 percent of the duty and import tax.
	Merchandise listed on an ATA Carnet can be imported to and exported from any of the member countries as many times as needed during the one-year life of the Carnet.	Need to research country participation/ acceptance.
	Works well when routing a trade show scenario or a temporary demonstration or evaluation of particular machinery in the U.S.	If any repairs or alterations are made to the equipment or product while in the U.S., the old parts must be retained and shipped back with the Carnet.
	No merchandise processing fee.	ATA Carnet's expiration date for remaining in the U.S. is one year and cannot be extended.
		A responsible party will need to ensure that the Import Department receives the "original" Carnet document. The original must then be given to an Export Department to be used when the shipment is finally to be exported out of the U.S.
		Goods imported under a Carnet (or TIB) may not be offered for sale.
TIB	Does not require having to track an "original" document as with the Carnet. If a broker is coordinating the TIB entry with Customs, they will be responsible for closing out the TIB for you.	Failure to prove exportation on a TIB (or Carnet) subjects the importer to liquidated damages equal to 110 percent of the duty and import tax.
	Has an exportation date of one year, however, can be extended with Customs.	Every item on the shipment must be tracked and recorded with a summary report provided to Customs to permit closure of the TIB prior to export.
	Merchandise listed on a TIB can be imported to and exported from any countries as many times as needed during the one-year life of a TIB. This works well for a routing trade show scenario.	Product from a TIB import that is required to be destroyed may need to be witnessed by Customs prior to destruction.
	Country does not have to be a participating country.	Goods imported under a TIB (or Carnet) may not be offered for sale.
	No merchandise process fee.	

then it may be worthwhile to have a regular consumption entry arranged since you will not be paying duties. You will, however, still be subject to the merchandise processing fee (MPF) if you decide to go with a consumption entry. Remember, MPF has a cap of $485 on a formal entry. In all cases, regardless of entry type and scenario, the harbor maintenance fee (HMF) is still applicable and must be paid.

SERVICE PROVIDERS HAVE BEST PRACTICES THAT CAN ASSIST AN IMPORTER

Continuing with the customhouse broker benefits, brokers may be delegated the responsibility of paying certain costs on your company's behalf that the import shipment may accrue; for example, collecting freight charges (depending on Incoterms) and documenting handling fees, as well as processing the duty payment to Customs. These transactions save your Accounting Department added work and reduce costs, since the department does not have to generate multiple checks to various parties involved with clearing and moving your shipment. As mentioned earlier in this chapter, another best practice is a total ownership concept for importers. Total ownership also eliminates the document turnover fee payment. This fee, paid by a broker to a forwarder for the import documents, causes delays, as it may take twenty-four to forty-eight hours to transfer the import documents from one service provider to another once the forwarder receives the check from your broker. When a separate forwarder is involved other than the broker, the forwarder may charge a document turnover fee to the importer (meaning you). This fee is to cover the costs of the forwarder having to supply your broker with the original import documentation. This fee can run between $15 and $100 per shipment and can really add to your costs if you have a high volume of imports. You may either negotiate this fee away with your service provider or have it reduced. However, under a total ownership program, you have eliminated the cost altogether as you are working with the same forwarder/broker company. This is a common area that is often overlooked and should be researched.

The broker cannot help you unless you keep them informed. Keys to a streamlined process include:

- The broker is aware of when and how the cargo is shipped.
- The broker gets all the necessary documents in advance of the arrival of the cargo.
- The broker has all necessary information for the carrier or themselves to transmit twenty-four-hour AMS information.
- The broker knows your deadline.

It is important to get the brokers to work for you. Another best practice for a service provider that would be worthwhile to their import customers is to keep them abreast of current events that affect their supply chain operations customers (for example, new security requirements, port congestion, seminars and conferences that are available to further educate importers, etc.). Brokers can communicate this information via circulating newsletters, e-mail, face-to-face meetings, and/or monthly conference calls. As the global supply chain continues to evolve, having a service provider who is on top of the game will benefit any company. Almost all brokers seem to have a newsletter that they circulate with current events that directly affect imports or exports. Get on their distribution lists and also have them contact you directly on anything that may cause havoc to your forecasted shipments. Have them make recommendations to you based on their experience working with other accounts that were successful. Learn what services will eliminate unnecessary company in-house efforts and costs. Have them present their ideas to you. You may be dispatching a refrigerated truck at a highly expensive rate, whereas your broker may have a local trucker that gives a superb rate because they are striving to continue business with your broker.

As an example, let us use our pseudocharacter Chuck, once again, to help explain the scenarios when the importer utilizes their own company-approved truckers or their broker's approved truckers:

- Chuck imports temperature-sensitive samples. On Chuck's first shipment, he requested a refrigeration carrier approved by his in-house transportation company. Let us say that Chuck imported ten shipments in one month. *His current monthly trucking cost: $1,200/run × 10 shipments = $12,000.*
- Chuck and his Import Department reapproach the broker to explore other truckers in the port to which Chuck's samples are destined. The broker offers three different refrigeration truckers, one of which is actively used by the broker for their other import clients. The refrigeration service is available through this particular trucker, while not compromising good service. *His new monthly trucking cost: $98/run × 10 shipments = $980.*
- *Chuck's overall trucking savings for ten shipments in one month: $11,020. Achieved just by inquiring.*

Some truckers have very good relationships with your brokers and are willing to offer you pretty close to a standard trucking rate, if they have regular runs in the area you require. Note that some carriers will not even move less-than-truckload (LTL) refrigerated cargo unless they have other cargo to piggyback on top of it or will make you pay the full truckload (FTL) rate. If you cannot find a carrier willing to give you a really good deal on LTL refrigerated rates, you will have to pay the FTL rate even if you only have a fifteen-pound product to transport. Remember to evaluate whether or not refrigeration or a special service is unequivocally needed. Do you even need the expense of a refrigeration trucker for a shipment that arrives in a U.S. port just three miles from its final delivery location, in the middle of the winter? Perhaps a standard truck could be utilized.

BUNDLING AND CHOOSING THE RIGHT PATH AND PORT AS A BEST PRACTICE

Do not stop at exploring cheaper trucking services via your service provider. Bundling as a best practice provides for huge savings. Consider that bundling your multiple air shipments into one ocean shipment may be feasible for cost savings if your inventory or customer delivery dates permit a longer traveling time. Work with your service provider as well as your foreign supplier to evaluate whether they are receiving a cheaper tonnage rate under their own steamship line contracts. As well, you may inquire if they are aware of routes that could be quicker. It is highly recommended that a firm research the routing paths of the various airlines and steamship lines prior to booking a flight or vessel. For example, a shipment destined to Chicago could stop first in the port of Long Beach, California and then transfer to rail for further movement. This could be because of costs or unavailable direct routing from one port to another.

Smaller U.S. ports may have a less-knowledgeable government import staff and adopt different port practices (even though they will claim they do not). Utilizing a larger U.S. port for import activity has its benefits. Customs and OGAs in New York, Chicago, San Francisco, and Charleston have experienced staffs and know the import drill well. We are not promising, by using these ports, that shipments will clear effortlessly, but there are advantages to having Customs in a particular port become familiar with your company's imported product line. If you have bundled imports routinely into the same port, Customs inspectors are assigned importer accounts and will grow familiar with your clearances. Taking all of the above into consideration, you may consider a trial import, follow the ABCs, and then evaluate the outcome of the overall import.

- ■ **A** — Act on a really good plan. That means, do a test run first before committing.

- **B** — Benefit from broker bundling as a result of their other businesses with importers.
- **C** — Cut costs as a result.

REVERSE LOGISTICS IN THE CONTEXT OF IMPORTING

The term "reverse logistics" represents import shipments that are manufactured in the U.S. and exported across U.S. borders, then returned to the U.S. for a particular reason, such as a customer rejection or complaint or perhaps a product returned from abroad after further manufacturing or repair. When a clearance process for reverse logistics is set up properly, duty payment is avoided. Returned goods are duty free under Customs law if the appropriate documentation is established. Setting up an efficient reverse logistics process will also expedite turnaround time and reduce compliance risks. A database covering all requirements for returned goods should be created to capture a U.S. contact name, import requirements, declarations, and forms to establish the reimportation of a product for U.S. clearance. The foreign supplier has an obligation to complete Exporter Declaration forms; the importer, as well, has an obligation to complete any Importer Declaration form coinciding with the returned product. The information on the form must be completed accurately and made readily available for clearance prior to its scheduled return date. The various returned goods forms can be found on the Customs website.

In the case of food-related U.S.-manufactured products, such as vitamins that are returned to the U.S. for quality control analysis, the shipment may be subject to the Bioterrorism Act and require a Prior Notice (Chapter 5) clearance even if the intended use is not as a consumed product. Contacting the Regulatory Affairs (RA) Department to review this situation will eliminate unnecessary shipping expense if the proper registration is not complete in the U.S. If you have a situation where a product is being returned for repairs and then will be re-exported back out of the country to the customer, establish a clear procedure with the same service provider.

LOOK TO YOUR SERVICE PROVIDER TO STREAMLINE THE REVERSE LOGISTICS LANE AND MANY OTHER NEEDED SERVICES

As mentioned, total ownership is a great way to consolidate functions for saving time and money and to ensure control. Trucking companies can offer a total ownership program for various international transportation lanes and that is another avenue to consider for supply chain requirements, aside from just importing. A well-established trucking company that has expanded its role beyond carrier deliveries is Advance Relocation Services. They have been in the relocation business for approximately twenty-five years and offer a premier transportation service and provide corporate clients one source for all their relocation, installation, expansion, and storage needs. A diagnostic company on the east coast utilizes Advance Relocation and has been one of its customers for many years. In the beginning stages of the growing partnership, manufacturing by the diagnostic company was confined to the New York region. Advance Relocation provided insight into how the relationship between the companies could grow through various stages and be mutually beneficial.

Ms. Michelle Stulberg, National Account Manager for Advance Relocation Services, states, "Advance Relocation's primary function was transporting manufactured systems to their end users in the U.S., handling customer returns to a New York facility, and making weekly trips from the New York plant to JFK airport for overseas customers. Over time, manufacturing was moved to Puerto Rico and ultimately Ireland. As that happened, Advance began learning some of the procedures for receiving overseas goods. In time, the relocation company became a third-party instrument warehouse, which encompassed distribution and final delivery to the end user."

Stulberg advises, "My personal focus is the final delivery. Bottom line, the goods need to get there safely and in a professional manner. Systems need to be uncrated and placed. These services must be coordinated with the customer and installation personnel. Follow-up services on shipment is part of the service. If it's a fairly new product, a driver, installer, or crew I have never worked with before, I make it a point to do so. We solicit feedback from our customers as we find this to be very useful. You can find out what techniques worked and what didn't work as well, and this helps for future deliveries."

Stulberg continues, "The final delivery is what the end user sees as its part of the product and the service that they purchased. The lab or hospital at the receiving end really doesn't care what it took to get it there. We strive to find out what you need in order to get the delivery done and then work backwards. We prompt our customers to advise when they need to have the goods and then we get it there in an economical manner. We also ask: What unusual requirements does the destination have that need to be addressed ahead of time? This takes a lot of communication with the sales and service groups."

"Safety and security is ranked topmost as a company priority and is a continued industry obligation as a result of 9/11," Stulberg informs. "Decisions are made with security and safety taken into account for all services provided. Growing technology has put further demands on the industry for precision. Twenty years ago we had no cell phones, no Global Positioning System (GPS), no satellite tracking, no pagers. We relied on drivers calling in on an 800 number to update us once a day on their progress and ETAs. Today's customers want down-to-the-minute ETAs. This allows both drivers and installation people to use their time more productively," she concludes.

Stulberg has been known to track government releases for her loads, such as an FDA approval, and work the timing of a pickup to coincide with the government release. She has also been known to visit trade show events with her customers to ensure that certain systems are connected correctly. Advance also actively assists companies in their reverse logistics lane, arranging foreign site pickups at the Canadian borders, delivering to a third-party location to complete repairs, and then returning to the foreign customer.

By establishing a strong relationship with your service provider and working together to streamline processes continually enables a win-win situation for both parties. Using Advance's example with the changes made by its diagnostic customer, Advance mastered untapped territory such as border clearance time lines and developed new distribution options for its customer. This helped Advance to evolve into a global service provider. For the customer, expectations were fully met, plus some, with new effective ideas for cost savings, better control and safety conditions, and improved delivery time lines. As stated earlier in this chapter, do not let the relationship with your service provider get stagnant. Seek out a company such as Advance who will continually work hard for you and your business.

WHERE CAN THE COSTS BE REDUCED?

Not only are there brokerage, clearance, and transportation costs to consider when thinking "outside of the box," there are elements of the entire process that can be revamped for cost achievements. Let us take a couple of case studies to analyze where the thought process is another element to improve areas.

Case Study No. 1

- **Interested importer** — John Casey. John works for a reputable diagnostic company in the U.S. He plans to import innovative medical diagnostic equipment and patient monitoring systems.
- **His challenge** — To improve efficiency and speed of supply chain while increasing customer satisfaction.
- **Solution** — Either via the broker or in house, establish warehousing facilities at a distribution center in Europe and Canada. Services include the set up of European stock availability systems at the order

processing location in France and the management of customs clearance procedures.

- **Results** —
  - ☐ Increased competitive position
  - ☐ Increased speed of order turnaround and delivery
  - ☐ Improved access to European market
  - ☐ Streamlined business processes

Case Study No. 2

- **Interested importer** — Jesse Bryant. Jesse works for a research company that focuses on diabetes. He offers diabetics a relatively pain-free alternative to traditional glucose testing.
- **His challenge** — Carve out a niche for a start-up in a mature market by ensuring efficient distribution to multiple marketing channels.
- **Solution** — A fully outsourced logistics network via the broker or another third-party provider that will include order and inventory management, transportation, warehouse and accounts receivable, and customer service.
- **Results** —
  - ☐ Focus on core competency
  - ☐ Successful launch of new product
  - ☐ Retain working capital

The case studies above offer "outside" thinking. The more business you give to your service provider, the more leverage you should have toward achieving reduced rates/fees. The ideas presented above can be achieved if discussed with your service provider for rethinking your new or current global process for your marketed product. The main area that must always remain in your control is the clearance process. A company should never outsource this activity. You may leave only the "transmission" to Customs and the OGAs for the broker to handle. All clearance activities should remain in house; provide the information to be given for clearance to the broker(s). Otherwise, you will place yourself at a liability risk that incorrect information will be used.

PERFORM A COST ANALYSIS: WHERE SHOULD YOU LOOK FOR COST BUILDUPS?

We are often asked: Do you really know how much you are spending on your total logistics operation? Global logistics-related costs are dynamic and do not readily fit with traditional accounting methods. The accounting difficulties become more pronounced when trying to determine costs for a particular operation, customer, or location, or to evaluate, outsource, or find gain-share opportunities. Importers need to identify and determine their logistics costs. In Chapter 2, we explained certain areas of costs involved with clearing and delivering an imported shipment. Further below, we will better describe some of the costs and additional charges that might be incurred to raise further awareness.

An Import Department can provide a cost analysis by gathering all charges incurred on an import and providing a complete breakdown of costs. You must then look to the agreed Incoterm, as explained in Chapter 2, as to who has ownership of what transaction (such as freight and insurance) and at which location. If you currently are procuring product from a foreign supplier who is delivering the shipment to your door and absorbing all associated costs, you should review the breakdown of the unit price total they charge you. Have the Import Department then provide the costs that would be incurred if you were to take ownership of the clearance and deliveries. Compare the costs. Does what the Import Department provides reflect a higher or lower total cost? You may be subjected to unnecessary added costs and an unfair unit pricing.

When preparing a request for proposal, it can be helpful to review the areas in which import costs are required to be paid. Then there is complete understanding between buyer and seller of how, why, and where you will be charged. Some companies utilize activity-based costing to help manage and benchmark their logistics costs. They may evaluate their logistics costs in total or by function. A third-party freight payment company can be considered to handle all your transportation and brokerage costs. Ensure that the payment company has your most current fee and rate figures and knows to reject any accessorial fees not currently negotiated on the fee structure. They should bring these accessorial fees to your attention to challenge and evaluate with the service provider.

In addition to paying for the product, an inbound supply chain needs to budget for freight, insurance, duties, and other taxes and costs on imported goods. Provided below are standard logistics costs to improve understanding:

- **Packaging** — Depending on the quantity and type of goods involved, you should check the cost of packaging for export to the U.S. The packaging may be carried out by the company that you purchase the goods from, or you may need to hire the services of an independent company to pack boxes or containers. Special packaging material outside the normal scope of standard packaging must be included and listed separately on the commercial invoice for Customs clearance with the fair market value, as it is a dutiable item for clearance.

- **Freight** — The costs of transporting your imported goods to your place of business may include several steps:
  - ☐ The transport of the goods from the foreign factory or distributor where you purchase to the point of departure; for example, a foreign shipping port where the product will be loaded onto a ship or to an airport for loading onto an aircraft.
  - ☐ The transport of the goods from the foreign country to the U.S. Observe the surcharge rates, as they can fluctuate frequently.
  - ☐ The transport of the goods from the U.S. arrival point to you; for example, from the U.S. port or border to your premises.
- **Carriers** — Carriers charge freight costs, handling, and servicing fees.
- **Storage, demurrage, port charges** — Hopefully, you will not have these charges, unless your shipment does not clear on time. Some service providers will not charge reefer storage at the U.S. port.
- **Insurance** — The goods will need to be insured during all stages of the process and you should ensure that there is a clear understanding between you and the company from which you purchase as to who has responsibility. For example, the supplier may agree to arrange insurance from their factory to the port, but expect you to arrange for insurance from that point on. If you, as the importer, are paying for the insurance, you cannot deduct the insurance value from the invoice value. In all cases, the forwarder must be insured in the event that one of the containers damages the steamship line's vessel. However, for damaged or lost product, either buyer or seller can have that cost secured via the agreed Incoterm. Larger companies may have a global insurance policy to cover any damage or lost freight; therefore, it is unnecessary to pay a supplier to secure additional insurance.
- **Duties** — The burden is on the importer for the payment of Customs duty. If you entrust money to a broker for the payment of Customs duties and these monies are not forwarded to Customs for any reason, the importer is still liable for the debt. If the product is not classified correctly, the duty rate assessed may be higher than what it should be. This area should be part of your broker audit. Request a report from the broker that states when a payment was made to Customs on your behalf. As the importer, you may also elect to arrange for payment directly to Customs on your own accord.
- **Customs valuation** — The value for duty of imported goods or "Customs value" is the amount on which Customs tariff duty rates are calculated. If the value is incorrect on the invoice, you may be overcharged duties since the duty rate is calculated against the entered value of a shipment; that is, value minus any deductions allowed by Customs.

(Dutiable additions and nondutiable deductions are discussed further in Chapter 7.) This amount may not be the same as the amount paid for the goods, as deductions from and/or additions to that amount paid are sometimes necessary. The foreign shipper, who purchases goods and sells them to a U.S. importer at a delivered price, shows the cost of the goods to his firm on the invoice instead of the delivered price.

■ **Security fee** — A security fee may be charged by airlines, steamship lines, truckers, and railways for the additional new security measures that must be put forth to ensure security, such as meeting Advance Manifest Ruling requirements.

■ **War risk surcharge fee** — This is another security measure that may show up as "ISS" on your airline or broker bill. ISS is an International Security Surcharge/War Risk Surcharge related to upgraded security since 9/11. Importers may have seen this charge on a broker bill as one line item for collectable freight charges, but carriers have now broken it down into more detailed charges. Not all countries are charging both a security "and" a war risk surcharge to importers. Depending on your business lanes, your costs should only show one ISS charge, which encompasses both the security and war risk surcharge. For security fees, you may not see all the charges broken out as some of the air waybills lump the totals to include: Pickup, ISS (War Risk Surcharge), Sec. Fee (Security), A/L FSC (Airline Fuel Surcharge), and/or ISC (International Service Charge) — all included in the air freight. The airline handling is usually billed out at cost, based on what the broker is billed at destination. You should investigate further if you see unfamiliar charges on a bill of lading/waybill. For example, if the airline handling fee is listed and then a separate airline document fee is listed, you should request that the broker verify accuracy and clarification with the airline, or you may contact them directly. Listed costs should be closely monitored as some may be bogus and have no basis. Standard fees incurred by airlines/steamship line providers are:

☐ Documents
☐ Airline handling
☐ Pickup
☐ Security fee
☐ ISS
☐ A/L FSC
☐ ISC

■ **MPF** — Informal entries have a reduced MPF payout as explained in Chapter 2. If you do take advantage of an informal entry when it justifiably applies to your shipment valued under $2,000, you may be paying more MPF than required. The minimum and maximum are different dollar ranges, depending on the entry being informal or formal. Work with your broker to identify qualified shipments for information clearance.

■ **HMF** — As explained in Chapter 2, HMF has no cap. This fee could be costly to ocean importers. Bringing your product into a U.S. port and paying high HMF fees may not be necessary when you could ship to a foreign port such as Montreal and transport in bond through Canada to a U.S. port for clearance. The Customs website lists all the qualified ports of entries. Since there is no cap on this fee, numerous individuals in the importing industry have attempted to have this tax removed, or have a min./max., only to be rejected by the Court of International Trade. The bases for rejected requests were technical in nature, relying on interpretations of several provisions in the U.S. Constitution. The court has rejected and continues to reject all importer arguments.

■ **Miscellaneous brokerage fees** — Watch for added fees not previously negotiated; for example, a 15 percent "effort" surcharge. Effort for what? Also, messenger fees of $15. Some brokers may charge this for just having a runner pick up your documents from the port. This cost should be part of their service and already incorporated into your final broker fee unless there is a special request outside the normal pickup route. Do not permit abbreviated, truncated, or coded payment descriptions. Do not permit the lumping of various charges together or insufficient backup documentation for anything paid on your behalf. You must have some type of audit process to ensure that you are being billed correctly.

■ **Product payment** — Ensure that your foreign supplier does not double charge. Under Incoterms, "Delivered Duty Paid" (DDP), the supplier is responsible for everything, including delivery to your door, and you pay for this amount in your unit pricing. You may still get billed separately for transportation costs, with the bill going directly to your Accounts Payable Department. Watch out for double dipping.

■ **Exchange rates** — Are the exchange rates in your favor this week? When the invoiced amount is in foreign currency, it will be converted to U.S. dollars at the rate in force on the day the documents are presented to Customs. U.S. Customs operates a two-week exchange-rate period, with the information published one week in advance. The information can be obtained from any Customs Service Office or by subscribing to a Customs news and information package.

- **Customs charges** — Customs may charge miscellaneous service fees; for example, if you had made a request to Customs to "expedite" a shipment or if your shipment was moved to an examination site. You will not only pay the transportation arrangements, but you will also pay for the Customs inspector's time in the event it was an examination brought on by yourself, for failure to meet all Customs requirements.
- **Regulatory costs** — The OGAs may also charge miscellaneous fees for inspections. If you request an expedited release with another government agency, it will also charge for the extra service. You may also need to register your product with a government agency for a fee.
- **Foreign supplier fees** — This fee refers to the same message as noted in "Product Payment," however, evaluate all costs that your foreign supplier charged you. Eye any "Exporter of Record" costs when you did not agree to that responsibility. Unless you agreed to "Ex Works" on your sales agreement, you should not see this fee. Routinely, even if the supplier advises you are the Importer of Record, in actuality, they were, as the shipper is required to be responsible. Advise them to refer to their Exporter of Record document, prepared by their forwarder, for confirmation. As well, if they charged special packaging costs, clarify that you had made this request or it was justifiably required to ship a certain product. Research any costs your foreign supplier may attempt to add to your unit pricing to see if you are already paying them elsewhere, such as packing or transportation costs.

WHERE ARE THE FUNDS GENERATED FROM THE SECURITY FEES PAID BY IMPORTERS APPLIED?

Increased security and war risk surcharges are on the rise. Security charges that service providers are charging are passed along at cost to importers. In addition, the DHS is now making a stronger initiative towards more port compliance/security and vessel security (read more on security in Chapter 9). This move equates to increased surcharges if implemented. Security costs are higher in certain ports of export, so there will not be one set fee. The fees are non-negotiable for importers and fluctuate depending on where you are exporting to the U.S. Every country has its own charges. The U.S. has a larger security surcharge than other countries, about $0.15 per kilogram. This procedure has been going on since 9/11. The reason for the charge is that the insurance cost for the airlines has increased so dramatically, it must be passed on to the consumers. The changes that are being or have been made are:

1. The TSA continues to update the security regulations for aircraft operators in order to improve the security in all the areas where cargo moves. This includes new computer systems for access controls; for example, swipe cards and enhanced perimeter security.
2. The TSA and the DHS have forced airlines and airports to increase security focusing on:
    a. Criminal background checks for all employees must now be run.
    b. Additional screening measurements must take place on those who have access to the aircraft for any amount of time.
    c. Stowaway screening.
    d. New security requirements for unattended aircrafts and the air cargo area (cameras, video, etc.).
    e. Recurring checks on existing employees.
3. Increased exams worldwide, both inbound and outbound. Some airports and airlines inspect more than 30 percent of the cargo they are moving.
4. Targeting of high-risk U.S.-bound cargo. Airports and Customs have increased staffing and training to target any potentially dangerous cargo coming into the U.S.
5. Implementation of X-rays for screening cargo (applicable to both inbound and outbound cargo).
6. Improved computer systems collaborating information of known and unknown shippers.
7. Effectively designed (improved) systems that aim to avoid the need to search every passenger or every piece of cargo.

In short, there are multiple improvements being made every day within the airlines and airports. The cost of the new computer systems, increased staff for security, and exams and screenings continue to increase both security and war risk surcharges. If you are an importer who has not experienced detainments, you are fortunate. Detainments may now slow down your cargo, as security has contributed to numerous delays with other shipments. With all the new security, procedures, obligations, and costs, a standard broker fee rate list can reflect a variety of items. To explain, let us examine a shipment from a foreign supplier located in the U.K. who is shipping to the U.S. port in Chicago, with charges in British Pounds (GBP). Involved items will include:

- Airfreight rate into Chicago £x.xx per kilogram
- Collection for next day daily truck £xx.xx plus xx pence per kilogram
- Special collection available on request
- Processing and handling £xx.xx plus xx pence per kilogram

- Fuel surcharge £x.xx per kilogram
- Aviation security £x.xx per kilogram
- War risk fee £x.xx per kilogram
- Storage in a temperature facility (strive to obtain free storage days from U.S. arrival)
- Trucking to a U.S. port to final destination (depends on weight)
- Entry fee $xx.xx (negotiate first two line items as free, then $x.xx per line item after the first two)
- FDA entry $xx.xx
- Terminal fee $xx.xx
- Handling charge $xx.xx
- Additional $xx.xx per day reefer storage fee, if applicable.

The above category rates would not include any local taxes or duties and would not include insurance, but would be subject to standard International Air Transport Association (IATA) regulations. IATA represents over 270 airlines comprising 95 percent of international scheduled air traffic.

You have just been supplied with areas in which costs are incurred and where they can easily become inflated if not monitored and controlled. It is important that you plan accurately what these costs are going to be and also plan your imports so as to avoid any "forgotten" entities that will delay your shipment. The following checklist provides the main items you should include in your budget.

- **Exfactory wholesale price** — The amount that you are being charged by the supplier for goods that you are importing.
- **Freight to ship** — The cost of getting the goods from the supplier to the main transport facility.
- **Documentation, Customs agent** — This fee is likely to be incurred before the goods leave the country of export.
- **Handling charges** — The cost of getting goods on or off the freight service onto the port; for example, moving a container off a truck.
- **Packaging** — If there is a large quantity of goods, or they require special packaging, then it is likely that you will either have to pay the supplier or another company to pack them for export.
- **Foreign bank charges** — Any fees the supplier's bank may charge to complete a transaction, which may be transferred to you.
- **Calculate the exchange rate** — This fluctuates daily, so you should make yourself aware of the rate when the transaction occurs.
- **International freight costs** — The cost of transport between countries; for example, airfreight or sea shipping. Fuel surcharges can fluctuate.

- **Marine (transport) insurance** — The goods must be insured while in transit.
- **Port charges** — Charged by the companies or organizations that handle the goods on arrival.
- **Custom duties or taxes** — Payable to the Customs Service before the goods can be released to you. This cost will include MPF and HMF (if applicable) and the amount depends on the duty rate determined by your product and country of origin.
- **Excise and/or income tax** — Depending on the port, if your company does not have a presence in that country or state, your product value may be subject to an excise and/or income tax. Research the U.S. port in which you intend to ship to determine if your product is subject to either tax. An excise tax is 6.6 percent of your product's invoice value. Puerto Rico is considered part of the U.S. domain for importing and applies these taxes. Tax exemptions and/or reimbursement can be an option and must be explored with the tax authorities in Puerto Rico.
- **Broker clearance charges** — Broker will charge a fee for each transaction.
- **Delivery and handling charges (from port to destination)** — This covers pickup of the goods from the ship or aircraft and delivery to your premises.
- **Bank charges (local)** — If you would transfer funds to a foreign bank, your own bank would charge a fee for the transaction.

All imported goods are subject to Customs requirements, which can include the payment of Customs charges. As explained in earlier chapters, the product must be classified, the origin of the product established, and the value of the products, insurance, and freight costs must be determined. On an invoice being used for Customs clearance, it is vitally important that the valuation be accurate on the declaration for all business transactions that may have a dutiable value. This matter is discussed in greater detail in Chapter 7 and should be studied by the Sales and Purchasing Departments. The sales price between the importer and foreign supplier must be captured and an invoice must be provided for clearance. In the event the product is a "free of charge" item, an invoice still needs to be prepared reflecting a valid Customs value for that product. This invoice is referred to as a "Proforma Invoice." Customs may audit certain areas of an entry and evidence of the following would need to be readily available: purchase invoice, manufacturer's costs, freight and insurance costs, product sample information such as catalogs or brochures, evidence of origin, proof of payment, etc.

SETTING UP METRIC PROGRAMS FOR COST SAVINGS

Let us assume at this point that you have become educated in all the fees for your inbound supply chain movement. You have completed a thorough cost analysis. Why not re-evaluate what you are currently paying? Compute the costs of various functions (for example, ocean freight costs, inland domestic trucking costs, current document turnover fee costs) and the savings if eliminated under a total ownership program with a service provider. Evaluate what your current costs are and reduce and eliminate those that do not apply. This may incorporate revisiting service providers, renegotiating contracts, or a simple request that a fee be removed. Lean on brokers to make improvements. Let them know your ultimate customer focus. "Premetrics" in a customer-focus world includes:

1. **Perfect order** — On time, complete, damaged free, customer satisfaction
2. **Total system inventory**
3. **Cash-to-cash cycle time**— Time you pay for the material to the time you get money back on that product
4. **ROI** — Return on investments
5. **Determined cycle times**
6. **Correct billing for seller, buyer, and ultimate customer**

AVOIDING THE HARBOR MAINTENANCE FEE: FEASIBLE OR JUST MORE COSTLY?

As stated earlier in this chapter, HMF costs can be high because there is no maximum limit on how much you will be required to pay. If your global procurement lane permits, consider importing into Montreal to avoid HMF. There are some pitfalls, unfortunately, with congestion at the railhead, so you need to weigh your options. It is not recommended that you ship via ocean if your U.S.-based inventory is running lean or you are expecting to meet a customer's tight ETA time frame. However, if the time frame turnaround is in your favor, shipping via a foreign port such as a Canadian port and then moving by truck or rail into the U.S. may save you big cash. As stated earlier in Chapter 2, an HMF fee is 0.125 percent and multiplied by your invoice or entered value. You may or may not be eligible for deductions depending on the Incoterm. HMF is considered an additional tax of which the funds are returned to U.S. ports.

The downside to railing is that intermodal railyards can become a freight transportation gridlock. Your shipment can either miss being placed on the rail because of too much congestion or it can be placed on the railcar and still not go anywhere due to strike or acts of nature. As described earlier in this chapter, a Senate Bill S. 2279 (the Maritime Security Act) that could successfully pass was introduced to put forth efforts that would require importers to have only five days for their containers to sit on the dock without clearing Customs before it is seized and placed into General Order. Routinely, fifteen calendar days are the allowance that ports make to importers to get their shipments cleared and on their way; however, there are the individuals who abuse this clearance window. Some importers take advantage of the situation and purposely leave their containers at the port so as to obtain "free" warehousing space via the port terminals or they may put off clearing the product and placing it on their inventory books to save on taxes.

Port staffs are not naive to these creative importers and their ideal scenarios that benefit them, but "security" is now the top priority for ports and proponents are trying to get the support needed from Congress to have the bill passed. It is unsafe for a container to sit unsupervised at a port, even if it is moved to a bonded warehouse off the pier for storage. However, if Customs will not clear the shipment within the five-day time span, what options are available for importers? Bonded warehouse storage could be an option and should be explored with your service provider if the bill should pass.

Security breaches can still happen aside from U.S. ports. As stated in Chapter 2, theft and vandalism have occurred in the centralized exam sites. Are importers able to recoup these costs? It all depends on the Port Director's evaluation. Importers will need to continue to remain abreast of the latest rules and regulations for U.S. ports, as well as railroads and steamship lines, that may very well begin collecting fines for intermodel equipment that overstays its welcome on terminal grounds. All of the loads preclear through the AMS, so in actuality, the railroads give away free days at destination when, in fact, many of the containers are already cleared.

BE AWARE OF PORT CONGESTION

Rail congestion, equipment shortages, and labor strikes have been the source of cargo delays as well. The ports have been relatively trouble-free in the past, however, as import volume grows, they are beginning to get hit with unexpected equipment shortages, intermodel rail congestion, and job actions by harbor truckers. If you currently are an importer, you may already be aware of how often port situations, such as congestion or strikes, have had an effect on your shipments. You may need to consider rerouting any pending shipments to the

U.S. This would not be considered "port shopping," which is the term Customs uses when importers have problems clearing shipments in a particular port and decide to switch their business lane to another in order to try to avoid delays caused by Customs or OGAs.

This situation does not reflect favorably on the importer, however, certain circumstances can justify the switch in business lanes. If your new route makes just as much business sense by entering through the port of Boston as opposed to New York, and your switch is based truly on logistics, then this would not be considered "port shopping." It may be worthwhile to see if you can save money on inland trucking moves, establish a distribution unit near the Boston port, or get closer to the new research facility. Certain railroad lines, from the west or east coast, can be badly congested with ocean carriers openly expressing concern about the ability of the west-east network to handle peak-season intermodel volumes. Total container volume continues to increase and some ports can handle the growth better than others. Approximately 772,000 consignees imported to the U.S. in 2004. This is a 35 percent increase in the total number of consignees from 1998 to 2003 (www.cbp.gov). Cargo volumes are projected to increase continually and several ports are up for major expansion projects. Terminals are implementing productivity technology, such as optical-character-recognition devices at the gates and computerized terminal-management systems in the container yards. They are also expanding their acreage for more space. A new problem that is becoming a concern is the steel shortage experienced in China in 2004. Most of the world's marine containers are manufactured in China and some factories reportedly were unable to fill 50 percent of their orders. Shipping lines rely on a steady influx of new containers to accommodate growing cargo volumes. If cargo import trade continues to rise, ports could be in a tenuous position to try to accommodate the expanding needs.

EXPLORE ALTERNATIVE PORTS

There are alternate ports that can be explored that still make good business sense and would not be considered "port shopping." Some ports advertise how much better it would be to import through their location. They offer congestion-free highway/rail transfer, open port gates twenty-four hours daily and seven days a week, continual truck turn times of about thirty minutes, warehousing storage, security, better rail equipment availability and transloading, etc. These services lead to quicker delivery turnaround, as your shipment will not be sitting in a particular port due to congestion. With all the advertised alternatives, it is worthwhile to consider other ports for any new or existing transportation routes.

HOW CAN IMPORT COSTS BE REDUCED AND DELIVERY TURNAROUND IMPROVED?

There are ways in which you can save money in transportation. More can be saved with air modes of transportation if you are flexible about your shipping dates to allow your carrier/agent to coordinate that you get on a full flight. Let us consider some commonly asked questions:

1. Why are the costs between transportation businesses so varied? Some transportation businesses try to attract business by offering a fixed, low price based on an optimal shipment. Since all transportation businesses are purchasing services from other providers on your behalf, your best option is to choose a shipper or service provider that charges a fixed agency fee and bills you the other charges at cost.

2. Is shipping safe for delicate instruments? Shipping delicate product is very safe if you have a reliable carrier involved that offers good packaging with an experienced loading and unloading staff. Some products may also require wider areas and take up more space on the airline, truck, or container. This will affect your rate. It may not be heavy by weight, but the dimensions take up the space, which means less room for other importers' cargo. The carrier will determine if your shipment will make a flight or vessel by the dimensions you provide. In addition, sellers and buyers should ensure that the shippers are aware of hazardous products or temperature requirements. These can be risk factors for a shipment, if overlooked, because certain carriers will not transport hazardous or infectious products. Other carriers may not be able to move hazardous products as a special certification or permit may be required for that carrier.

3. What risks are involved with importing? While hundreds of products are moving by air, ship, rail, or truck each week, expecting to arrive without impairment or damage, there are still risks in transporting your products. Usually when something does go wrong, it routinely is associated with inconveniences due to weather, carrier scheduling, freight bumped from a confirmed shipping date, and carrier or exam delays. The more serious problem, lost freight, is always a possibility. These problems can increase importation costs.

4. What should you look for when choosing an agent, carrier, or service provider? Your choice should be based on recommendation and reputation. You should expect to pay a fair price and expect excellent service and communication from their departments. A written estimate should

be provided by the agent, carrier, or service provider detailing what is and is not included.

5. In what type of equipment should you arrange for your product to be shipped? For the inland move from the U.S. port to the final destination, determining the type of trucking service to be used is the responsibility of the buyer, to be relayed to the carrier. If an odd-sized shipment requires a flat-bed trailer or an air ride trucking service, this needs to be arranged even prior to the shipment dispatching from the foreign supplier, as the equipment may not be available. Also, you need to verify with your Receiving Department that they will have the man-power to offload the shipment and have adequate warehousing space available. Special bracing requirements should also be relayed to the carrier so they may arrange to reserve the equipment needed for your load. Certain bracing can loosen and fall down or become uneven under pressure. In any case, while a product is en route is not the time to introduce new packaging requirements. Some products require thermal blankets to assist with temperature control. A carrier or even the broker may purchase them for you and warehouse them until utilized. Thermal blankets used for an export need clearance when returned. The broker may offer to take ownership of the import and export clearance pro-cesses as part of their service. Any items shipped should be well marked, as missing equipment can be a problem. Include a packing list in your paperwork.

6. What else can speed things up? When using overseas transport, have the purchase order indicate that the bill of lading will be issued as an "ex-press" bill of lading as opposed to an original. An original bill of lading must be made available at the U.S. port. If not mailed to the correct address, your shipment cannot be released from the port and will be detained until the original is located and routed to the port.

DELIVERY TURNAROUND

Importers need to understand how long it will take to get their shipment re-leased. Entry clearances turnaround depends on the type of entry filed, what the merchandise is, whether or not it needs to be examined, and how many errors were made by the importer, broker, or foreign supplier. An airfreight perishable item can be cleared and delivered within twenty-four to forty-eight hours or can take three to four weeks. Know when your shipment is going to arrive. In the first two chapters, we discussed the benefits of prealerting your Import Department and ensuring that all checks are done prior to order placement. Establish the "prealert" system as a preparatory requirement for your global supply chain procurement efforts.

MISCONCEPTIONS OF DELAYS

Misconception as to where a delay has occurred is very common. If you have an internal company Import Department based in Pittsburgh and your product was physically imported into the port of New York, certain individuals might perceive that their product is physically in Pittsburgh. Further adding to the confusion, if the product is being detained by Customs, individuals may be of the impression that your company's Import Department is holding it hostage. Communication is important for those striving to understand the holdup on their import purchase order. Is it Customs? Did the shipment even leave overseas at all? Is it lost? If you are a requester and are looking for your product, it is best not to make assumptions, but to contact the appropriate parties, usually the Import Department, to trace where the detainment actually exists.

Foreign suppliers should also ensure that their shipment has left the port of export. Often times, a shipment is produced and trucked to the port of export only to be bumped from its scheduled sailing date. Other times, a requester in the U.S. is waiting for the product, only to learn that the delay is not due to Customs or port congestion, but that the foreign supplier was behind on their manufacturing schedule and did not notify their buyer of the delayed production.

ESTABLISHING TIME LINES

Reports are great to establish in order to view where time lines are and which process area or action items take the longest time. They also help people to understand where the delay is occurring. For example: on 12/21/04, Stanley, of the Sales and Marketing Department, with the assistance of his Import Department, developed a tracking report for all his import shipments from Australia since the beginning of the year. The report was forwarded to other planners involved in the marketed product to provide them with receiving details and results of each shipment. Stanley elected to prepare this report to support his argument with a certain supply chain planner who was placing the blame for customer dissatisfaction on the company's internal departments — perhaps within the RA, Receiving, or Import Departments, but not the Procurement or Sales Departments.

Recently, there have been multiple backorders with certain customers. After reviewing the report, it became evident that all shipments were shipped, released, delivered, and received into inventory within an acceptable time period. It also became obvious that the supply chain orders did not correspond with what the customer had placed. As a result, not enough material was ordered. The moral of this story is to avoid making quick assumptions as to what you believe is occurring and also avoid "finger pointing." It will benefit all parties involved to verify each process time line and to eliminate the areas in which questionable delays exist.

Digging to the root causes of the problem can save time and money. Far too often, supply chain gaps are misunderstood and can continue to snowball into larger problems on future shipments. A healthy best practice for any supply chain operation is to communicate and work together as a team to avoid assumptions where missteps are generated that can escalate unnecessarily. In Chapter 4, we will discuss where other internal company departments still exist as missing links in supply chain planning and how by instituting "communication" as a best practice, a firm will create a strong global supply chain operation. As well, time lines are further covered for registering regulated products to ensure an accurate ETA to the ultimate customer.

4

OTHER DEPARTMENTS THAT PLAY AN IMPORTANT ROLE: THE MISSING LINKS IN GLOBAL PROCUREMENT SUPPLY CHAIN PLANNING

An importer's supply chain system is critical to a company's success. You need a trusted partner who will be with you every step of the way, especially one who has walked the path before. The sharing and dissemination of key information across every step of the product's supply chain is crucial. Success begins with knowing the types of services available within your own corporation. Why is this important? Because these services, groups, and departments have methods to reduce supply chain costs and ensure reliable delivery quotes, while keeping the company in compliance. Not knowing that these internal resources exist has been an obstacle for many large organizations, but this obstacle can be overcome. Communication is the key. Conversation is "free" and can open the gates and allow the flow of knowledge between the various departments, promoting an understanding of each other's purposes and processes.

Why is it that some departments choose not to communicate? Trudy Cole, MA in Counseling Psychology, has over twenty years of experience working within "systems" such as the Army, Health Maintenance Organizations (HMOs), and county government. Her assignments have provided her with the opportunity to observe how subsystems communicate and interact with one another. Cole provides professional insight into the corporate world mentality and why departments tend to not network properly. She begins by explaining, "Individual departments want to be individualized, because to do otherwise would mean more work. Working as a team requires much effort on everyone's part, starting from the top. Although working as a team has its pros and cons, it usually means additional responsibilities and keeping boundaries. Whereas working individually requires being responsible for one piece of the information. Working individually also means standing apart from others, which can create competition between departments. Some companies would rather have each department responsible for its own piece, so if a problem surfaces with a product, one department can take the blame. If all departments work together as a team, all members will be held accountable."

"Additionally," Cole continues, "communication is an art. While communication is important, not everyone can communicate effectively. As a result, miscommunication, misunderstanding, misperceived messages, and looking foolish in front of peers may come to pass. As a society, we can have difficulty communicating to our own family members, let alone communicating to strangers. So to ask for departments to communicate to one another, it can be done, but it takes great communication skills, open mindedness, and effective listening. In meetings, there usually is the one colleague who does not censor anything being said, but will chatter continuously. Then sits the "mouse" colleague, from a different department, who does not say a word, but has much to offer. Periodically, it can feel like extremes in the work environment. Where is the balance to bring the departments together? It begins with each individual, regardless of their role or title, to be a leader, role model, and to take personal accountability and perseverance to get the communication flowing. Individuals in a supply chain operation should identify, within themselves, their strengths to advance the operation to a new plateau. Equally important, they should identify any of their weaknesses that could impair a supply chain. It takes a team to build an empire, but only one person to render the operation ineffective."

Some companies will take various levels of management, such as team leaders, to an off-site location and basically psychoanalyze their personalities. Will they work well as a team? Will the department(s) and overall company benefit from their alliance? Are their visions in sync with each other? Do they have different work ethics, habits, or processes they have adopted that collide with their work partner when making department or company decisions? Other companies have circulated surveys on management or departments to other internal departments within the company. This is an opportunity to receive feedback on how others view the performance of a particular department and its management style. Often, it helps to raise awareness within the company that such a department exists. Conducting an evaluation and soliciting feedback within supply chain operational departments would allow for better understanding of the roles and possibly produce fresh new ideas.

GET THE MEETINGS STARTED:
THE FIFTEEN- TO THIRTY-MINUTE CHATS

As a very easy first step to ensure a successful outcome of a global procurement project, arrange a meeting with the right individuals to flow-chart and diagram the involved processes and services. Networking groups that search for new ideas or an improved process are, more then ever, playing pivotal roles in the development of implementations and solutions. Whether it be for a new capital project or revisiting an already-established supply chain operation, arranging "spot-check" or "touch-base" meetings is highly advantageous. It not only puts everyone on the same page, it also helps to identify missing links in the processes. Does someone in the Planning Department know someone in the RA or Environmental Safety Department that might need to be involved with a global project involving chemicals or pharmaceuticals?

Arrange supply chain meetings with your internal and external counterparts. Include the forwarder, broker, trucker, planners, foreign supplier, Import Representative, Transportation Representative, Procurement Representative, etc. Ensure that everyone understands the steps involved. When building a diagram of the processes, assign names and responsibilities to each process step. In Chapter 6, you will learn the importance for each of these individuals or departments to make good decisions, as it will have a winning effect on others involved in the supply chain operation. If you cannot meet face to face, have monthly "touch-base" conference calls. Even if there is a mutual sense among the responsible parties that everything is flowing smoothly, and another meeting or conference call is not worthwhile, still make the effort to speak, even for fifteen minutes. You will be surprised how topics surface that may assist or even further improve a process.

IDENTIFYING THE OTHER CAST OF CHARACTERS

As we move further into the import and procurement process, you are being provided with the specific areas that will help your existing inbound supply chain operation or being exposed to a first-time global procurement project. The first level of detail is essentially oriented around people. Knowing who they are and how they can be identified can be one of the hurdles to overcome. What can they do to streamline or add value? How important are they to the global procurement project? Picture yourself for a moment, sitting in a meeting discussing your future or current international supply chain process. You are analyzing the steps involved and evaluating the costs and turnaround times. Are all the right players in the room with you? Let us consider cost and compliance concerns. If compliance is not met and clearance and transportation costs are not preidentified and negotiated, the global supply chain project is not going to work efficiently, or may not even break ground. Are the individuals who can provide the best representation for these areas in the meeting room with you?

Procurement efforts strive for the best price and delivery turnaround, but multiple factors play a role in detaining the import process and inflating costs. When importing, one major factor is compliance — before transportation — even before procurement. It must be ensured, secured, and adhered to or a company will not even possess the import privilege needed to procure products globally. These detainments and delays directly affect the success and outcome of product distribution. The authors bring forth the "unsung heroes" in such meetings, those who strive to guarantee the continuous import privilege while reducing delivery turnaround and costs. Some of these individuals, for example, handle the FDA when this particular government agency elects to "drop by" unexpectedly for an inspection. These individuals also play a part with the other government agencies (OGAs) in determining your delivery turnaround, as they hold the key to a successful product registration. They know what makes a product "regulated" by another governing agency such as the FDA and how this will affect your "time lines." The "unsung heroes" are the individuals within a company's own RA, Import Operations, Compliance, and Transportation Departments. Far too often these departments are not consulted in a global procurement project.

Conversely, when these departments work together with a global supply chain operation, whether or not for regulated products, a company can save time, money, aggravation, and unnecessary steps and avoid noncompliance issues to ensure a continuous inbound supply chain course. Let us begin with discussing these various departments.

THE REGULATORY AFFAIRS DEPARTMENT: WHO ARE THEY AND WHAT ARE THEY ALL ABOUT?

A company's RA Department works to ensure that regulated products and activities comply with regulatory requirements such as drug listings, investigational research activities, medical device regulations, etc. in the U.S. and abroad. In partnership with the Quality Assurance Department, RA participates in the product launch and implementation of an international supply chain operation, monitors upcoming regulations and standards, and works with industry groups on issues that affect a company's activity. As mentioned in Chapter 1, a regulated product is anything with which another government agency, aside from Customs, must be involved in order to secure clearance. How would you know if another agency is required to clear your shipment? Generally, if it is anything other than a spare part or article, consult your RA, Health and Environmental Safety, and Import Departments. These departments can identify clearance and inland Department of Transportation profiles for a regulated and/or hazardous product.

Ordering a regulated product from a foreign supplier is not a hands-off task. There are shared ownership responsibilities that must be brought to the forefront of the process.

Jean Mazet, Regulatory Affairs Manager for a global health-care operation, has been in the regulatory industry for many years and has become an expert in her field. She offers advice to individuals involved with importing a regulated product line who wish to shorten their lead times to customers. Mazet states, "The biggest challenge when procuring product for a global supply chain operation is getting your company counterparts to tell RA what they are doing. The RA role isn't about telling a supply chain how to do its business. RA wants to help grease the wheels to 'make it happen.' Look to RA for regulatory import clearance consulting. The bottom line is if you prepare for the import, you'll have a much better chance of achieving success. Communicate, plan, and develop a rapport with the people you service, so they can provide you with the information you need before the government agency asks for it. When the importer understands what you must do to facilitate the entry, such as register their product for international business, and the benefit, they will join the team. A system should be established that puts RA in the planning process when a new product is being imported. This applies to both small special-research and quality-controlled samples, as well as production quantities. The most satisfying reward is when, after total training, the process is understood by all partners and a seamless, swift import is achieved."

The global sourcing professional must learn to approach RA early and find out what information is required. RA will work directly with the appropriate OGAs on your behalf to facilitate your entry. These agencies may include the FDA, USDA, CDC, EPA, etc. and they all speak their own languages and have their own best practices. Mazet explains, "The greatest challenge in meeting regulatory requirements for regulated products when working with regulated agencies is deciphering the 'Agency Speak.' For example, an import could be put 'On Hold' by an FDA Inspector, who will cite it as 'mislabeled' or 'mis-branded' as the reason for detention. That could actually mean 'they can't find it on the computer' or 'someone used an abbreviation on the entry and/or invoice document' and the FDA Inspector cannot match the abbreviation with the regulatory listed name."

RA speaks the government regulatory language, and with the input of the Import Department, breaks down the communication and zooms in on the clearance rejection. RA will also designate the key person to resolve the issue with the FDA directly, once the Import Department has confirmed that the clearance rejection was not due to a clerical error or hardcopy documentation request from the OGA. It is surprising how many imported products may have to receive clearance with any one of the OGAs. These agencies and what they essentially rule over are discussed further in Chapter 5.

Since 9/11, government requirements have been implemented that further challenge the RA Department. More specific information is required for each submission that may ultimately suspend the import planning. New bar-coding requirements for investigational blood samples and new Bioterrorism Prior Notice clearance for food importers (both discussed in Chapter 5) are typical examples.

"An example of the impact of new government regulations post 9/11 would be the new Bioterrorism Act (BTA)," Mazet comments. "Prenotification for the new BTA regulations are presenting a challenge as the products companies import may be subject to this regulation even if it is a single bottle for testing. That material may require the same prework as if it were a production quantity. Appropriate registrations and documentation must be created and wholly incorporated into the process."

Government agencies can audit a company at any given time. Mazet advises, "The FDA can audit anything it wants; but traditionally, they audit areas which present the greatest risk. The FDA will also audit the data provided by other departments to confirm that your data reflect what is actually being done. Their visits to your site can be an impromptu review. With this FDA best practice, they will perform a 'Risk-Based Assessment.' RA routinely will accompany the FDA at all times, as will representatives from the department being audited. The FDA will also visit foreign manufacturing sites from whom you import. In certain cases, this may be a prerequisite to accepting the goods into the U.S.," Mazet concludes.

Automate the Communication

RA can assist a supply chain in shortening clearance lead time by proactively identifying the requirement needed. In order to accomplish this, RA needs the requester's, purchasing agent's, and suppliers' assistance. By giving RA assistance, you help yourself. An automated purchase ordering system can accomplish this feat. Prior to placing an order with the foreign supplier, a requester or purchasing agent would complete an electronic import purchase order checklist form (IPO Form). The IPO form would consist of a product description, product composition, quantity, manufacturer, supplier, intended use, permits, and so forth.

The form would be considered a checklist for the requester to ensure that all import information required was captured. For example, if you are a pharmaceutical sample importer and your samples are ready to move to clinical trials, an Investigational New Drug (IND) Code is required. On the IPO Form, an "IND Code" would be a field referenced on the form as a checkpoint. If an IND Code applies for the particular imported product, the requester marks "yes" next to it (in the event the requester possesses that level of knowledge; otherwise, RA would determine this via the product description and intended use). The blank space next to the IND Code would be where RA would provide the actual IND Code for the requester. The requester would complete the IPO form and then hit "enter." The IPO form would electronically link to the Regulatory/Import Department's shared product listing database to cross-reference if the product was shipped previously and has the regulatory profile already established for the *same intended use intentions*. If the database does not find a match, the product is considered "new" and the database instantly creates a new record template for this product and the IPO form electronically continues on to RA. Also, if the "intended use" of the product is different, the database will consider this "new," as an intended use change from research to distribution could now entail a drug listing application requirement. In this situation, the requester's product is new and RA receives the IPO form. RA completes the regulatory information on the IPO form, which is then routed back to the requester with a prealert copy to the Import Department.

The requester is obligated to ensure that the field marked "Approved for Order" is marked prior to order placement. If it is not, RA provides an explanation. For example, the IND Code field is marked "yes," but the requester notices that an IND Code was not provided and a comment stating "IND Code application being processed" was inserted. The requester is reminded that he/she cannot import the product until RA successfully obtains an IND Code. This could take several weeks.

Automate the Regulatory Documentation

Some organizations may not have the luxury of automation available. An IPO form can still be routed via a manual process. An IPO form may be completed via a word-processed document and then may be scanned or faxed. First, it goes to the RA Department to review for regulatory information or to the Import Department in the event the product is redundantly ordered and does not have an intended use fluctuation. The requester would be responsible for ensuring whether or not the product being ordered is new or has changed its intended use from previous imports. It is ultimately the responsibility of the requesters to ensure that the Import Department has the required information to provide to the broker for clearance. It is also their responsibility to ensure that their foreign supplier is aware of what they will need to provide with the import documentation they prepare, such as an FDA End-User letter or USDA Guideline Declaration (Chapter 5).

Any regulatory information and requirement should be logged into a "shared" database, to which RA and an Import Department would have access. RA would log any new regulated product information into the database for the Import Department to utilize. All departments, outside of RA, would have "viewing" access only to the shared database. Field requirements would prompt for the product description, quantity, packaging, intended use, manufacturer's information, government requirements, etc. An electronic system is the recommended way to communicate regulatory information. It permits crystal-clear documentation and record retention of the transmission of information. Elimination of typographical errors or miscommunication if RA verbally provides regulatory information to the requester and Import Representative is one possible improvement. It also serves as a solid and reliable communication process for clearances in the event of a Customs or OGA audit.

Form an Alliance with Import and Regulatory Affairs Departments

A formed alliance between a company's Import and RA Departments would essentially streamline the process, since regulatory information must be transferred from RA to the Import Department once it is established. It is a great first step when a requester has been proactive by arranging and receiving product import registration via their RA Department, but a requester must guarantee that the process keeps going.

You proceed and have your product ordered and shipped, only to realize that an equally important second step was missed. The individuals responsible for the clearance process of your shipment, those who must provide the regulatory information to the OGAs, do not have the regulatory information. These people belong to the Import Department. Your shipment arrives and the government agency rejects your shipment. It may risk having to be re-exported back or destroyed under Customs' supervision. A best practice would be to develop a manual procedure or, more desirably, an automated database that transmits the information as presented on page 110 and ensures that the product import profile is complete. Automation would be the most recommended route because e-mails can get lost. Benefits include:

- Assurance that all needed information is in place at the time of importation.
- Reduced import and regulatory process cycle time.
- Product is delivered in a more timely fashion to the customer.
- Paperless systems are more convenient for reporting purposes, record retention, and audits.
- Ensures that compliance and regulatory issues are met.

Where Else Can a Regulatory Affairs Department Assist Me?

An effective RA Department will research and provide strategic plans for any development program, including full range of Investigation New Drug (IND), to New Drug Applications (NDA), to Medical Device Listing (MDL) regulatory services. It will offer both hands-on assistance and serve as an FDA liaison service, providing regulatory consulting throughout the regulatory process, from pre-IND planning and agency meetings through regulatory submissions (IND to NDA) and postmarketing activities. A good RA Department should be focused on obtaining the earliest regulatory approval possible. The sooner you consult with your RA counterpart on your global procurement project, the sooner you can begin business. A standard regulatory list of services would involve:

- Strategic drug development planning and consultation
- Product registration and follow-up of government approval and recording
- IND development, filing, and updates
- Drug master files
- Labeling requirements
- NDA planning, document review, and submission
- OGA liaison, such as the FDA, USDA, DEA, etc.
- Audits
- Coordinate FCC/RAD forms for computer/monitor imports
- Maintenance of current registration information and preparation and submittal of annual reports
- General regulatory services including labeling reviews and confidential internal document and facilities audits

Understanding Time Lines with Product Registration

As Jean Mazet mentioned earlier in this chapter, understanding the "Agency Speak" is vital. Equally critical is avoiding miscommunication, as it can often be a reason for poor planning. Whenever a global procurement project is planned for a regulated product and you have done all your legwork to avoid missing links, do not assume all work is complete. Just because RA has submitted the needed documents does not mean that all is well and the FDA received, approved, and loaded it into the Operational and Administrative System for Import Support (OASIS) database. (OASIS is an automated FDA system for processing and making admissibility determinations for shipments of foreign-origin FDA-regulated products seeking to enter domestic commerce. It is important that the information for a regulated product be complete and match the shipping documents at the port, including shipping labels.)

RA submitted the proper registration, provided you with an estimated time line of FDA approval for your product launch, the registration made its way to the FDA and, after FDA approval, the data made their way into the FDA database. However, just because RA mailed the product registration application does not always guarantee that the FDA received it or, if they did receive, did they approve? If they did approve, did they load it into their database? The FDA does not provide confirmation back to RA. It is important that RA follow up that the FDA completed all product registration steps for pending new imports.

When dealing with time lines for listed products, Mazet advises, "The FDA has annual company listing updates each January and June. RA is required to submit their company's most current listing information to the FDA twice a year. However, at this time, when an agency does listing updates, there is a backlog. This may mean your filing gets buried and takes the agency longer to get to your product registration. This is not the best time to submit a drug product listing. Avoid this hectic period, as it can cause an additional six (6)-week delay to your product launch. One technique that can be used is to send notices with special Post-it® notes on the documents written with colored pens to catch the registration agent's attention. A polite note stating 'Please Expedite' or 'Product – Import – Product,' will go a long way. FDA staff will try to accommodate you as long as you alert them to your situation. Also, remember the difference between an urgency and emergency. If you exaggerate your need, one day it may not be heeded," Mazet cautions.

Describing the Process to Describe the Time Lines

To continue describing time lines, let us consider medical device importers and the registration time lines they are up against. RA can identify whether registration information is required for your medical device–related product, which can be a chemical analyzer and/or reagents to an analyzer. RA can also assist in moving a product closer to an earlier product launch. The notion that medical device companies must maintain robust quality assurance systems to achieve regulatory compliance is not a new one.

What is new, however, is the opportunity for medical device companies to transform regulatory compliance from a diversified set of cost center activities to a core element of their most strategic and profit-focused product initiatives. Numerous medical device companies are leveraging collaborative solutions from automation for FDA compliance to drive profits through faster time-to-market and streamlined quality assurance and regulatory compliance. By developing a single information environment that ties together all product-related data and supporting documentation, some medical device companies are earning higher margins on the products they deliver and insulating themselves from costs arising from noncompliance.

Ken Edds, Sr. Director of Regulatory Affairs for a major in vitro diagnostics company, has worked from the ground up to streamline RA activities to achieve a quick turnaround with FDA product registrations. Edds advises, "A general goal of all companies is to enter the market quickly, while looking for automated solutions to make things happen more easily. Industry needs to understand that the FDA has the same goal and both parties keep metrics on that goal. If we count the number of days to clear a product registration, industry averaged around 100 days in 2003. A top-notch supply chain operation working with the RA Department could achieve this in fewer than sixty days. There is an incentive to get things done quickly."

Edds continues by explaining other areas that also affect time lines. He states, "When listing a medical device, a problem that can surface is RA keeps a list of products that are 'listed' and the FDA keeps a similar record. In this particular instance, a company's medical device information on the 'list' can quickly become a problem if your database differs from the FDA list. A company that alters any information from its 'list' may immediately put the FDA's 'list' out of date. Anytime a firm updates its medical device information, it causes a mismatch between the databases. For example, if the company name doesn't match with the FDA's list, your shipment doesn't clear Customs. A Manufacturer's Identification (MID) Code is transmitted at the time of entry as part of the clearance requirement. This MID advises Customs and the OGAs, such as the FDA, EPA, etc., which company is the 'ultimate' manufacturer of the product (not just the shipper). The MID Code and the Medical Device Listing name may need to be matched. Agencies are sometimes stretched thin and may be asked to audit and monitor dozens of products, so their tolerance for inaccurate information is small."

As a result, Edds developed a best practice to ensure that current information held by the government agencies such as the FDA is accurate. He explains, "The FDA advises us to go to its website and look up a Medical Device Listing (MDL) Number. You will find in this website a 'what to do and when to do it' list. The link is http://www.fda.gov/cdrh/devadvice/342.html. The FDA has really good Internet coverage for most topics. Keeping up to date with what the FDA wants to know from each medical device manufacturer is critical when you are involved with supply chain planning. The FDA wants to know if you are a manufacturer, what kinds of products you sell, etc. The FDA lists their regulations in 21 CFR, Parts 862–892. In those parts, different categories of devices are described. The FDA might want to know if you make a clinical chemistry analyzer, for example, and that is one of the categories in 21 CFR. RA will register your product category with the FDA by submitting a form to it. A company might make various chemistry analyzers and when they market the first one, RA will have registered the device and received an FDA Product Code and MDL Number. Once a company has done this, the FDA understands that you manufacture, distribute, or sell chemistry analyzers. You do not need to register new ones. When you stop marketing the analyzers, you need to have your RA representative contact the FDA and advise them that you have discontinued this part of your business and cancel the MDL Number."

"Working to obtain product registration prior to a product launch," Edds advises, "the registration form should be with the FDA at maximum thirty days after you begin to sell it." He provides the step-by-step process of an FDA approval process:

1. On the very top of a clearance letter is the FDA Product Code for the product.
2. Determine if you already have that code listed. If that category of code, for example, for chemistry analyzers, is already listed, you do not need to list it again.
3. To list a new code, contact the FDA for a prenumbered form. The number on that form is the MDL Number. The FDA uses a three-character product code. This causes confusion sometimes when an FDA Product Code needs to be entered for Customs clearance by the broker. The field for an FDA Product Code is seven characters. To fill in the other four characters, RA must go to the FDA Product Code Builder located on the FDA website (http://www.accessdata.fda.gov/SCRIPTS/ORA/PCB/PCB.HTM) to complete the FDA Product Code for entry.
4. Instead of using prestamped forms, you can use the electronic forms program on the FDA's website. Each electronic form generates a new

number. Fill it out on-line, print it out, and send it in. Unfortunately, you still need to mail a hard copy. The link is http://www.fda.gov/cdrh/comp/fda2892.html.

5. Mail it, in either case, to the FDA at the address on the form within thirty days of device clearance.

6. *Ensure that the FDA has it in its system list.* The FDA does not send back any acknowledgments. This is problematic because when you think it is registered with the FDA, it could actually not be in its system. The FDA has now farmed this activity out to a third-party contractor. The hope is that the contractor lists the appropriate code for your company with zero chance of a typographical error that will cause your shipment to be rejected.

7. As a precaution, periodically have the FDA print out all MDL codes for your site. It is worthwhile to use the list to check against your own records.

Another element that medical device manufacturers must track is the 510k Number. Products for distribution require an MDL Number and may also require a 510k (K) Number, if the regulations require it for that product. If your intended use is for research and development only, you would not need these K Numbers, but would still require an FDA Product Code and MDL Number for Customs clearance. This, again, would be built via the FDA Product Code Builder or by contacting the FDA directly for assistance. When a company submits a 510k, the FDA assigns a K Number with six characters. The first two characters represent the year it was submitted. The remaining four characters represent the sequential number of submissions received that year. The FDA will send you a letter of acknowledgment with the K Number, and that K Number follows that device for the rest of its life.

Edds concludes by advising, "While there may be electronic solutions to filing some of this information with the FDA in the future, currently RA must provide detailed information on any registration form. This applies whether the firm is the manufacturer, distributor, labeler, repackager, etc. RA needs to specify the company's activities as they relate to a product, for example, whether your company is the developer or the manufacturer. Accuracy of this information is essential for product registration and clearance through Customs."

Having an understanding of the registration steps and requirements will ensure precise understanding for estimating timely distribution options the moment the product is ready for market. Include your RA Representatives in your planning. They will provide time lines that are crucial to the supply chain expectations and planning.

IMPORT AND COMPLIANCE DEPARTMENTS

From reading the first few chapters, you have learned the responsibilities of Import and Compliance Departments and the added requirements to be met for global buying as opposed to domestic means, due largely to the differences in languages and customs, magnified by greater geographical distances and lead times. Distances between the original manufacturer and end user create a longer pipeline, which requires a greater commitment to advance planning. This is an incredibly crucial component to truly understand and comply with. Domestic procurement habits have purchasing agents placing orders with no awareness of how to meet government obligations. The backlash of not meeting all import requirements and checkpoints can be costly and time consuming. Postorder services are more complicated because of currency fluctuations, identifying methods of payment adjustments for goods and services, the need to deal with U.S. Customs, and the involvement and utilization of import brokers and international carriers.

Foreign suppliers do not pre-establish every product for export to the U.S. It is the obligation of the purchasing agent to advise U.S. requirements to the foreign supplier. An import "clearance requirement" template must be created and adhered to. The Import and Compliance Departments cannot negotiate the product price, but will provide the answers needed to develop such a template. They can respond to questions raised on costs, transportation, and compliance. An Import Department can also aggressively investigate import shipments that have added expenses; for example, when refrigeration or "hot shot" (an immediate delivery) inland trucking services are requested by the planners/requesters. Sometimes this is not necessary and the Import Department can take a more proactive approach by specifically identifying the pricing involved and clearly capture the added costs for such requests. The cost findings can then be presented to the requester to revisit their anticipated need. Hot shots can be avoided altogether if preplanning is arranged. As well, hot shot expenses may be found to be unnecessary, as a company's receiving warehouse may not be able to receive the inventory. A supply chain can contact either department to solicit advice or clarification on any aspect of meeting compliance, transportation, and receiving recommendations.

WHAT DOES A TRANSPORTATION/LOGISTICS COORDINATOR DO FOR A SUPPLY CHAIN?

You understand how to utilize your service providers to assist in coordinating the movement of your shipments. You know you can contact your Import

Department for recommendations on which service provider to utilize. But who is ultimately identifying and acquiring the service providers? Who is negotiating their rates for your company? Do you know if you are truly receiving the best rate for the best move? Are you fully aware of all the best move options for your inventory cycle? Air? Sea? Truck? Rail? A Transportation/Logistics Department can assist with answers for all of these questions. If you work closely with such a department, the premier routing of your product can be achieved.

The Transportation Department can assist with watching the bottom line, particularly when added costs are ultimately out of control; for example, when the Port of Long Beach tariff rate increases by 5 percent. The rate hike includes wharfage, dockage, storage, and demurrage. Other U.S. ports are hoping to implement tariff increases. They point to sharp increases in infrastructure and security costs as reasons for seeking a rate advance. Transportation experts remain abreast of such increased rates and negotiate directly with ports, steamship lines, airlines, etc. to mitigate rate increases. They will review current rate structures with the various service providers and advise what is already included in your ocean rates.

You may also reduce delivery turnaround via tracking and auditing a current business lane with your Transportation and Import Departments and then revisiting the same lane after you have made some enhancements, such as a total ownership program (using only one service provider for better control as discussed in Chapter 3). Obtain pre- and postdelivery turnaround time line statistics from these departments to evaluate the new business change cost savings. They will also work with you and the Import Department to move your product successfully from the shipper's door to your customer's door. Ultimately, this department would negotiate the total ownership program rates and fees for your business lane.

Another area would be with "working the bugs out," literally. Customs rolled out an awareness in 2004 with implementation in 2005 of new regulations for the importation of unmanufactured wood articles. The regulation calls for wood packaging material to be either heat treated or fumigated with methyl bromide, in accordance with the regulation guidelines, and marked with an approved international mark certifying treatment (see Figure 4.1).

The regulation is for controlling pests in wood packaging material used in global trade. Recent U.S. requirements for wood packaging material were not fully effective, as shown by analyses of pest interceptions at ports that show an increase in pests associated with wood packaging material. For further information, you may visit the website at http://www.aphis.usda.gov/ppq/swp/. A Transportation or Logistics Representative in the movement of cargo could assist you by appropriately alerting your foreign suppliers to such new requirements.

(a) Inspection agency logo
(b) Unique number assigned by the National Plant Protection Organization
(c) Represents either HT for heat treatment or MB for methyl bromide fumigation
(d) The ISO country code

Figure 4.1. Approved international mark certifying wood treatment (www.cbp.gov).

WAREHOUSING/RECEIVING DEPARTMENT: INCREASED SECURITY RESPONSIBILITIES POST 9/11 — OVERAGES, SHORTAGES, AND BROKEN SEALS

From a compliance and security aspect, it is important to know when your Receiving Department received an overage or shortage shipment and to arrange for linking a point of contact for the Import Department with all the Receiving Departments. An overage or shortage in the quantity of the shipment's piece count may affect the duty payment made to Customs. If more product was shipped than declared on the invoice, you may owe Customs more revenue because the value was not accurate. Your shipment must be received according to the purchase order. Equally important is to report immediately to your Import Department if your Receiving Department notes any seals on containers that appear to have been tampered with or broken, with no indication on the import documentation from Customs or OGA that they had inspected the container. The Import Department will contact Customs to determine if an inspection was conducted on that shipment and what actions need to be taken if Customs has no record of an inspection. As a result of 9/11, an internal company security procedure should be in place for any received piece-count discrepancies or tampered freight.

For damaged containers, an evaluation of the product's stability should be assessed. If it is found to be worthless as a result of the damage, the product should be quarantined immediately and your Import Department notified. They can arrange for a claim to be processed via your company insurance policy, through the party at fault, or through Customs if the product was still in Customs' territory at the time of damage or theft. Company insurance deductibles should be considered before venturing into a claim as it may not be worthwhile for the value of the product.

This is a good time to point out why it is equally advantageous to provide the fair market value of your product in the event of a claim. If the invoice reflects an undervalued amount in the attempt to save on duty payment, this would be the value of your claim including the items listed earlier in this chapter (duties, taxes, transportation, storage, etc.). A shortages/overage/damage communication report should be created and circulated from your distribution/ warehousing locations to the Import Department and any other key individuals within the supply chain. The report should capture the bill of lading, container number, or air waybill number to quickly identify the entry within the Import Department to review for the discrepancy or to calculate the value of the potential claim. An example of a shared piece-count discrepancy report is illustrated in Table 4.1.

As we learned from our character Chuck in the earlier chapters, it is important to communicate to your Warehousing Representative any shipment that must be received. Let your warehouse know which shipment is yours and if any special conditions must be arranged prior to its arrival, such as refrigeration. Warehouses can have bottleneck situations arise. Requesters may incur the added expense of paying for expedited trucking service at prime rates, only to learn that their Receiving Department cannot accept the load due to various conditions.

Table 4.1. Communication Table.

	Bill of Lading #	
	XYZ123	PRRM123
Date received	12.3.04	06/18/04
Vendor	Isaac Roy Wiring	Anthony's Conduits
Purchase order no.	101601	96784
Requester	Lauryn Grace	Alexander Michael
Item ordered	40504	12594
Quantity ordered	10	10
Total ordered cost	$10.00	$20.00
Item received	40504	12594
Quantity received	10	10
Total received cost	$50.00	$0.00
Reason/comments	5 pieces damaged	Wrong item #, vendor will reship

CONSULT YOUR CLAIM OR INSURANCE DEPARTMENT FOR REIMBURSEMENTS

Customs will recoup your duties if the product is stolen or damaged while still in their territory. However, if not within the control of Customs, you can submit a claim through your insurance company. The value of the claim should be calculated to include all costs of the shipment. Your Import Department and service providers can provide backup of payment for those areas. If you receive a damaged product, make certain that you hold it in quarantine until the insurance adjuster can examine the load.

Below are charges for which you should seek reimbursement:

- Value of product
- Customs duties/taxes (including MPF and HMF fees)
- All transportation costs (including U.S. inland trucking)
- Brokerage costs
- Any miscellaneous fees, such as storage, demurrage, etc.

RAISING THE AWARENESS THAT "ADDED VALUE" DEPARTMENTS EXIST

For those of you in the Missing Link Department category, or in the supply chain operation, who want to assist in raising the awareness to better your company, this section is for you. You want others to know that you exist. You strive to advise that you can help, but the company size is overwhelming, with too many individuals involved with global procurement. You can begin your awareness campaign in a piecemeal fashion. For starters, prepare presentations and organize training symposiums. Title the subjects to grab the audience, for example, "Product Supply/Imports/Regulatory/Logistics Symposiums." Recruit the other Missing Link departments to participate, such as a representative from Imports, RA, Compliance, Environmental Safety, Procurement, and/or even Exports for the reverse logistics business lanes.

Provide your process overview, flow charts, and written standard operating procedures to serve as guidance. Include regulatory/drug or MDL process/documentation, time line and cost factors, compliance requirements, etc. in your training mission. Have a Procurement Representative provide input on the import ordering and distribution requirement. You can learn from them as well by understanding their processes and customer commitments. Seek out an alliance person from the Warehousing Department. Give them an opportunity to share receiving protocol.

Why not solicit your service provider to share insight into the clearance and transportation process? Take the whole entourage and make a road show that travels throughout the corporation. Limit the symposium time to a few hours. Continue with your awareness campaign using other related themes. Make posters, create websites, dispatch company-wide e-mail messages. Prepare and mail handouts. Go out and train using the handouts. Get your nose in the supply chain plans. Find out who the players are and network with them. Do not forget the foreign suppliers. They struggle to learn the U.S. regulations as well. Develop a "How Do I Export to the U.S." handout geared to their requirements. Train them on it via teleconference and/or conference calls.

Everyone will benefit from an awareness symposium training process. Providing a platform to educate and guide everyone to the same page is extraordinarily beneficial to individuals, departments, and the corporation. If you stumble on newly found import volume, identify the core person and coordinate another training symposium, with a face-to-face or conference call meeting with the entire supply chain operation including the foreign supplier and service provider. Smooth out obstacles in current import procedure. Results are rewarding and provide the open communication that is so necessary where cost avoidances and improved time lines can be gained.

NEW PRICING AND TIME LINES FOR FORMERLY PROCURED DOMESTIC PRODUCT

Basic domestic purchasing differs greatly from international purchasing. As we are reminded, global procurement has its own share of added requirements. This requires added departments to be involved. Let us visualize the very basic import cycle details. The illustration below indicates the basic steps involved from buyer to seller.

Step 1
Buyer — Buyer sends request for quote/price — Seller makes offer to buyer The buyer requests a large piece of machinery.

Step 2
A request for quotation/product offer checklist is created, depending on product and terms and conditions of a sale. Do you have a representative for each of these categories?

- Product specifications
- Factory location
- Product identification codes and complete description

- Type of product: is it a raw material, component, part, finished product, other
- Product valuation
- Manufacturing lead times
- Construction, fabrication, and/or material breakdown
- Country of origin of product
- Origin markings and/or labeling regulations
- Harmonized code number
- Regulatory registration
- Shipping requirements
- Number of units
- Packaging requirements
- Labeling requirements
- Invoice requirements
- U.S. government agency requirements
- Government information declarations
- Transportation requirements

Step 3

If you are in a position in which you have procured product domestically and are moving to procure the same product internationally for a distribution in the U.S. market, you need to consider the added costs you will absorb and adjust your current unit pricing to your customers. It is very important to speak with all the "missing links" in your newly formed supply chain operation to ensure that you have captured all your new costs. Before you finalize a pricing structure, you should meet with your new "resources" within your own company, do a test run of the first import, and evaluate your new costs and time lines.

SUMMARY

The planning, design, and development of major infrastructure projects is undergoing drastic changes throughout the world. The tragic events of 9/11 have resulted in an even greater set of risk considerations and security requirements as well as for both existing or newly proposed infrastructure projects. What was a multitrillion-dollar annual global infrastructure market now has new cost parameters that are undergoing rapid assessment and change themselves. Transformations are now rapidly occurring worldwide all along the project development, delivery, and operations continuum for all forms of global groundwork. Included are transportation, production, distribution, added resources, communication, building facilities, new financials, and delivery and receiving systems.

Linking the right players together into an effective supply chain is crucial. Do not let the lack of communication cause the demise of a flourishing company global vision. By analyzing your entire global supply chain activities on a regular basis, you are one step closer to meeting the customer's expectations, reducing costs, reasonable care, informed compliance, and a continued import privilege under U.S. Customs' watch.

Continue on to Chapter 5 where you will be educated on the "other government agencies," their purposes, and how they can affect your time lines, cost, and planning.

5

THE OTHER GOVERNMENT AGENCIES: THE "OTHER BUREAUS IN CUSTOMS' NEIGHBORHOOD"

The clearance process starts with the buyer and seller contacting each other and forming a sales contract. When the price and the quantity to be shipped have been finalized, the importer may open a letter of credit in favor of the exporter's bank as a guarantee of payment for the goods. The exporter ships the goods on confirmation of the letter of credit and sends the original shipping documents to the importer's bank. Through whatever arrangement the bank might have with the importer, the original documents are released on some sort of understanding. It is at this stage that the broker comes into the picture. The original documents are handed over to the broker and he/she begins to trace the vessel, prepare the bill of entry (if applicable), and perform the necessary formalities leading to the clearance of goods from the airport or seaport. Clearance is made five days out from the arrival of a vessel. Customs permits clearance while the vessel is still on the water. The FDA elects not to do so. "Who is the FDA?" you may ask. You may have experienced this same dilemma and asked yourself: "If it was cleared through Customs, I should be done, right?" Wrong.

The U.S. benefits from a governmental structure of the Judicial, Executive, and Legislative branches, all of which play a role with saving a company money on their global procurement costs via tariff and trade bills aimed to reduce or eliminate duties on certain commodities. These branches evaluate and decide on all aspects of a bill. Tariff and trade are discussed further in Chapter 8. There are other governmental structures that can assist a company with saving money and time while ensuring the safety of U.S. citizens.

As discussed earlier, U.S. Customs and Border Protection does not run the show alone. In Chapter 9, you will learn how Customs had a facelift and redesigned government agencies. For now, let us discuss the "other government agencies" (OGAs) as they have become known and how each may have clearance authority on your shipment. Some of these federal and commission agencies are independent U.S. government agencies, directly responsible to Congress. Many of these agencies are undergoing new changes as they are seeking solutions to enhance or replace existing operations and methods. Customs has taken some criticism over the money spent on the Customs-Trade Partnership Against Terrorism (C-TPAT) and Department of Homeland Security (DHS) to incorporate safety features that must eventually branch and connect to the OGAs that are overseen by the DHS. The deployment of a completely new centralized system is far into the future. Eventually, Customs and the OGAs will be automated under one system. A complete list of the federal agencies and commissions is located in http://www.whitehouse.gov/government/independent-agencies.html.

The U.S. government has its own best practices and innovations since 9/11. A list of the "primary" government agencies that would likely be involved in your clearances will be provided. We will also consider what type of paperwork and company and product information is needed for these OGAs to obtain successful "paperless" releases the first time around. As the FDA states on their website: "Our lips are sealed." Any information requests that importers make to an OGA, such as the FDA, must be denied due to the confidential nature of the data. FDA employees are prohibited, by law, from divulging information considered either proprietary or confidential. For example, FDA employees cannot release any information on unapproved drugs unless the manufacturer has given the agency permission or has already released the information to the public. Importers should not be concerned about personal company secrets being leaked when providing detailed company and product information to an OGA.

A member of a global supply chain operation should ensure that the homework was completed by the RA Department with the OGAs for any regulated imported product. Glitches can surface easily from any of these government bodies that will detain your clearance turnaround and add unnecessary costs to your bottom line. The most problematic issue in dealing with an OGA is the slow response time. It could take weeks for you to reconcile a delay with a particular agency.

Import and RA representatives should be the main point of contact with these OGAs. RA must also know the urgency of your required purchase and delivery. Creating and providing complete and accurate clearance information to the OGAs is the "make or break" factor. Knowing how much time and cost is involved to establish a profile and registration for a product, and understanding what other departments within your company are involved, can help your inbound supply chain. A product registration may require a site inspection of yours or the manufacturer's facility, which could take weeks to complete by an OGA. Who could you turn to for assistance to bring your supply chain product into compliance? A rule of thumb would be: If you find that a government agency is behind the implementation of a new requirement, immediately refer to your RA Department (as discussed in Chapter 4). If your company does not have one established, you should evaluate your existing supply chain to incorporate a knowledgeable person in the regulated field and create such a department. If that option is ruled out, then your Import or Compliance Department can assist by directing you to the correct representatives in the government agencies.

Why would the Import or Compliance Department not just deal directly with the actual product issue? RA responsibilities incorporate, as part of their background to work directly with the OGA, any product registrations and commentary of profiles. Import/Compliance is more of a logistics, clearance compliance, and governance position. You want to be working with experts in the regulated field who are responsible for knowing the full parameters of a product's makeup and purpose in the U.S. Let us begin by describing some of the most standard government agencies involved with the imports into the U.S.

THE FOOD AND DRUG ADMINISTRATION

The Food and Drug Administration (FDA) is an agency within the Department of Health and Human Services and consists of eight centers/offices, which are identified on the FDA website (www.fda.gov). The FDA mission is: To promote and protect the public health by helping safe and effective products reach the market in a timely way; to monitor products for continued safety after they are in use; and, to help the public get the accurate, science-based information needed to improve health. The majority of regulated products must be cleared through the FDA. If you are unsure as to whether or not your product is subject to FDA clearance, your RA or Import Representative can clarify this issue.

The hardcopy Harmonized Tariff Schedule (HTS) book does not show a flag for OGAs to indicate if the FDA is required for clearance. However, Customs did create a list of HTS codes that are flagged for all OGAs, including the FDA. You may contact Customs or your broker to obtain the listing. The broker may also query the HS Number assigned to the product directly in the Automated Broker Interface (ABI) System to learn from which government agencies you must obtain releases. An FDA flag indicator in the ABI System is reflected as an "FD1" (optional entry with FDA; therefore, you can override FDA submission) or "FD2" (mandatory entry with FDA). The ABI System is used by brokers to transmit import information electronically to Customs and the OGAs for clearance.

When a product is indicated as being regulated by the FDA, the entry must be transmitted to Customs as well as the FDA. The FDA is responsible to review and grant a release. If the FDA is not satisfied with the information electronically provided in the ABI System, they will alert the broker via ABI by keying in the term "FDA Exam" to relay their intent to review the hardcopy documentation. The broker will send a runner to the FDA office to provide the documentation. Importers should know that the FDA will look for an FDA "End-User" letter to accompany the import documentation. Also, when an entry is flagged for the FDA, an FDA Product Code (described below) must be transmitted for every flagged line item. Depending on the product and intended use, additional information may be required for FDA entry approval. (The FDA has implemented two more flag indicators since 9/11, for food imports. This has been a source of detainments for nonfood products and has reduced the number of electronic/paperless FDA releases.)

FDA Product Code Builder: What Is It and How Do I Use It?

When a shipment has been transmitted and the FD2 indicator appears, the broker is required to transmit an FDA Product Code for that product. An FDA Product Code would be provided to the broker by the importer via their broker instruction letter. The FDA Product Code is created within the FDA's Product Code Builder located on their website. It is an on-line web-based product code builder and tutorial. The link is http://www.accessdata.fda.gov/SCRIPTS/ORA/PCB/PCB.HTM and importers or brokers can access the database to search and build the appropriate FDA Product Code. An FDA Product Code better characterizes the commodity to the FDA and provides an avenue to accomplish this by creating a coding system that "builds" a general profile of what is being imported, such as antibiotics, human/animal, penicillin, prescription or nonprescription, liquid or extended release tablets, etc.

An example FDA Product Code would be 55YY-99. It is a seven-character reference number that the code builder will create for you by the selections you make. Each character represents a description or packaging of the product. It should be noted that when a company applies for a Medical Device Listing (MDL) Number, a three-character FDA Product Code is provided by the FDA to the registered party on the MDL form. This three-character code must be further completed (through the FDA Product Code Builder) prior to forwarding to the requester and the Import Department. You may refer back to Chapter 4 regarding FDA codes for medical device products. A company's RA Department should have ownership and responsibility for creating the codes for FDA clearance and providing them to the Import Department. At times, the FDA Product Code may be the source of an FDA rejection if not properly built for the commodity imported. In this case, the importer, not the broker, will work directly with the FDA to reconcile the confusion.

FDA's Notice of Action Letters: Do Not Wait for the Hardcopy

Resolution turnaround is the greatest challenge when dealing with this agency. When the FDA detains a shipment/entry, this information is not communicated immediately to the Importer of Record (IOR). The FDA issues a hardcopy to the IOR address, a "Notice of Action" letter, when a shipment is placed on hold. The letter will reference the entry number to the shipment. The FDA will also update the entry status on the shared ABI system. This first letter simply indicates to the IOR that the shipment/entry is placed on hold. The usual turnaround for an IOR to receive this letter is approximately two weeks from the date of entry. Then the FDA will issue a second letter explaining the reasoning behind the delay within four weeks of the shipment's entry date. For any importer, this turnaround can be detrimental to a supply chain operation.

The broker and the Import Representative should be closely monitoring any pending FDA release. If an entry does not obtain an FDA release within the first forty-eight hours of the entry date, either the broker or the Import Representative should arrange a call to the FDA. The FDA offers a Help Desk line that will provide information on the status of your shipment. The entry number to the shipment is used for reference to the FDA. If a Notice of Action letter was issued, the FDA Help Desk should be able to provide the rejection reason. An example of an FDA reject would be if the IOR's registered company name differs from the registration name on the drug listing codes submitted on the entry.

Shipments should always be completely released by all government agencies prior to final delivery. A broker should not dispatch any shipment to the trucker until the FDA release is reflected in the ABI system. The broker should provide a printout of this release to the importer for record keeping. Only in a dire situation should an Import Department have the broker dispatch a shipment pending an FDA release. The FDA will allow a shipment to be dispatched for delivery if the location is within a certain mile radius of the FDA port. Your Import Control Officer (ICO) or Import Representative would need to confirm this agreement with your FDA port officer. Written commitment by a designated individual at that receiving location should be secured, prior to delivering, that documents a guarantee that the product will be held in quarantine until they are notified in hardcopy form of the FDA release. The FDA still has the authority to request a "Redelivery Notice" for shipments up to thirty days after a release was already granted. This has been a debate among importers with the FDA as the majority of a shipment's inventory is no longer available for return with this time span.

FDA Clearance Template for Improving Time Lines and Clearance Turnaround

Jean Mazet, Regulatory Affairs Manager, offered us insight into the regulatory functions and touched on the issues when dealing with the government in Chapter 4. She now expands on interactions and time lines under the FDA, which could descend on any IOR's regulatory activities. Mazet begins by explaining, "Turnaround with the FDA can be a barrier; however, if you establish a clear submission calendar, you can avoid delays and unnecessary added work. The agency can take a minimum of three weeks to get a new item into their system. If the supply chain operation is running neck-to-neck with an import, you must make this a time line factor. Remember also that each change in package size and new labeling must also be submitted. RA and the supply chain must be clear on when the material is expected to ship to the U.S."

Mazet continues, "If the product does require FDA drug listing or update, you must avoid running your registration requirements simultaneously with FDA's best practice of semi-annual review, which takes place in January and June. Every company involved with regulated products sends drug-listing updates for the product changes representing the last six months for the FDA to review. A supply chain should be aware of this as FDA will be further inundated with workload issues and your company drug registration could get caught in a pile on someone's desk at the FDA. Your supply chain product plan could be caught in this quagmire and add unnecessary costs with huge delays. Avoid this time frame. Sometimes the FDA will permit an importer to send a product listing in with a cover letter that a shipment is forthcoming and request FDA to 'please expedite.' Of course, this should be preceded by a call to the FDA and be mailed by an overnight courier."

"The Bioterrorism Act and the subsequent FDA regulations were published as a result of 9/11 to address the hazard risk to our food supply. Now foods are also undergoing the close scrutiny that drugs experienced all along. Most importers have their ducks in a row with their previous product imports. Now, all must work with the FDA to provide equal security for the food industry supply chains," Mazet concludes.

Mandatory Bar Coding for Nondistributed Products: Are You Ready?

In 2004, the FDA published a final rule that required bar coding on drugs, including over-the-counter (OTC) and biological products. This ruling aims to protect patients from preventable medication errors and helps to ensure that health professionals give "the right patient the right drugs at the appropriate dosages and time." Bar codes, similar to those on food packages and other consumer goods, are required on most prescription drugs and certain OTC drugs. The rule also requires machine-readable information on container labels of blood and blood components intended for transfusion. The FDA estimates that the rule will help prevent nearly 500,000 adverse events and transfusion errors while saving $93 billion in health costs over twenty years.

Jean Mazet advises on the purpose and steps involved to ensure that the bar-coding requirements are met. Mazet begins by explaining, "Ramifications of what the FDA is doing with requesting bar coding for prescription drugs serviced to hospitals is very valuable, but this does not mean all drugs should be bar coded. The over-the-counter (OTC) industry had a concern with products that already had a Universal Product Code (UPC) symbol on its retail package. Retailers currently scan bar codes on OTCs. These are already used universally and would not benefit from any additional bar coding. Bar coding enables the hospital to positively identify the patient and the product."

"Not all OTC medication is marketed to the hospital setting. If the stock keeping unit (SKU) is marketed to the hospital, it is appropriate to bar code; however, it would not need a retail UPC. This, however, could cause chaos in a retail setting. Fortunately, when the FDA published its final rule, they determined that only product SKUs that are marketed directly to hospitals need comply," Mazet informs.

Taking this new regulated requirement into account, who should be responsible for keeping abreast of such requirements within a company and finding solutions to institute new procedures to accommodate the government? A case in point would be with our fellow importer Chuck from earlier chapters. Chuck may find the need to import various samples that include blood-derived specimens. These types of samples may be directly affected by this new requirement. Who would be responsible for advising Chuck correctly? Or should Chuck be responsible for areas that would directly affect his imports? A supply chain should have a designated team of individuals responsible for identifying all aspects of the imported product. This includes consulting RA, Imports, Legal, HES, and Transportation.

The government has developed new rulings such as the bar coding of blood samples in the past several years, necessitating that importers comply quickly. Identifying the correct and previously involved individuals and departments is essential in order to develop processes that would work with your supply chain. Taking the new bar-coding example, an RA would be the most knowledgeable party to have already been aware of the correct procedures. The RA Department responsibilities include reviewing new regulations and changes and then determining their impact to the company's supply chain. They would then advise the affected parties accordingly. The existence of an RA Department should be known throughout the company. Written standard operating procedures would clearly document such responsibilities. Chuck's RA Department would contact him to review this new requirement and also advise that RA would perform all steps necessary to fulfill the new government criteria.

FDA's Radio Frequency Identification Pilot Programs

The FDA is moving toward newer technology. In 2004, the FDA announced its intention to exercise enforcement discretion until December 31, 2007, concerning certain regulatory requirements in order to facilitate the performance of feasibility studies and pilot programs involving radio frequency identification (RFID) tags for drugs. The FDA will use RFID technology (discussed in Chapter 11) in an effort to protect the U.S. drug supply from counterfeiting. The enforcement discretion is designed to allow industry to gain experience with the use of RFID technology to ensure the long-term safety and integrity of the U.S. drug supply. In a report issued on their website entitled "Combating Counterfeit Drugs," the FDA identified RFID technology as the cornerstone in the fight against counterfeit drugs and announced its intention to facilitate the adoption of RFID technology by participants in the pharmaceutical supply chain.

Coping with New Post 9/11 Requirements for Importing Food Products

The most significant post 9/11 requirement to arise for importing was the new food Bioterrorism Act (BTA). The Public Health Security and Bioterrorism

Preparedness and Response Act of 2002 directed the Secretary of Health and Human Services to take steps to protect the public from a threatened or actual terrorist attack on the U.S. food supply. This new ruling came in two separate intervals.

"Registration" of Food Facilities

To carry out the provisions of the BTA, in 2003, the FDA published an interim final regulation, Registration of Food Facilities, requiring domestic and foreign facilities that manufacture/process, pack, or hold food for human or animal consumption in the U.S. to register with the FDA. Under this interim final regulation, all existing affected facilities must have been registered by December 12, 2003. In the event of a potential or actual bioterrorism incident or an outbreak of food-borne illness, facility registration information will help the FDA to determine the location and source of the event and permit the agency to notify quickly those facilities that may be affected. There is no cost to register. An RA Representative can identify whether or not your product line is affected by the BTA. Additionally, on the FDA website (www.fda.gov), there is a list of the commodities subject to the BTA, such as dietary supplements and dietary ingredients, beverages, infant formulas, dairy products, raw agricultural commodities, snack foods, animal foods, etc.

An owner, operator, or agent in charge of a domestic or foreign facility that manufactures/processes, packs, or holds food for human or animal consumption in the U.S., or an authorized representative, must register that facility with the FDA. A domestic facility must register whether or not food from the facility enters interstate commerce. A foreign facility must designate a U.S. agent (for example, a facility's importer or broker), who must live or maintain a place of business in the U.S. and be physically present in the U.S., for purposes of registration. The FDA website provides guidance on who must register, how often, registration numbers and how they are assigned, and what the consequences are for not registering a required facility.

"Prior Notice" Clearance of Imported Food Shipments Prior to Dispatch to the U.S.

The BTA requires that the FDA receive registration information of food imported into the U.S. Information required to be submitted to the FDA is usually transmitted by the broker, but can be done by the importer. Under the BTA, this information must be provided to the FDA in *advance* (prior notice) of an imported food's arrival into the U.S. The FDA will use this information in advance of the arrival to review, evaluate, and assess the information, and determine whether to inspect the imported food. The FDA and Customs have collaborated on the implementation of the Prior Notice (PN) interim final rule. Nearly all of the current imported food shipments can comply by using Customs' Automated Broker Interface of the Automated Commercial System (ABI/ACS). An HS Number query can advise an importer if the product will be tagged for PN submission, even if the product is not a food-related product that is ingested. Some HS Numbers have been flagged incorrectly and can be rectified by working with the FDA. If your product is flagged for PN, it may also mean that it does qualify justifiably under the BTA for PN submission even if the product is not digested. It could be a return of a vitamin for quality and assurance valuation.

A listing of all the BTA-regulated importations that require PN regardless of value are also found on the FDA website as well as any exemptions (www.access.fda.gov). It will provide guidance on how to submit PN. The website also will advise PN time frames in which the PN must be to the FDA for the various modes of transportation. Each mode has its own time line to meet prior to the product arriving into the U.S.

The BTA and PN are prime examples of where RA and Import Departments are essential. Internal company RA databases may need to be altered to accommodate new fields for the BTA information for clearance. RA will register the required information with the FDA and provide the registration numbers to the Import Department; for example, the registration identification of the submitter, transmitter, firm information, manufacturer, grower, shipper, country of production, ultimate consignee, etc. The RA or Import Department will then populate the necessary fields with the registration numbers within their housed database of regulatory information for a product's profile. The product's profile can also be flagged internally for BTA PN.

For importation, once the PN is transmitted by the broker to the FDA and approved, the carriers will need the PN confirmation number on arrival. The broker can arrange for the transmission of this information. The broker will also take this PN confirmation number and enter it into the ABI system to show Customs and the FDA that the shipment was precleared.

For a PN that is submitted through the ABI/ACS interface, the PN confirmation number together with a "PN received" message will be made available to the filer through the ACS/ABI interface. If PN is submitted through the FDA PN system interface, then the transmitter will receive a confirmation on-line as soon as the submission is confirmed. To make it easier for the carrier or individual at the port, the carrier should have a copy of the confirmation, which includes a PN confirmation number in his/her possession. For international mail packages, the PN confirmation number must accompany the package. For food carried by or otherwise accompanying an individual arriving into the U.S., the PN confirmation number must accompany the food.

Foreign suppliers should note that, most likely, R&D samples and hand-carried samples, if applicable to the BTA, need to go through the process of prior notification. Foreign suppliers should confirm to their customers that they have programs in place to meet the new prior notification requirements, if applicable. The FDA has also issued booklets on both registering and on prior advance notice. Regularly updated information on registrations and this prior advance notice are available on the FDA's website at http://www.fda.gov/oc/bioterrorism/bioact.html.

You *CAN* Assist Your Shipment's Clearance Turnaround via an FDA End-User Letter

The FDA requires a written End-User declaration letter to better assess the commodity you are importing. This letter is a vital part of avoiding delays for your import documentation. It can assist an FDA compliance officer's understanding of your business lane in the event that your shipment is randomly selected for a "spot" exam. The letter should state what the product is, what it is derived from, its intended use, the type of research, from whom it shipped, and the name and address of the end-user in the U.S. (which is routinely the consignee). This letter should be prepared by the foreign shipper on its original letterhead to accompany the shipment with a copy forwarded to the Import Department *prior* to exporting from abroad. A purchasing agent should arrange to have the FDA End-User letter information included in the terms and conditions of the purchase order.

Who Is Considered the "End-User"?

The "end-user" of a product for FDA clearance would be whoever will be using the product. For example, even though certain pharmaceutical products ultimately are distributed to various hospitals, the End-User letter would still have the "consignee" on the bill of lading as ultimate end-user. This is based on the consignee doing something first to the product prior to domestic distribution, whether it be packaging, relabeling, palletizing, reformulating, or getting it ready to be shipped to the ultimate purchaser. When a product is shipped directly to a customer or research university, then the End-User letter would need to state that name and address. The FDA will assist any importer on clarifying who the ultimate end-user will be for a shipment.

FDA's Import for Export Program

For the purchasing agent who procures drug products, or for the company who has a foreign manufacturer of a drug product, all its "intended use" stages must be registered with the FDA. At the various stages of a drug product, the FDA will assign codes; that is, if your drug compound has moved to clinical trials, then an Investigational New Drug (IND) Code is assigned. Once the potential drug is moved to a marketing stage, but not yet distributed, it receives a New Drug Application (NDA) Code. Once the drug is ready to be sold in the U.S., a New Drug/Drug Listing (NDC/DLS) Code is assigned, all of which RA will manage. For drug products procured from a foreign drug manufacturer, the "foreign" drug listing code must be used for U.S. clearance and not the domestic drug listing code.

In the latter part of 2002, an FDA Import for Export Program went into effect. The FDA Export Reform and Enhancement Act of 1996 (Export Reform Act), Public Law 104-134, amended section 801(d)(3) of the Act to allow the importation of certain articles that are *unapproved* or otherwise do not comply with the Act (products that have not received their NDC/DLS Code). The provision was that those imported articles are further processed or incorporated into products that will be *exported* from the U.S. by their initial owner or consignee in accordance with section 801(e) or section 802 of the Act or section 351(h) of the Public Health Service Act (PHSA).

Importers should be aware of the Import for Export Program as certain products may be subject to the U.S. Customs Temporary Import Bond (TIB) entry type or other bond instruments as required by U.S. Customs, under the new section 801(d)(3)(A)(ii) and remains subject to section 801(a). A TIB entry (discussed in Chapter 3), which differs from a normal consumption entry, entails that the product being cleared into the U.S. can achieve duty-free status, but must be re-exported within a one-year time frame unless granted an approved extension by Customs. Every piece count of the product must be accounted for even if destroyed. Customs may need to witness the destruction.

Any follow-up regulatory actions regarding the failure of the initial owner or consignee to meet the requirements of section 801(d)(3) should be referred to the Division of Import Operations and Policy (HFC-170) for handling. The FDA is utilizing the TIB program as a vehicle for tracking and reporting of the product during its stay in the U.S. Depending on the port, an FDA compliance officer may request a hardcopy of the secured single bond. If your shipment was entered using your company's continuous bond, the Customs entry summary 7501 reflecting the entry type code "23" which indicates "Temporary Import Bond," must be provided to the FDA office at the designated port to show evidence that a TIB entry was opened for the shipment. The FDA will then clear the shipment. Once it is time to re-export the finished product back out of the U.S., a company's Export Department must provide to Customs, prior to actual exportation, a report that summarizes the activity status of every piece count from the original shipment. The TIB would then be closed out with Customs via the broker and shipment re-exported. The link to the FDA's Import for Export Program website is http://www.fda.gov/ora/compliance_ref/rpm_new2/ch9impex.html.

THE U.S. DEPARTMENT OF AGRICULTURE

In 1862, when President Abraham Lincoln founded the USDA, he called it the "People's Department." In Lincoln's day, 48 percent of the people were farmers who needed good seeds and information to grow their crops. The USDA remains committed to helping America's farmers and ranchers. Under the new Customs facelift, the USDA falls under the DHS and they are responsible for screening and clearing every imported shipment into the U.S.

Following 9/11, the USDA took immediate steps to secure sensitive facilities and examine vulnerabilities throughout the food chain, and it conducted assessments to identify the critical needs to fill security gaps. The USDA continues to take the necessary steps to ensure that its programs and services are responsive to potential biosecurity threats. USDA programs aim to meet two very important objectives: first, to prevent the entry of plant or animal diseases and second, to contain and eradicate the problem if we do face an emergency. The Department's efforts on homeland security are based on a long-standing commitment to food safety and to securing the food supply and agriculture from threats. For example, in 2001, the Department dealt with the threat of foot-and-mouth disease as a widespread outbreak occurred in the U.K. and other parts of Europe. The USDA strengthened surveillance and response systems as it dealt with the threat of this disease.

Since 9/11, the USDA, along with the FDA, is examining threats to our food supply. Key homeland security activities include protecting the food supply and agricultural production, as well as protecting USDA staff and facilities and ensuring emergency preparedness. Some of the key biosecurity enhancements being implemented include the following:

- Security has been increased at appropriate USDA facilities.
- At ports of entry, personnel are conducting intensified product and cargo inspections of travelers and baggage to prevent the entry of animal or plant pests and diseases. The Agricultural Quarantine Inspection program has been strengthened and an automated system of inspections was coordinated with Customs. The USDA has purchased rapid pathogen identification devices and hired additional inspection personnel. They have also doubled the inspection dog teams. Port inspection responsibilities were transferred to the DHS.

■ Food safety inspectors (FSIS) were given additional guidance to be alert to any irregularity at food-processing facilities. The USDA constantly reviews and updates its biosecurity procedures as laboratory methods and science improve. FSIS has increased monitoring, provided training to inspectors, hired additional inspectors for imported meat and poultry, and expanded technical capabilities.

New USDA Post 9/11 Programs Add Work, But Improve Turnaround

The USDA clears imported shipments via the electronic Automated Manifest System (AMS) transmitted by the airline/steam shipping lines. If the manifest description of the product is too generic, it is placed on hold. For security purposes, companies tend not to list a product name to avoid their competition having knowledge of the shipment. When clearing imports with the USDA, it is more of a manual process than with the other OGAs. They are linked to the ABI system, but they communicate to the importers via hardcopy documentation and utilize the bill of lading number as reference. As archaic as this system is, we have seen this government agency provide quick turnaround for importers when inspections or delays are involved. They have a reputation for always being readily available to discuss any importer's shipment.

When they reject a shipment, they place a cover sheet onto the importer's import documentation, indicating why they rejected it. They place this paperwork back into the broker's bin at the port for pickup. The broker retrieves the paperwork and faxes a copy to the importer to provide the information needed for clearance to the USDA. An example of why the USDA may reject your shipment would be that they believe a USDA permit is required or they are looking for the declaration letter.

You *CAN* Assist Your Shipment's Clearance Turnaround via USDA Declaration Letters

As with an FDA End-User letter, if your product is *not* derived from any plant or animal source, providing a separate letter to the USDA declaring what the product is, what it is derived from, and its intended use will assist a USDA inspector in understanding your product. This letter is to be prepared by the foreign shipper on its original letterhead to accompany the shipment with a copy forwarded to the Import Department. The same statement on the invoice should be noted as the USDA looks for the phrase "not derived from any plant or animal and is not infectious."

Customs and the USDA are always involved with any import clearance into the U.S., even if the shipment is a spare part. Importers should note that if one product in a full container is to be inspected, the entire container would be detained. Since 9/11, the USDA has increased their demand for a letter from the foreign supplier declaring what the product is and what it is derived from.

USDA Guideline Letter or a USDA Permit with a Declaration Letter?

If your product *is* derived from a plant or animal, the USDA does not always require a permit for U.S. entry. When an actual USDA permit is not required, a "Guideline" letter may be requested. Specific text must be provided on the letter, which an RA Representative would need to identify for you. The letter must be provided from the foreign shipper and an "original" letter may be required depending on the USDA guideline. Certain USDA permits require an "original" declaration letter from a foreign source depending on the product, for example, certified veterinary. You can find specific USDA guideline and permit information that apply to varied goods on the USDA website (http://www.usda.gov). A company's RA Department will research if a USDA permit, guideline letter, or just a declaration letter will be required for clearance depending on the origin and nature of the product.

If a USDA permit is identified as being required to enter the U.S., this could take several weeks to acquire. A purchase order should not be placed until the permit is secured and provided to the foreign shipper to supply with the import documentation. A copy should also be provided to the Import Department for clearance. The USDA Inspector at the U.S. port will see the permit and/or original guideline letter with the import packet. This may assist with gaining a quicker release.

Different Port Practices Can Surface and Mislead Importers

Different government port practices lead importers to believe certain requirements are not mandatory. If the Chicago FDA port office, for example, does not request an End-User letter for FDA clearance with every entry, then importers are led to believe that it must not be required. However, in the other FDA ports all over the U.S., it is requested. Chicago just does not enforce solicitation. It is better to get into the habit of providing declaration letters because, eventually, other ports will catch up with the port best practices and begin to request them.

THE U.S. DEPARTMENT OF TREASURY

The Treasury Department is the primary federal agency responsible for the economic and financial prosperity and security of the U.S. They will never be involved with clearing your shipment, but are responsible for a wide range of activities including advising the President on economic and financial issues, promoting the President's growth agenda, and enhancing corporate governance in financial institutions. In the international arena, the Treasury Department works with other federal agencies, the governments of other nations, and the international financial institutions to encourage economic growth, raise standards of living, and predict and prevent, to the extent possible, economic and financial crises. The Treasury Department is organized into two major components: the departmental offices and the operating bureaus.

The departmental offices are primarily responsible for the formulation of policy and management of the Department as a whole, while the operating bureaus carry out the specific operations assigned to the Department. The bureaus make up 98 percent of the Treasury work force. The basic functions of the Department include:

- Managing federal finances
- Collecting taxes, duties, and monies paid to and due to the U.S. and paying all bills of the U.S.
- Producing postage stamps, currency, and coinage
- Managing government accounts and the public debt
- Supervising national banks and thrift institutions
- Advising on domestic and international financial, monetary, economic, trade, and tax policy
- Enforcing federal finance and tax laws
- Investigating and prosecuting tax evaders, counterfeiters, and forgers

A records disclosure program was administered in the Treasury Department that is in compliance with the Freedom of Information Act (FOIA) and the Privacy Act. The FOIA gives any person the right to request access to records of the Executive branch of the U.S. government. The records requested must be disclosed unless they are protected by one or more of the exempt categories of information found in the FOIA. Records that generally may be protected from disclosure are properly classified material; limited kinds of purely internal matters; matters exempt from disclosure by other statutes; trade secrets or commercial or financial information obtained from a person and privileged or confidential; internal agency communications that represent the deliberative, predecisional process, attorney work product, or attorney-client records; information that would be a clearly unwarranted invasion of personal privacy; law enforcement records to the extent that one of six specific harms could result from disclosure; bank examination records; and similar information. Your company is permitted access to its own FOIA report for its import activities. This would assist in reviewing what has been used under your IRS Number and for reconciliation purposes with Customs for entries.

THE ALCOHOL AND TOBACCO TAX AND TRADE BUREAU

Previously a bureau under the Treasury Department until 2003, the ATTB is responsible for enforcing and administering laws covering the production, use, and distribution of alcohol and tobacco products. The ATTB also collects excise taxes for firearms and ammunition. These products, on importation, are subject to this tax *in addition* to the Customs duty charges. Certain HS Numbers aside from just firearms and ammunition may flag for ATTB clearance. If your product does not apply to ATTB jurisdiction, you may have your Import Department contact them directly and advise the content and purpose of your shipment in better detail.

THE ENVIRONMENTAL PROTECTION AGENCY

Since 1970, the EPA has been working for a cleaner, healthier environment for the American people. The EPA works to develop and enforce regulations that implement environmental laws enacted by Congress. They are responsible for researching and setting national standards for a variety of environmental programs. The EPA also delegates to states and tribes the responsibility for issuing permits and for monitoring and enforcing compliance. At laboratories located throughout the nation, the Agency works to assess environmental conditions and to identify, understand, and solve current and future environmental problems. They also integrate the work of scientific partners (such as nations, private sector organizations, academia, and other agencies) and provide leadership in addressing emerging environmental issues and in advancing the science and technology of risk assessment and risk management.

A company's RA or HES Department should be responsible for determining the Toxic Substance Control Act (TSCA) declaration for your product. In turn, this information should be forwarded to the Import Department to indicate on the broker instructions and TSCA stamp the invoice accordingly. In the event courier shipments are utilized, the Import Department should be consulted to obtain TSCA determination for the foreign supplier to indicate on their invoice in lieu of a stamp. This will enable the shipment to clear paperless with the courier if all information has been supplied by the Import Department to that courier.

THE FEDERAL COMMUNICATIONS COMMISSION

The FCC is an independent U.S. agency, directly responsible to Congress. The FCC was established by the Communications Act of 1934 and is charged with regulating interstate and international communications by radio, television, wire, satellite, and cable. The FCC's jurisdiction covers the fifty states, the District of Columbia, and U.S. possessions. Most people know that if they watch television, the FCC is part of their life due to its role in regulating interstate and international communications by radio, television, wire, satellite, and cable. What people may *not* recognize is the extent to which every area of their life is intertwined with the communications technologies the FCC has responsibility to regulate. For example, because almost all electrical and electronic equipment emits radio frequencies, FCC equipment authorization rules protect you when using computers or laptops, when you swipe your debit card, use your garage door opener, or a radio-controlled toy. Since 9/11, the FCC's role in modern America reminded the country of the importance of reliable, easily available, and interoperable communications, both for emergency personnel responding to a tragedy and individuals checking on family and friends.

When Is an FCC Form Required for Importing?

The FCC requires specific documentation to be submitted at the time of import clearance. The FCC requires an FCC Form 740 (a statement regarding the importation of radio frequency devices capable of causing harmful interference) for completion for any FCC-regulated product for import clearance. A sample can be obtained via website http://www.fcc.gov/Forms/Form740/740.pdf. The FCC ID Number is found on the device, located near the FCC logo; if the FCC logo does not have a number in close proximity, it indicates that the device is self-certified by the manufacturer. *This requires the manufacturer's address for import clearance.* For example, if you had accidentally left your laptop abroad during a foreign visit, your laptop would need to be imported and cleared by U.S. Customs. Before having it sent back to you, someone would need to read this information to you from the back of your laptop in order to complete the form. The form would then need to be provided to the Import Department to accompany the broker instruction packet to the broker. The RA, HES, and Import Departments must establish written procedures for maintaining these forms. The FCC has provided U.S. Customs with a list of tariff numbers that require submission of the FCC information (tariff numbers can be screened via the Import Department). The merchandise normally requiring submission of this information consists of items that contain radio frequency devices.

The FCC works with Customs to enforce the regulation of FCC Form 740 at the U.S. ports. Penalties and/or imprisonment for failure to produce the form and/or produce inaccurate information for FCC/RAD (see below) are a liability involved with signing. If a shipment is received into a U.S. port without the proper FCC form, Customs may approve a "manipulation" on an import that already arrived. A manipulation term means that Customs will allow the broker/ importer, under Customs witness, to open your shipment.

Center for Devices and Radiological Health

In conjunction with the FCC requirements for electronic imports, a "RAD" form may also be required. The Electronic Product Radiation Control (RAD) provisions of the Federal Food, Drug, and Cosmetic Act (the Radiation Control for Health and Safety Act of 1968) requires that all imported electronic products, for which applicable radiation performance standards exist, shall comply with the standards and shall bear certification of such compliance. *Before* the products can be permitted to enter the U.S., importers are required to submit, with each shipment, certain import entry papers through the District Director, U.S. Customs Service, to the appropriate FDA district office. These importations of electronic goods are regulated by the CDRH, a branch of the FDA Center for Devices and Radiological Health, which requires specific documentation to be submitted to the Department of Health and Human Services. The importer or consignee must establish written procedures for maintaining control and final disposition of these products.

The CDRH requires that all products imported into the U.S. provide proof that they are safe from a radiological standpoint. This typically means that, for example, CRTs do not emit dangerous radiation and that laser devices do not pose a safety hazard. The CDRH requires a Form 2877 to accompany these products. This form is filled out with the accession number for the device in question. The accession number is not found anywhere on the product, nor is it a matter of public record. The manufacturer of the device is required to submit a report for each device, on a yearly basis, to the CDRH. Once the CDRH has approved the report, they assign it an accession number, the number required on the Form 2877. For further information on how to market a product in the

U.S., please refer to the Device Advice website at http://www.fda.gov/cdrh/devadvice/overview.html.

Movement of uncertified products in U.S. commerce is a violation of Section 538(a)(1) of the Act. Violations will result in voiding this exemption for the responsible parties and are subject to civil penalties. Providing false information to the U.S. government is a violation of the U.S. Code, Title 18, and subject to criminal prosecution.

What Specific Products Would Need FCC and/or RAD Forms for Clearance?

Imports that are regulated by the FCC and/or RAD provisions of the Federal Food, Drug, and Cosmetic Act (the Radiation Control for Health and Safety Act of 1968) require declaration forms to be provided for the following types of imports prior to the shipment's arrival into a U.S. port:

- Computers
- Monitors
- Laptops
- Bar-code scanners
- Printers
- Disk hard drives
- Diagnostic workstations with computers
- Keyboards
- Servers
- Modems

A company's RA Department could arrange for the regulated forms to be completed. The requester would be responsible for ensuring that all required information for the form is provided to the RA Department for form completion and signature. *The foreign shipper cannot complete the forms as the U.S. importer is responsible for the accurate information and signature.*

Add FCC/RAD Fields to Your Import Purchase Order Routing Checklist

FCC/RAD requirements for electronic imports (computers, monitors, bar-code scanners, etc.) should be an added element to the "routing" checklist database. Linking the database to RA to review for FCC/RAD requirements and form completion will save a company time and money in delays by the FDA. Work to have a separate database automate the access to these forms, once completed, for the foreign suppliers to obtain and supply with the shipment and provide a copy to the Import Department with their invoice and bill of lading paperwork.

Import Process for a Regulated Product

As you have learned, the import process, as shown in Figure 5.1, begins with the importer or filer submitting the necessary entry information to the local Customs district office. For those entries not filed electronically, a paper entry consisting of the commercial invoice, Customs entry forms 3461/3461ALT and/ or 7501, or documentation would need to be provided by the importer or filer. For products regulated by OGAs for U.S. clearance, a flow chart is provided to depict the process and to provide a visual.

THE DRUG ENFORCEMENT AGENCY

The mission of the DEA is to enforce the controlled substances laws and regulations of the U.S. The DEA brings to the criminal and civil justice system of the U.S., or any other competent jurisdiction, those organizations and principal members of organizations involved in the growing, manufacture, or distribution of controlled substances appearing in or destined for illicit traffic in the U.S. In carrying out its mission, the DEA's primary responsibilities include:

- Investigation and preparation for the prosecution of major violators of controlled substance laws operating at interstate and international levels.
- Investigation and preparation for prosecution of criminals and drug gangs who perpetrate violence in our communities and terrorize citizens through fear and intimidation.
- Management of a national drug intelligence program in cooperation with federal, state, local, and foreign officials to collect, analyze, and disseminate strategic and operational drug intelligence information.
- Seizure and forfeiture of assets derived from, traceable to, or intended to be used for illicit drug trafficking.
- Enforcement of the provisions of the Controlled Substances Act as they pertain to the manufacturing, distributing, and dispensing of legally produced controlled substances. Not to be confused with the TSCA, this law is a consolidation of numerous laws regulating the manufacture and distribution of narcotics, stimulants, depressants, hallucinogens, anabolic steroids, and chemicals used in the illicit production of controlled substances.

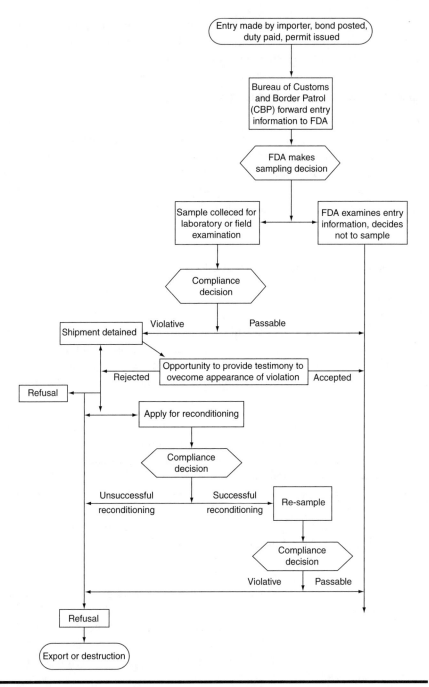

Figure 5.1. Import procedures flow chart for regulated products. (Compliments of www.fda.gov.)

- Coordination and cooperation with federal, state, and local law enforcement officials on mutual drug enforcement efforts and enhancement of such efforts through exploitation of potential interstate and international investigations beyond local or limited federal jurisdictions and resources.
- Coordination and cooperation with federal, state, and local agencies, and with foreign governments, in programs designed to reduce the availability of illicit abuse-type drugs on the U.S. market through non-enforcement methods such as crop eradication, crop substitution, and training of foreign officials.
- Responsibility, under the policy guidance of the Secretary of State and U.S. Ambassadors, for all programs associated with drug law enforcement counterparts in foreign countries.
- Liaison with the U.N., Interpol, and other organizations on matters relating to international drug control programs.

DEA-Regulated Products Must Be "Prenotified" Prior to Importation

There are threshold quantities of which certain DEA-regulated products may enter the U.S. without an official DEA entry and tracking of the product. A company's RA Department will determine if the regulated product is subject to DEA, such as List 1 products, pseudophedrines, that are popular with illegal drug manufacturers. Official prenotification is required to the DEA as well as follow-up information on the shipment after U.S. entry. The DEA tracks any product regulated by its agency. For example, a "hand-held" tablet press would make for a valuable gadget for street drug dealers. The DEA strives to ensure that these types of imported products remain unavailable to those not using it for legitimate means.

THE DEPARTMENT OF TRANSPORTATION

The DOT, a cabinet-level executive department of the U.S. government, has a mission to develop and coordinate policies that will provide an efficient and economical national transportation system, with due regard for need, the environment, and national defense. It is the primary agency in the federal government with the responsibility for shaping and administering policies and programs to protect and enhance the safety, adequacy, and efficiency of the transportation system and services.

On 9/11, radical Islamic extremists with the group Al Qaeda, hoping to sow terror and confusion among Americans, commandeered four American domestic airliners and transformed them into missiles that were used to destroy the

World Trade Center in New York City and to hobble the Pentagon in Arlington, Virginia, killing thousands. The DOT managers and FAA air traffic controllers performed a Herculean task by bringing the rest of the fleet down safely. Responding to this new form of terrorism, Congress passed the Aviation and Transportation Security Act and on November 19, 2001, President Bush signed it into law. This act called for the establishment of a completely new Transportation Security Administration in the DOT to increase security at airports and other transportation venues.

What Requirements Do Importers Need to Meet for the DOT?

Truckers who transport material on U.S. roadways must have appropriate paperwork reflecting the DOT description, such as if the product is a hazardous liquid or solid. This entails prescreening the inbound product and establishing the DOT profile prior to arrival into the U.S. port. Hazardous chemicals must be classified according to the DOT for inland domestic moves from U.S. ports to final destinations. A Material Safety Data Sheet (MSDS) is required, to be supplied by the requester to the Safety and Transportation Department, to complete the inland bill of lading profile required for moving freight in compliance with the DOT.

The DOT has a new programming tool for electronic Hazmat incident reports. In the event of an accident that involves a hazardous spill onto a roadway, the appropriate Hazmat team would need to be notified immediately. Each bill of lading should reflect the 800 phone number for contacting the Hazmat team. At the end of 2004, the DOT Research and Special Programs (RSPA) announced the availability of the programming tool for companies or individuals to use to file Hazmat incident reports electronically. The new electronic format may only be used for reporting incidents that occurred on or after January 1, 2005.

THE U.S. FISH AND WILDLIFE SERVICE

Through its international programs, the Fish and Wildlife Service works multilaterally with many partners and nations in the implementation of international treaties, conventions, and on-the-ground projects for conservation of species and the habitats on which they depend. These divisions, through the Wildlife Without Borders initiatives and Multinational Species Conservation Funds, seek to strengthen the capacity of interested local conservation and natural resources managers, institutions, and communities in regions around the world to conserve wildlife (including species conservation) and their habitats.

From time to time, you may have one of your shipments rejected for clearance due to Fish and Wildlife flagging. Even if your shipment had no involvement with this agency, the HS Number to your product may be flagged for clearance with this agency. You can either advise Customs by letter why your shipment is not qualified for Fish and Wildlife clearance or you can re-evaluate your HS Number to determine if you classified it correctly. If so, you may review with Customs why your product does not fall under Fish and Wildlife jurisdiction. Customs may revisit the HS Number and reconsider the necessary flagging for this agency.

THE CENTERS FOR DISEASE CONTROL AND PREVENTION

The CDC is recognized as the lead federal agency for protecting the health and safety of people at home and abroad, providing credible information to enhance health decisions and promoting health through strong partnerships. The CDC serves as the national focus for developing and applying disease prevention and control, environmental health, and health promotion and education activities designed to improve the health of the people of the U.S.

By charting decisive courses of action, collecting the right information, and working closely with other health and community organizations, the CDC has been putting science into action to tackle important health problems since 1946. The CDC seeks to accomplish its mission by working with partners throughout the nation and world to monitor health, detect and investigate health problems, conduct research to enhance prevention, develop and advocate sound public health policies, implement prevention strategies, promote healthy behaviors, foster safe and healthful environments, and provide leadership and training.

If your product line involves an infectious disease, human plasma, etc., consult your RA Representative to learn if your product is subject to a CDC permit, which could take several days or weeks to secure. At the time of entry, the FDA will determine if your product is subject to CDC requirements or not.

SUMMARY

Most companies that are impacted by "other government" regulations have already spent a lot of time and resources in proactive internal planning to meet the requirements. However, a critical part of the planning process involves the ability to self-assess and then fix any gaps that each may have in their current process. Furthermore, prior to forging ahead for a new product line, allow for the necessary time and training to occur for both importers and government officials under a new and relatively untested business lane to achieve a workable process that satisfies government and customer obligations. Ask yourself what affect does this OGA have on my turnaround? What can I do to speed things along and still be in compliance? What do they like to see for clearance? Any OGA will meet with importers to develop a strategy plan to avoid any wasteful efforts for both parties. Consider a developmental meeting with the agency with the jurisdiction over your clearances. This will assist you in deciding what course of action to take before making the contract commitment with the supplier. Identify in Chapter 6 what creates good or bad decisions on courses of action for a global supply chain and its planning.

6

THE EFFECTS ON DECISION MAKING

Every job function or task requires a decision and a direction. Whether the decision encompasses establishing a process for continuous functions, tasks, responsibilities, or those everyday unexpected occurrences, decisions need to be made. Judgment and evaluation are required to arrive at the best decision for budgets, costs, responsibilities, pricing, liability, distribution, packaging, when to purchase, when to ship, how to ship, what to market, what to warehouse, etc.

Each decision has a counterreaction to another element that coincides with the area in which the decision is made. One could decide to have product shipped via ocean to save on costs, yet the just-in-time inventory will be directly affected by this decision. How do you know if the decisions made for global procurement are the right ones? The answer comes with learning by trial and error or just by taking the time to dissect out all the elements involved that could/would have a positive or negative effect from a decision. If each decision is researched carefully and accurately *"before"* the contract or purchase order agreement is signed, the desired outcome may be achieved each and every time. Streamlining the individuals involved with decision making is the starting place. We have discussed the various individuals, departments, and responsibilities that must be involved with the international procurement business, but what if these departments are not linked together? In this chapter, we will discuss the various side effects to the decisions one can make and how to maneuver your outcome effectively to ensure that the right practices and decisions are instituted.

SMART FIRST-STEP DECISIONS IN PLANNING TO PROCURE PRODUCT GLOBALLY

Correct decision making is enabled by following a step-by-step procedure.

A. **Get your in-house act in order** — "The first and most vital step is to make sure your in-house act is together and in working order," according to Robert Rudzki, President of Greybeard Advisors LLC. He advises, "You have to ensure that there is a willingness inside your company, at all locations and divisions, to bundle your buys for volume leverage. You can't start to source outside your home country until you have your domestic house in order. That requires understanding your needs and specifications. You must have a good sourcing process in place, which is widely understood and utilized. You need discipline with bundling and negotiating. Presenting one face to the supplier and 'speaking with one voice' to your suppliers is central to that focus. And, you must encourage receptivity to suppliers' ideas. The more flexible you are in allowing suppliers to creatively respond to your requests, the more opportunity you have to find and negotiate the best possible deal."

B. **Select the right team members** — Another step to making a good decision is selecting the right team members. Rudzki counsels, "Select the right team members because you do not want 'corporate' trying to represent all points of views for all locations for all business divisions. Make sure you fully understand all your cost components and obstacles related to international procurement. By virtue of going beyond the borders of your residence, you are incurring different costs (not necessarily higher) and different risks." Rudzki offers the following examples that are cost and risk factors:

1. Transportation costs are likely to be different and more complex and transportation time lines are likely to be fairly lengthy.
2. Import/export rules and regulations and fees.
3. Foreign currency risks.
4. Sovereign country risks. There is always a risk that the foreign country could stop trade with the U.S. (because of a political debate within that country) or experience internal turmoil, which disrupts business commerce.
5. Credit risks of the foreign supplier itself. It can be more difficult to gain the information needed to assess the credit worthiness of the foreign supplier.
6. Storage and trans-shipment costs and time lines.

C. **Select the right process** — Rudzki concludes his remarks by advising, "Have the right team members and right process in place so that you fully understand all the costs and components relating to international procurement. Ensure that all those costs are compared on an apples-to-apples basis. It is commonly believed, for example, that American-based companies can save an enormous amount of money by outsourcing their IT activities to India or Eastern Europe. In a recent study by a major U.S. company, it was confirmed that the hourly rate in India for IT development was lower than in the U.S. However, outsourcing that work to India required more management oversight and the efficiencies and productivity of the outsourced work product was not as good. That had the effect of significantly reducing the apparent cost advantage of outsourcing. That particular example highlights the need to identify and assess all implications of a decision to source internationally."

THE FAILURE FORMULA

With a grasp of the first steps for global procurement, you need to connect all the elements to avoid bad decisions. Forming a solid base foundation for effective productivity has a chain reaction. How do you influence individuals and/ or departments to network and formalize such a base? Analyzing quotes, the competition, interest rates, territory, and customer interest are all elements that are spread across various departments. Ultimately, sales, procurement, manufacturing, and distribution departments connect to one goal: Make money while maintaining customer satisfaction. Individuals who are bad decision makers need to be identified quickly or the firm risks not reaching this goal.

The individuals who can cripple a supply chain vision are the ones who feel that researching cost or risk factors may be too time consuming and instantly making a decision will suffice. They may feel that this reflects a strong presence in the supply chain by someone who can make quick decisions with confidence in order to keep the process flowing. It is getting the job done and moving on to the next task that they feel will ultimately benefit the customer. In the realm of global procurement, such thinking can be a dangerous habit. So many elements and factors of every decision may have a boomerang or rippling effect and ultimately fail to meet the commitment to the customer and to the government. It may also negatively impair a corporation's name as a responsible importer.

If you are a company that is decentralized into various operating companies, then the international business decisions made in the Import Departments of those operating companies will have a rippling effect on the overall company name. Centralizing your international operations is a best practice avenue to ensure that the same methodology for decisions is being conducted throughout the entire global procurement process. Customs and the OGAs ultimately view the company as a whole and not the separate operating companies. They will evaluate reasonable-care performance by the "parent" company. It is imperative for importers to perform in the same systematic method with the government agencies. Customs and the OGAs will pick up on a shoddy operation where the company has too many different types of decision makers on what the best approach is to meeting compliance in a given situation.

A corporation's Compliance Department should set the baseline for what decision is to be made in a given situation, such as for valuating "free of charge" sample products, country of origin markings, trademark and copyright situations, etc. A Compliance Department should be responsible for conducting internal audits to ensure that the same methodology is evident with all global procurement import transactions. This is known as "Internal Control."

EVADING THE FAILURE FORMULA

Companies may predict and calculate the amount of failure an individual will experience by the following formula: Supply chain operations fail in equal shares due to their willingness to accept socially acceptable excuses for failure and lack following "known" operating procedures. Individuals may be negligent when researching facts required for a successful supply chain operation. Some may even default to pass off the decision or task to another department to formulate the necessary prerequisite. If those across the entire supply chain strive to avoid the failure formula in all cases, cost negotiations and accurate compliance information will be secured. What will be achieved is a thorough understanding of all costs and time lines to protect the company from hidden costly reparations and exposure to liability. The outcome of the actual entry process will be seamless clearances and deliveries to satisfy your customers (see Figure 6.1).

From the same line of reasoning, seeking out the token fall person is wasted effort.

The moment an inbound shipment goes awry, a grouping of the minds should be orchestrated immediately. Research to the core of where the problem may have occurred, evaluate what went wrong, and track back to the source of the problem. Sometimes the fatal error of a shipment is not caused by the actual mishap, but with the lack of identifying the core problem. Valuable time will be saved by avoiding the first reaction of joined groups, making assumptions

COOPERATION PAYS

Figure 6.1. Working together to achieve the same goal.

on who or where the source of the error belongs. Instead of succumbing to the urge to find the "token fall person or department," a supply chain should implement corrective action measures with key individuals who know how to provide the best guidance. However, if you know what went wrong, another fatal error is the refusal to accept personal accountability.

Individuals should not feel unworthy of positions that may have involved an error with the importation of a shipment. There are so many aspects of the global procurement and clearance domain that new information is surfacing almost monthly. Admitting to the mistake and correctly moving forward is the noble decision. Focus on the negative *and* the positive. What have you learned from this wrong decision or error? What was your best learning experience? How can you incorporate a process that eliminates the reoccurrence of this particular noncompliance or costly event?

In Chapter 3, we provided examples where misconceptions of mishaps within the transportation and clearance lane exist. Donel Accorsi, Import Specialist for a large U.S.-based company, has many years of experience in the international field, allowing her to witness a medley of various misunderstanding circumstances. Accorsi provides an example in which wasted assumptions can be made by noting, "Misunderstanding with the source of damaged freight has been known to be a time-consuming effort to capture where the fault resides. If a shipment is received into a warehouse showing evidence of damage, some people assume the inland trucker is the one at fault. However, it could have already been damaged overseas, en route, at the port, or within your own receiving area. Importing, as a whole, is misunderstood by many and it is unquestionably important to involve the right departments to determine conclusively where the impairment originated."

"Damage to a product may because a temperature-sensitive product was received at room temperature. Miscommunication between the foreign supplier and the forwarder on temperature requirements may have been the cause. Perhaps, it was decided to ship the product via a courier service as opposed to a commercial airline to achieve quicker turnaround, thus eliminating the need for temperature-control requirements. Unfortunately, a delay in the clearance process could surface, allowing the product to sit longer at a U.S. port than expected. Any number of incidents can befall an import and must be researched with an unbiased preassumption opinion, corrective actions identified and, most importantly, those corrective actions must be adhered to moving forward," she concludes.

THE OVERSEER AND THE LOGISTICS TROUBLESHOOTER

Appointing someone to be the overseeing guidance person and a logistics troubleshooter would be another suggested best practice. This person or persons should be involved with monitoring, evaluating, and offering suggestions to a new or current import procurement process for a global business lane. This best practice recommendation may be considered one responsibility or two separate needs, for which one or two individuals would be responsible. In some companies, a representative from a Compliance Control Unit (CCU) (defined in Chapter 7) is a good tool to place strategically within supply chain operations. The CCU Representative would have knowledge of the international business, transportation, purchasing, distribution, etc. The CCU Representative would not be a decision maker, however, he/she could attend a supply chain meeting and serve as a mediator and guidance counselor.

A CCU Representative can assist with linking the supply chain with the other departments within the company that may also need to be decision makers for an imported product. For example, RA would advise if the product needed to be registered for importation. This would cast an important time line component into the planning. It is beneficial to have a CCU Representative of an upper-position level within the management tier structure. Such a person serves as the influence factor to motivate individuals to execute the right decisions and guarantee that required tasks are accomplished in a timely manner, prior to the purchase order placement. The added support of a CCU Representative would offer the influence where needed in a supply chain.

A logistics troubleshooter should originate from an Import Department. Import Control Officers within an Import Department have an aerial view of the entire supply chain flow. They have direct dealings with the supplier, forwarders, shipping lines, airlines, truckers, government agencies, regulatory, procurement, accounting, and receiving locations. A logistics troubleshooter would do just what the title implies, troubleshoot potential problem areas and/ or surfacing quandaries. They can provide a line of prevention scenarios as well as assist with identifying where a problem evolved. By arranging to appoint an overseer and/or a logistics troubleshooter representative(s), a global supply chain operation would be privileged to have a direct resource for all and any questions or issues.

THE "SIX SET" ELEMENTS TO A SUCCESSFUL GLOBAL PROCUREMENT OPERATION

To be a top-notch global sourcing company, you need to get to the company's rock-bottom values and beliefs. When procuring globally, any organization should strive to incorporate six elements:

1. A quality or unique product
2. Secured compliance
3. Proper timing
4. Adequate budget
5. People resources
6. Effective management

Customers like to deal with a company they can trust. They need to know that the company has the expertise to meet their requirements and provide them with good quality. If a new global procurement acquisition is in the works and one of the above elements is not 100 percent ensured, a seamless path, proper timing of introduction into the marketplace, and the customer confidence could be placed in jeopardy. There is usually a good chance that an untapped, useful resource exists within every company to help avoid missing any of these elements. The problem is finding the people and responsibilities that have the potential to better build and brace these six elements and add value to a procurement process and/or any supply chain operation.

Through honed best practices and a sound strategy, a powerful global supply chain operation with secured longevity will emerge. Greybeard Advisors' President, Robert Rudzki, offers another six elements for a successful and strong future international course:

1. Effective leadership, the most important ingredient. Having someone in a leadership role that cannot lead is a harbinger of disaster.
2. Understand and implement best practices, regardless of the geographic scope of your sourcing activities.
3. Be willing to identify and adopt stretch, quantifiable objectives that are relevant to the company's bottom line. Link individual objectives and incentives to those stretch objectives.
4. Invest in the most important asset you have, people. Devote time and attention to the ongoing development of your employee base. Make training the last item to be trimmed at budget time.
5. Never shortchange yourself on professional resources. The pennies you save on salaries can easily be overcome or overwhelmed by lost opportunities or costly errors if you do not have adequate resources or properly trained resources.
6. Select the best technology. Some companies put technology at the top of the list, but technology is actually an enabler that helps all the other items listed above.

Deciding on global procurement processes for contract or purchase order agreements can involve huge milestones. Know all your costs for importing and liabilities associated with a particular U.S. port. Carefully analyze your steps and communicate your intentions to the right departments before committing to long-term projects. A solid foundation is built through the efforts of honest, responsive-reactive, good decision-making individuals, departments, and management.

CONTINUED TRAINING OF PERSONNEL CAN SPARE EXCESS SPENDING

Rudzki states that you need to have the right team members and right processes. This statement holds true for having the right team members for the right *responsibility*. The decision to cut back on the training budget can ultimately cost the company more in damage control expenses than for the cost of a seminar or training class. Ensuring a generous training budget that also allows for travel is a worthwhile decision. Far too often, a departmental position becomes vacant and the new recruit is expected to assume the responsibility with a transparent transition into their new role to the external departments.

These individuals strive to figure out their new responsibility without making any detrimental decisions that could halt a supply chain operation. For example, a person departing a position in RA that encompasses decisions on required regulated product information for U.S. clearance should properly train their successor. If the new recruit has not had the time to get proper training, they may generate invalid information simply because they do not know what resources are available. What has become a common "un"best practice in corporations is the lack of sufficient training for newcomers.

Heather Rohaley, Logistics Specialist, works for a major health-care company and has vast experience in the international logistics field. She has worked with a myriad of individuals who struggle to identify what their roles really entail and where they can seek guidance to handle the responsibility delegated to them appropriately. Rohaley states, "Many times, individuals are placed in positions to carry out compliance responsibilities and commission decisions that directly affect whether or not a product can make U.S. clearance. These individuals may not always be fully qualified for the responsibility they have undertaken. They may have been placed into their new roles either to fill an unexpected void in a given department or the new position was recently identified as a requirement and management did not understand the magnitude of the responsibility. The person who was bestowed a given function quickly finds themselves in unfamiliar territory. Most likely, they are unsure as to what they are to do, what their scope of responsibilities entails, how specific regulatory information is being used once passed on, who their resources are, or what their decisions affect."

Companies may find in-house training already available at no cost to a budget for a particular department function or individual need. If internal training does not exist, it may be time to decide on developing your own training program. Companies who house a Compliance Department offer internal training classes in the importing and exporting field. Individuals in supply chain operations that involve global procurement should take full advantage of this type of training. As Motorola's CEO George M. C. Fisher, succinctly put it, "We find it necessary to continually train all of our workers."

Each employee has a right to training and retraining when technology or requirements change. Figuring out just how to conduct the training is not always straightforward. If a company develops internal written standard operating procedures (SOP) for the import activities, a rollout of training on these SOPs should be conducted throughout the organization. A Customs Compliance Manual (CCM) should be created and implemented by a Compliance Department in conjunction with the Import and Law Departments. How a CCM fits into the importing arena and how it can be offered as a training tool is discussed in Chapter 7. Each procedure of the manual would explain all areas of importing and the areas of greatest concern to a global supply chain, for example:

- Valuation
- Classification
- Country of origin
- Marking requirements

Each topic would be geared towards training a particular audience such as sales, marketing, procurement, research, distribution, warehousing, etc. Raising the awareness and educating those individuals involved with inbound procurement will eliminate risk to not addressing vital areas that may prevent your new product launch from surfacing or detain your shipment. You will also save yourself time in postwork having to retrieve and prepare information for a Customs audit to justify actions and decisions you had chosen.

MAKE GOOD DECISIONS WITH NECESSARY DETAILS

When administrating a formal procedure system, it is important to decide on the amount of information to include. The level of detail included will have a direct affect on the amount of administration necessary to maintain procedures reflective of current practice. Diane Lewandowski, a manager in a major U.S.-based health-care corporation, has administrated procedure control systems for over twenty years. Lewandowski recommends utilizing written procedures as a foundation for a strong documentation system. She states, "They serve as a valuable tool for training new employees and serve as great references for existing employees." In her history, she has been responsible for administrating, reviewing, and approving over 1,000 procedures. "Procedures," Lewandowski continues, "should be detailed enough to capture all the critical points. However, don't make it such a burdensome ordeal that they are rarely utilized. Procedures can work to your advantage if they strike the appropriate balance between control and flexibility."

"It's helpful to separate procedures into two or three levels," she advises. "The highest level of procedures documents the interdepartmental functions, general work flow, and clarifies which departments/functions have responsibility for decisions and work output. The next level covers individual department processes with enough detail to describe the process, but not so much that a revision is required every few weeks as small changes are made. The third tier of procedures is the most specific one. These are often referred to as desktop procedures."

Lewandowski continues by advising the following procedure rules:

1. Use controlled (numbered, reviewed, approved) procedures in a consistent format.
2. Never use names of individuals in procedures, only use titles/functions.
3. Revisit procedures at least every two years. This "catches" the small changes that may not have been recognized as requiring a procedure revision.
4. Assign this periodic review to the individuals most familiar with the content. The benefits are twofold: it spreads out a tedious task to many so that no one individual is overwhelmed, and over time, users become very familiar with procedures, which further ensures compliance.

Lewandowski adds, "In an organization with moderate to high turnover, written procedures are important in maintaining consistent work flow by using them for training and then for reference. For stable organizations, procedures provide a solid framework to build upon. In many regulated industries, the requirement for written procedures is sometimes regarded as a necessary 'evil.' However, the benefits of a documented, flexible procedure system far outweigh the effort required to maintain such a system."

It is essential for those in the decision-making position to identify the individuals who do *not* know what their job entails, as well as the individual who does not know how to do the job required, or someone who is interfering with his/her ability to complete the job task. Providing the written procedures, guidance, and training will make all the difference in a person's confidence and ability. Companies, moreover, need to ensure that they have proper documentation as a result of new post 9/11 company security requirements and participation programs such as C-TPAT, the Sarbanes-Oxley Act, government audits, and for ensuring nothing steps out of the bounds of procedures that affect the bottom line.

DECIDING ON ONE FACE TO THE GOVERNMENT AGENCIES

Any part of the U.S. government can probe into your global inbound supply chain operation on a whim, more so by reason of the 9/11 events. Unfortunately, when Customs or any OGA approaches your company with an inquiry or an impromptu audit, there is no option to respond to them "at a later time."

Various types of Customs inquiries have deadlines, to which importers must respond. Failure to meet these deadlines results in fines, penalties, and/or possibly imprisonment. It is a wise decision to identify someone within the corporation who would be responsible for researching what is needed for Customs and provide prompt responses. At the same time, you must limit the number of individuals who would be permitted to work directly with Customs and/or the OGAs.

A best practice to follow would be to provide "one face to the government agencies." This person would be familiar with the "response act format" that Customs desires. This area is another in which a conformity process should be taken each time when working with Customs or any OGA. You will receive a quicker response turnaround if they receive the information solicited in the desired format. Every time a shipment is detained for release, a company incurs unnecessary costs, a customer deadline is missed, storage charges may accrue, examination charges may be applied, additional fees by the service providers may surface, damage to the product could occur at the port site, and if a noncompliance issue is identified, it may mean fines and penalties.

TESTING THE WATERS

Testing the waters for any internationally procured product for the first time is a worthy decision and always makes for a shrewd best practice for new start-up launches. It is advisable to run a sample-size test shipment to work out the kinks. This will allow everyone involved to witness the flow of the process without running any risks of missing a live customer deadline or bottom-line costs. Prior to approving any contracts or blanket agreements, wait for all the final bills to come in to calculate the true costs because many hidden expenses can descend on a shipment that affect your original cost expectations. You may need to re-evaluate your pricing and terms and conditions of sale. Since different U.S. ports have different requirements, running through the process before signing any contractual agreements with your supplier will bring overlooked areas to light. For example, Puerto Rico is considered part of the U.S. domain for importation activities, but not for exporting. Unlike other U.S. ports, if your business lane requires clearances into Puerto Rico, an additional excise tax (for example, 6.6 percent of your invoice value) and/or income tax may apply to your merchandise. This is in addition to your Customs tax, MPF, and HMF costs. You may not have thought to question any added taxes. (Further on in this chapter, a new tax savings concept, Triangulation, is introduced.) If a tax applies to your merchandise, have your Import Department research with Customs and the Puerto Rican authorities to see if you are eligible for an exemption or reimbursement. You may also have to register your activities with the local government. Insist on a "transitional service" clause in any long-term contract that would obligate your supplier's continued cooperation in the event your first few shipments encounter obstacles.

Always allow time in your planning for researching. If an unsuspecting problem surfaces with a live shipment, a key individual who would have the resources to resolve the dilemma quickly may be unavailable. This preferred path of researching the step-by-step process serves as a best practice as knowledge is always gained from observing a total process.

TRIANGULATION

The dynamics of today's marketplace support the need for strong business solutions that help companies manage the increasingly complex global supply chain and the risks associated with global trade. Compared to other application areas, global trade management has struggled to gain traction, in part because of the lack of holistic and integrated solutions. If you are deciding on ways to fortify or increase your company's global supply chain performance arrangement and to optimize your business procurement processes, a fairly new concept may offer assistance.

Marlene Russo, Manager of International Service Operations for a large global agricultural firm, has worked in innovative ways to gain controlled, cost effectiveness for the company via new venues. Russo has accomplished the fresh trend of Triangulation, a process that can assist a company in restrategizing the location where the purchase order is secured for tax advantage optimization. She shares the systematic theory by explaining, "In International Logistics, Triangulation is a financial concept which offers tax savings benefits to a corporation with worldwide global affiliates, but also has implications where material management is concerned."

Triangulation can provide a multinational company with a triad of benefits: (1) an ultraefficient transfer pricing mechanism, (2) tax benefits, and (3) duty savings. Duty savings may be realized by following the "first sale" premise that is upheld in the U.S. by the infamous case of *Nissho Iwai American Corp. v. United States*. Duty savings based on the "first sale" premise are discussed in detail in Chapter 7.

"Typically, the Triangulation Center (TRIA-Center) is located in a European country, for example, Germany or France. The TRIA-Center receives purchase orders from one of its global affiliates for goods, which are produced by another affiliate. The sale in this case is between Country Customer and the TRIA-Center. They have an agreed-upon established transfer price."

"The TRIA-Center then will place their sales order with the global affiliate who produces the goods. The sale in this case is between the Producing Country and the TRIA-Center. They also have an agreed-upon transfer price."

"The Producing Country," Russo continues, "is instructed to ship the goods directly to Country Customer. The Producing Country then invoices the TRIA-Center and, in turn, the TRIA-Center invoices the Country Customer. In Shipper's Export Declaration (SED) terms, the Producing Country is still the Exporter of Record because they realize a financial gain from the transaction. The goods, however, will clear customs in the destination country on the invoice from the TRIA-Center, because the sale is between the Country Customer and the TRIA-Center."

"Many companies opt for running this type of business transaction in concert with a Global Demand Planning scenario. Where all countries concerned have access to a global demand-planning tool, transparency is achieved regarding advanced forecasting. Strategic materials can better be allocated and the production planning process becomes more efficient," she concludes.

Within the Triangulation framework, the scope of a project includes the creation of a globally harmonized and optimized order management process for a given company. A global company should involve their tax, customs, and credit authorities and legal counsel to ensure proper development of such a framework. In certain European countries, legislation mandates strict documentation of intercompany value flows. This requirement forces companies to develop a harmonized transfer price policy within the legal framework that retains written, streamlined order management process procedures to avoid any business risks and obstacles.

GETTING HELP WITH KNOWLEDGE
AND DECISION MAKING

Triangulation and other cost-effective opportunities are available for global decision planning. How can one begin to identify and understand global opportunities? Who out there can help you to understand the overall picture? An actively involved Procurement Department that works with its internal Import and Compliance Departments will always be a good source of information for a global supply chain, but there are other external resources that can help you overcome decision-making concerns and barriers. Various industry and global groups are cropping up yearly that can be consulted by foreign sellers and U.S. buyers.

One particular support network that is leading importers and exporters to the next era is the American Association of Exporters and Importers (AAEI). This organization's purpose is to assist exporters and importers with a vast array of useful methods. They are actively involved in the latest issues rolling out from Congress and the multiple regulatory agencies that have a direct effect on companies in the international industry. AAEI has been around for eighty-one years and has a member roster of approximately 500 and growing. AAEI sponsors a variety of seminars yearly, which include various speakers and topics from companies in the exporting/importing industry. The organization provides multiple industry scenarios, via skits and presentations, of obstacles that members and organizations have encountered and what they did to resolve these situations. An example of knowledge one would gain from an AAEI seminar would be the "Trade, Compliance and Security: Turning Challenges into Successes" that featured government and private-sector speakers providing insights into coming changes and practical steps for surviving and thriving in today's rapidly changing trade environment.

AAEI's President and CEO, Hallock Northcott, elaborates on how involved the AAEI has become in international issues, how they have grown over the years, and the foundation and support for major changes to government rules and regulations that are now in place today. Northcott begins with this scenario, "You are sitting in the port of New York. Now, for a moment, think about the distinction between 9/11 pre and post. This is now the world our members live in. Post 9/11 is now the big-picture stuff. Members consider 'facilitation' in making the system work and getting the product from one end to the other end and that involves customs modernization and all other pieces and processes that need to work to facilitate other operations. The fact that people talk about a paradigm shift and what has happened to our industry is an incredible example of the dramatic shift in thinking that was not known and not widely discussed."

Northcott continues by describing the government's priority: Ranking differences between pre and post 9/11 and how it has a direct effect on companies' options for global procurement decisions. "Okay, we are going to play a game for just a second. You be 'the trade and supply chain industry' and I'm going to be 'government' and we're going to agree on a ranking scale of import issue priorities pre 9/11 on a scale of 1 to 10. There are four things we agree to rank:

1. Drugs
2. Revenue
3. Facilitation
4. Security

Prior to 9/11, the big variable with importing was drugs. Drugs had a ranking of 1, but moved to 7 and to 9 and back again. So, let's talk about 'stability' on the same 1 to 10 ranking scale. For the government and the

Treasury Department on their scale, the first priority is going to be 'revenue,' again, on the same 1 to 10. But you are important and your industry cares a lot about 'facilitation' and, as a result in a pre 9/11 world, this ranks about 3 on the scale. Then we have 'security.' In pre 9/11, this factor hit the scale as a level 3 priority for the government, but was focused largely on product theft and loss. Post 9/11 happened and 'security' was instantly redefined to focus on terrorism and became the number 1 ranked priority for the U.S. government."

"No longer ranked number 1, 'revenue' slipped down to number 5 or 6. It is still important and it is vital for government, but is nowhere near the importance which security now has captured. What happened to 'facilitation'? Facilitation is what AAEI and our industry had been all about. You tell me where it went on the scale," challenges Northcott. "Some people will argue it's not on the scale at all. AAEI thinks it not only should be on the scale, but it needs to be a whole lot higher. If facilitation doesn't become a priority, it works against the economy and the AAEI members."

"Okay, now to the second dimension of the paradigm shift — and that is the system itself. You remain the industry and I'll remain the government. Pre 9/11, if you've got a problem getting something into the country, the government has people in the Department of Transportation where you've got friends there that can help you. Now, you have a purchase order that is difficult to import, so you go to your resources in the Department of Justice. You have a problem with a classification holdup that doesn't make sense, a regulatory difficulty that you need to resolve, so you go to Treasury and get a resolution. Pre 9/11, you have department after department within the government that can help to get it done. Now it's post 9/11 and your world has dramatically changed. All the government people have gone into other functions not at all related to what they used to be. They are now within the Department of Homeland Security (DHS). Not only have the questions that we addressed changed dramatically, but also the places where we address them," Northcott concludes.

HOW DO YOU KNOW IF YOU QUALIFY TO JOIN SUCH AN ORGANIZATION? AAEI'S DOORS ARE OPEN TO ANYONE

Deciding what organization(s) best meet(s) your needs and visions can be laborious. You strive to identify with a group that understands your business process obstacles and the barriers you experience. You look for a group or association that can provide consultation, seek answers, brainstorm, and work to make changes needed for industry improvements. The AAEI is constantly evolving its agenda to tackle the most current issues facing global supply chains in a post 9/11 era. The AAEI has been behind many great feats that reconstructed the way companies conduct and benefit from international business.

Hallock Northcott reflects on some of AAEI's greatest accomplishments, "There was a great deal to do thirteen years ago as AAEI was a leader on the passage of the Modernization Act. AAEI put in time and money and coordinated much of the overall restructure. Multiple 'instant' groups must become involved to try and make anything happen. AAEI, essentially, was heavily involved in pulling together the Private Sector Coalition, which helped drive the adoption of the harmonized code and the way the Modernization Act is today. AAEI was a principal driver."

"Anyone in our industry can be a member. There is a division that all members within AAEI are equal of all rights and obligations. We recognize and serve, but do not distinguish between three categories of members, that is, importers/exporter, retailers/distributors, and service providers," advises Northcott. "People have come out of Customs who are now working in the importing/exporting arena in corporations. Some became AAEI members. We are a variety and in terms of servicing the business needs, we are from soup to nuts of industry players, AAEI is it!" (www.aaei.org).

LEARNING DECISIONS, CONSEQUENCES, AND BEST PRACTICES

When meeting with trade groups in the industry, one of the many perks is to have the opportunity to mentor or to be mentored. Having the avenue to meet individuals with a wide array of industry processes is priceless. Multifaceted ideas and approaches are available. Similar procedures and requirements for international procurement are widely spread among members. This allows you to take a new outlook or direction, even for the most common task, back to your job.

Below are several fictitious examples that can raise the expertise level of basic arrangements that affect the supply chain process. They are provided to educate those securing the purchase order agreement and establishing the time lines. Multiple factors must be considered along with the price negotiations to remain in compliance for Customs clearance, such as, assists, free of charge samples, etc.

Do Not Try to Beat the System: Scenario Number 1

The Sales Department Representative of CTB Company lands a blanket agreement with a foreign company who will supply repetitive imports of fabricated components. The agreement involved a decision to include a clause that once a certain amount of components are purchased, CTB Company will be given a dozen components "free of charge." Did the Sales Department appropriately disseminate this information to CTB's internal Import Department? Why should they? The answer is that any free imported items that are "thrown in" with your shipment as an added perk from your supplier must have a dollar value and must be clearly indicated on the invoice as to what the product is and its intended use. Otherwise, when Customs stumbles on this purchasing agreement area, CTB will most likely be penalized for failure to justify substantially why these products and values were not made evident on the invoice. Chapter 7 provides more insight on what is mandatorily required on an invoice as a result of various types of sales agreements.

Registration: Scenario Number 2

A company launches a new regulated product line of an over-the-counter (OTC) medication that already has an approved Drug Listing Number established with the FDA for the manufacturing site in France. A decision was made to move the OTC production site from Company A in France to Company B in Spain for better manufacturing conditions. A decision was also made to move the product launch date for domestic distribution and begin imports immediately. All tasks have been performed efficiently to import the OTC product into the U.S., or have they? The regulated OTC product arrives into the U.S. and is processed through the FDA for clearance. The FDA rejects the shipment and advises that the product is not registered.

Why does the FDA determine this? Because the FDA does not show the product registration information in its database with "Spain" as the country of manufacturer. The drug listing shows "France" as the manufacturing and registered facility. Should someone within the supply chain have verified that the FDA did "indeed" receive the revised registration information? The answer is "yes." A decision was made to begin the process without ensuring that all tasks were completed. Even though the RA Department provides the FDA with registration information, it is imperative that follow-up be conducted with the FDA to ensure that they receive any revised registration information and have loaded it into their system prior to any purchase order release for the U.S. Numerous weeks could be involved with resubmitting the registration information to the FDA in the event the FDA misplaced it. The revised registration company name and address must also undergo an entirely new approval process and data entry adjustment by the FDA.

Rushing: Scenario Number 3

A research group based in Santa Ana, California called Roth Company embarks on a product line of new base metal spare parts and sources from a foreign supplier in Brazil. Roth Company learns of some tough competition existing on the east coast for the same product. A decision is made to get the product launched as quickly as possible by any means. Roth advises the Brazilian company to ship the first batch immediately on expedited clearance and transportation arrangements. The shipment arrives into the U.S. Since these are spare parts, only Customs and the USDA are involved with the clearance. The shipment is cleared and delivered in record time. Roth Company then receives the bill. It is 40 percent over the original estimated costs as a result of requested expedited privileges and services with Customs and the transportation providers. Roth paid dearly for their urgency.

BENCHMARKING AS BEST PRACTICE

Various companies participate in import benchmarking consortiums. It is beneficial to allow yourself to be gauged against someone else's similar activities. How are they handling their processes? What are their results? What has been the biggest benefit? Do you have a colleague in the global procurement industry whose supply chain operation is similar in nature to yours? Similar means that the purchases are of the same magnitude, that is, large or small in comparison. Or are they regulated by OGAs? Do they require Prior Notice, same customer expectations, similar technology systems and processes, etc.? Benchmarking as a best practice for your international business against another company's similar or identical business lanes is a creative way to stay abreast of current technology, requirements, procedures, etc. This can be achieved via seminars, conferences, benchmarking organizational groups, or self-organized efforts. Benchmark your operation. Perhaps you will find that your company's organizational processes are in need of a facelift or you realize that you are a forefront runner with a superior operation.

TAKE THE TIME TO STREAMLINE

Streamlining all tasks improves efficiency, effectiveness, cycle times, costs, and ultimately, reduces stress. The decisions that a specific area of a supply chain makes have a direct effect on other aspects of the tasks involved. Ultimately, an implementation of an automated system would assist in streamlining tasks, capture decisional material for documentation purposes, and network the required departments. This is what some companies elect to do. Through technology, they can link their systems together with their service providers. It ties their entire company processes together. Let us provide an example of how deciding to automate can work well to streamline processes.

A total ownership program (discussed in Chapter 3) with a particular broker can provide for the streamlining of events. Having the broker granted access to specific areas of your systems can provide an efficient, paperless process. For example, an automated development resource system is the new wave for companies to link their entire business through one funnel system. This type of automation can be built to manage your company's entire operation from procurement to accounting to receiving. It weaves its technology throughout a company's processes through a variety of Internet portals that enable true collaboration. External service providers can tap into your system to complete various transactions, such as dispatching freight. A company will begin a process in the system, such as order entry, and the service provider will tap in at a certain transaction to complete the process, which could be delivery dispatch information.

Mark Dailey provides expert supervision to an Import Staff Department of a global brokerage firm. He has many years of experience working in the international field and with meeting customer's expectations and visions. Dailey offers the following perceptiveness into the connecting technology with importers and service providers. "I feel constant progression with technology will enable both companies to provide leaner and more streamlined operations. The nature of the technology industry itself is constantly evolving and it is essential that both importers and service providers alike identify and adapt these changes in order to remain at the top."

Dailey continues, "Let's say we have two customers, one that provides access to their system for documents and one who does not. In the situation where the customer provides access to their system, a broker is able to access the information when required, thus, enabling a quicker turnaround than the customer that does not. Ultimately, when a broker is in charge of an account, the broker would want to have access to as much of the process as possible. The more the broker can control and react to unforeseen circumstances within the customer's virtual environment, the more the broker can ensure the process keeps flowing. As a result of this, the broker can identify issues, whether current or in the future, which can delay or halt the process."

"With a reliable service provider, the advantages to an importer would be with having a broker who may be able to provide more insight into the importer's process rather than having the importer be solely responsible internally for this insight creativity." However, Dailey cautions, "the danger with this same model is the importer only having visibility to a certain aspect of the supply chain operation. Department of Transportation (DOT) documentation for domestic carriers, for example, can be incorrectly processed without an understanding of why and what the effects of it are."

"Supply chains can be effectively managed when the 'big picture' is understood," Dailey states. "Having a service provider you are comfortable with and possesses the experience can very effectively help you understand this big picture. In my experience, the customer who requests that we access their system for this documentation has the level of comfort and confidence I was referring to. From past experiences, before importers switched their supply chain platform, we informed them when information was incorrect and/or what delayed the process flow. Using the same example, DOT information for domestic carriers can be incorrect when passed to the broker. We would also recommend against certain domestic carriers selected from the importer due to the carrier's lack of service or not even providing the service they were required. I believe importers learned from this to help re-evaluate current decisions. When the new platform was in development, they used the past to plan for the future and assigned the task to the service provider."

"When a service provider has access to an importer's platform, there are issues that should be identified and both the customer and service provider should agree on who is responsible for them. This should lessen or eliminate blame on either part when these issues arise as I have witnessed this firsthand," Dailey states. "My recommendation would be to roll out new platforms in stages. If you are an importer, implement the new platform with the smallest division. This way, if issues with the change (employees who are unfamiliar, hence reduced productivity, programming of the platform itself, etc.) arise, your whole system and customers are not affected."

JOINING "DISTINCTIVE" PROCESSES MUST REMAIN IN HOUSE

Various tasks are outside the realm of the broker and necessitate being prepared in house. Let us consider the shared Regulatory/Import product database discussed in Chapter 4, in which regulatory information must be managed in house and not outsourced to a service provider. This routing-linkage technology can be taken a step further to include tabs and fields to populate the DOT fields for the inland movement from the U.S. port to the final destination. Hazmat descriptions can be built out in the same shared database by the company's Safety and Transportation Department and can be an added routing link to the import purchase order form. When the product is classified by the Compliance Department for the proper HS Number, again, a tab and fields can be developed within the same database to be routed and populated accordingly. The entire import purchase order form could then be routed back to the requester with a copy to the Import Department to serve as a prealert. The system would have allowed the purchase order to go full circle to obtain all required information to complete the product profile via this technology.

BUILDING YOUR RELATIONSHIP
WITH YOUR FOREIGN SUPPLIER

Procurement Departments have their own supplier selection best practices that involve various attributes for the decision process. Once the supplier of choice is made, the relationship building should begin. The expectations and the life-cycle perspective of the commitment between buyer and seller will influence your costs and time lines. When procuring from a foreign entity, post 9/11, foreign suppliers are further involved and responsible for fulfilling U.S. Customs requirements for exporting to the U.S. Forecasting, planning, and manufacturing commitments are routine foreign supplier prerequisites to complete. New security and government regulation requirements for the foreign supplier to fulfill must be met to participate in the U.S. market. Working closely with your foreign supplier is an orderly decision to make your relationship strong and ensure a continued import privilege. If budgets permit, arrange a site visit to your foreign supplier. Also, further extend the relationship-building concept to your Import Department with your foreign supplier. It makes for a quicker process if the Import Department and foreign supplier interact directly to speak the "international" jargon.

The foreign supplier is required to provide vital information for a successful paperless clearance with the government agencies. By providing guidance to your supplier, a win-win situation will be achieved on each and every shipment. Utilize the purchase order/pricing agreement to provide clear, precise information needed for transportation, clearance, delivery, and payment. It will eliminate any misunderstandings and prompt shipping and import reminder requirements. The supplier will help any importer through any government audit if all the pricing and clearance information matches completely across all paperwork. Customs audits the pricing uniformity from what is reflected on the purchase order to the invoice pricing for clearance to the price actually paid by Accounting. All pricing must match; otherwise, explanations and justification will need to be solicited from the supplier, procurement, and accounting representatives.

A Compliance Department may decide to conduct their own "mock" audit in order to be proactive in preparation for a "live" audit conducted by Customs. Along with pricing information, the systems and/or databases utilized to access and process pricing information are also among the items that will be researched. The basis for accurate valuation for Customs is to ensure the correct calculation of duty payment to Customs. If you are undervaluing a product, that is less revenue for Customs if the product is dutiable. The duty rate is multiplied by the entered value to arrive at the correct duty amount due to Customs.

DEVISING NEW LOGISTICS TRENDS: FOREIGN SUPPLIERS PENETRATING THE U.S. MARKET WITH NO WAREHOUSING INVESTMENT

Let us reverse, for a moment, the business process to the foreign supplier. What options are available to them for U.S. trade? Foreign suppliers and/or manufacturers involve larger spectrums of procurement, compliance, and transportation decisions that the U.S. manufacturer may not necessarily need to make. They have broader areas in which to think outside the box and try to tap into the U.S. market. The most prominent question, however, for a foreign supplier not having a U.S. agent would be: Can I keep inventory in the U.S. instead of having to arrange exports to the U.S. per order? Warehousing has undergone a major facelift in the global supply chain world. Companies are starting to expand their product markets globally without the added weight of materials management, warehousing, and distribution costs — and without adding staff in new markets. Let us provide a unique idea from EGL Eagle Global Logistics' President and CMO, E. Joseph Bento, who provides the following concept from his article "Penetrating the U.S. Market With No Warehousing Investment" in *Inbound Logistics*, April 2004.

Middle East to U.S.:
An excellent example of this new logistics trend is a Middle East manufacturer of ready-to-assemble consumer PVC storage sheds and buildings. With these products growing in popularity in the home improvement industry, the company wanted to penetrate the U.S. market and quickly expand its presence and market share. In order to have the lowest possible overhead, it had to eliminate its

warehouse inventory and its own distribution to name-brand U.S. retailers. It also had to eliminate direct involvement in overseas shipping. To leverage this new supply chain business model, the manufacturer took the following steps:

- Outsourced certain steps of the supply chain from production in the Middle East through distribution in the United States.
- Hired a logistics provider to manage the entire process.
- Eliminated product warehousing, resulting in considerable savings.

This innovative process can work for any foreign company that wants to penetrate the U.S. market with virtually no warehousing investment. In fact, companies can initiate a test project for a year, or several months, to see if the U.S. market presents a profitable opportunity for their specific product. For the portable building manufacturer, the logistics provider set up a national logistics/distribution process with five strategically located warehouses. Upon stateside delivery of each shipment the logistics provider clears each container through Customs, bar codes, and downloads the data to its warehouse management system. Twice daily, that information is uploaded so the retailer can see inventory levels to determine needed replenishment. In this case, as many as 10 to 20 containers are typically needed to feed the re-supply requirements of more then 1,000 store locations nationwide. This end-to-end reshaping of the supply chain allows the Middle East company to focus exclusively on its core competencies: manufacturing and sales.

Maintaining Flexibility:
Within this newly emerging business model, the logistics provider has certain distribution hub flexibility. Although distribution is currently optimized at the five central locations, it can readily expand to include many more national locations. For practical purposes, the manufacturer is tapping into the provider's carrier network, facilities and infrastructure, including the information technology (IT). With virtually the entire supply chain operation conducted via the Internet, thus dramatically reducing the cost, the manufacturer has total visibility of all products in transit. The IT component, although not the magic bullet envisioned by many, is critical. The key is a keen understanding of the physical flow and processes, then layering the information and financial requirements.

Inventory in Motion:
In the new supply chain business model, the ultimate goal is not necessarily to see how much warehouse space a logistics provider can acquire in order to "spin" it for stocking more customer inventory. Instead, the goal should be to continually bring in inventory, keep it constantly in motion, and get it as close to the customer as quickly and efficiently as possible for final delivery just-in-time, while squeezing out every last ounce of cost in the process. So, how is the portable building manufacturer doing since the first shipment in January 2003? Its business has increased by double digits. And what about the logistics provider? It went from delivery product to each store every two months to delivering to the major retailer's chain once a week.

MAINTAINING THE U.S. VISIBILITY

Global companies can conduct business via multiple venues. Offshore procurement can be through the purchase of imported material from a U.S.-based foreign company agent, import merchants, wholesalers, or trading firms. Having the U.S.-based site in control of the government clearances and delivery removes real or potential roadblocks, but a drawback is that unit prices are higher than domestic buying. However, for the U.S.-based buyer, it may be the only method to take advantage of more competitive pricing or locating a qualified supplier. When foreign buying is continuous and the value of commitments is substantial, direct foreign purchasing can enhance cost-reduction opportunities, despite the complexity that global procurement brings forth.

With the importer assuming all responsibilities and risks involved in buying foreign materials and making deliveries, it is critical for global companies to retain a U.S.-based site for visibility to the U.S. consumer and to maintain internal company and U.S. government control. Foreign suppliers are often not familiar with U.S. rules and regulations and the ever-evolving new requirements that arise. A global company's internal control must be on the U.S. side for import U.S. procurement.

The enticement can also exist for global businesses to outsource U.S.-based jobs to the foreign parent company or create a new foreign-based site for the U.S. market. A danger exists when foreign-site managers observe a creative process that seems to work well in one culture and then attempt to transplant it mechanically to their own environment abroad without understanding how cultural differences may affect the process. The most difficult problem of starting a foreign office is in staffing. Finding qualified bilingual candidates can be a challenge. Another problem is that foreign governments are extremely protective of their workers. Some countries promote "lifetime" employment policies and the laws require that "unnecessary" employees receive termination pay equivalent to two years' salary. As a result, global companies may tend to consider downsizing U.S. jobs and outsource the process to the foreign-affiliated country. It would seem to be more advantageous to eliminate the U.S. jobs since disposing of the foreign "lifers" is more expensive.

When relocating U.S. employees, titles used in the U.S. and salary practices cannot be exported to foreign countries. Soon the resentment and decline in morale among U.S. employees begins to surface as the fear of losing their jobs to foreign soil escalates quickly. While the concept may work for a global company deciding to make such changes, the compliance factor still exists. A company's IRS Number must be in full control by the U.S.-based site and must represent the foreign affiliate to the U.S. government as its U.S. agent. A continued import privilege will be the reward.

A GOOD LIFE IS MADE UP OF GOOD DECISIONS

The statement that a good life is made up of good decisions holds true for managing a company and a successful global supply chain operation. There are multiple players, requirements, and expectations to manage and all require decisions. A decision maker does not always have to achieve the "best" decision, however, in most cases, it is the decision maker that must decide which course is best. If the foundation and steps are built correctly and are based on good decisions, the obstacles and barriers that are within your own company's control can be safeguarded. When a company pours equal amounts of "money making and saving ideas" and "compliance requirements" through the same funnel, the outcome for any company can be victory each time! Chapter 7 provides insights into where your money-generating ideas must intertwine with compliance.

7

THE MONEY GENERATOR AND COMPLIANCE PORTAL

Importing is a "privilege." It is not a luxury or a means to choose from global procurement alternatives at a company's discretion. The privilege can be revoked by Customs if they feel that the company is not practicing reasonable care. Special government rules and regulations affecting importation, moreover, have developed as a direct result of 9/11 and impact importing procedures. Immense responsibilities, for example, have been placed on importers to ensure internal controls of their company IRS Number for importing.

From another aspect, the Sarbanes-Oxley Act, enacted in 2004, surfaced as a result of such business improprieties as the Enron fiasco. Companies now have to prove they have sufficient internal controls. Financial statements are no longer the only auditing factor used to satisfy investors that a company has secured internal control for all operations. There must be evidence of the kind of controls that prevent another large-scale impropriety. This act did not exclude international business. Compliance also has to define clearly how a firm's internal controls are structured and in place.

How does a company begin to embark on "ensuring" internal controls for its international business? How do you ensure that the firm is meeting all of the new requirements? In this chapter, we will provide practical advice for building and managing the entire "compliance process," where both costs and compliance funnel through the same pipeline. We will explain how developing and adhering to a structured importing process and supply chain operation will provide payoffs of reduced costs and a continued import privilege option.

Many areas of the importing industry have been directly affected by new post 9/11 regulations, which stretch from transactions arranged at the foreign supplier's door through to the U.S. customer's door. Today, Customs has an active interest in knowing from whom you are procuring product globally, how well you are securing your company's containers, what transportation access lanes are being used, and if the clearance process is being properly managed. Supply chain operations are equally anxious to bring forth their imported products and begin making money. However, a company's IRS Number must be secured first. Companies have an obligation to Customs and to the citizens of the U.S. to ensure the safety of their freight destined to U.S. locations. If the compliance factor is not embedded in a corporation's planning, no matter how great that price bid might be, a company will not have the option to import.

A CUSTOMS COMPLIANCE PROGRAM IN THE POST 9/11 ENVIRONMENT

In order for a company to eliminate risk, avoid added costs, ensure just-in-time delivery, and comply with all appropriate governmental regulations associated with the movement of material to, from, and within facilities worldwide, a compliance structure must be developed. A well-organized compliance structure that is intertwined with the supply chain is now an essential element of any supply chain involved with importing products in the post 9/11 security-conscious era. Sometimes, a company may have informal compliance programs in place, but somehow they have fallen to the wayside and are the forgotten entities with product launch planning. A typical question is: When was the last time you invited your company's Compliance staff to your newest product's launch planning meeting? Were you even aware they existed? Are they a checkpoint in your company's written procedures or process for new product launches? A Compliance staff holds the knowledge of what can go wrong, while explaining what can add to your costs and what can affect your just-in-time deliveries. Have they been consulted?

If compliance is not secured, the very option to market new imported products is null and void. Delays, added costs, damage, and added liability can occur on any given global purchase agreement. This chapter explains how building the correct foundation and educating the buyer and seller will position a company to ensure trouble-free movement of product at the original projected cost and timely arrival. We will raise awareness to what unnecessary duties or penalties can surface in an import supply chain operation.

Readers will learn ideas on how to institute a compliance structure and establish internal controls that are both cost and compliance effective. For example, a team of compliance experts is essential to an inbound supply chain operation, as they can provide information on how to reduce or eliminate duties on global marketed products via tariff and trade. As mentioned in Chapter 1, the Customs Modernization Act of 1993 (Mod Act) switched the burden for Customs compliance from Customs to the importer. Enforced compliance then surfaced that required the importers to be fully obligated to use reasonable care when importing their products or be subject to possible fines and penalties or even revocation of import privilege. The combination of the Mod Act requirements and the post 9/11 increased scrutiny and examinations of imported merchandise makes Customs compliance critical to the success of your global sourcing operations. U.S. Customs is steadfast and fully charged to engage in whatever actions are necessary to ensure the safety of the U.S. citizens.

WHAT RULES ARE IMPORTANT TO SOURCE A PRODUCT INTERNATIONALLY?

Let us begin covering the Customs import compliance basics that are critical for companies in case Customs should elect to audit your import records. Not only can noncompliance in the following areas cripple a company during such an audit, but it will also contribute to the risk of experiencing detainment in your import supply chain, or more severe, subject the firm to fines, penalties, and forfeitures. At the root of import compliance are the following four principles:

1. Valuation
2. Classification
3. Country of origin
4. Marking requirements

Valuation can be a difficult area in which to determine and capture all areas of the sales agreement properly. It is probably the most complex and most frequently violated of the Customs compliance requirements. It is crucial for individuals within the various areas of the supply chain who are involved in the price negotiations to understand valuation, as the terms and conditions of a purchase order may be lacking Customs-required "valuation" information. A best practice for any company would be to create purchasing guidelines that incorporate a valuation checklist as well as to arrange for training that can be provided by an Import or Compliance Department, per the following.

Customs Value

Customs does not allow importers to value their merchandise in an arbitrary or fictitious manner. No business can just assign a minimal value to everything that is imported to avoid paying duties and fees. You can equate valuing your imported merchandise improperly to cheating on your taxes by lying about your income. If you made $100,000 last year and only declared $10,000 to the IRS, you may pay significantly less taxes that year, but you run the risk of paying fines or going to jail. The same premise holds true for how you value your imported merchandise, which is the basis for how many duties and fees you must pay. Sales and Marketing personnel should be made fully aware of the elements of a sale. The elements need to be captured on the invoice being used for clearance.

For example, if you send a mold overseas to be used in the manufacture of a product, the value of the mold must be incorporated into the declared value. There are four methods for appraisement that Customs allows importers to use for valuing their merchandise. The U.S. Customs regulations pertaining to appraisement of imported merchandise are based on the World Trade Organization's agreement on Customs valuation and can be found in 19 CFR § 152. We will discuss each of these methods in some detail. These four methods are:

1. Transaction value
2. Transaction value of identical or similar merchandise
3. Deductive value
4. Computed value

Customs requires that an importer select its appraisement methodology from these four methods and in the order listed. If one of these four methods does not work for you, Customs also allows a fifth method, known as the "other reasonable method" or "derived value." This methodology is not widely used as it can be very complex to arrive at an accurate appraisement. However, it may need to be utilized if the business situation dictates its use.

Transaction Value

Transaction value can be simply stated as the price paid or payable for your imported merchandise. This is Customs' and most importers' preferred method of appraisement. You place a purchase order for merchandise from a foreign vendor and that vendor invoices you for the goods that you are importing. It is the vendor's invoice price to you (the price paid or payable sometime in the future) that serves as the transaction value. Transaction value may only be used as the appraisement method if the following conditions are met:

1. There are no restrictions on the disposition or use of the imported merchandise by the buyer other than those that are imposed or required by law, that limit the geographical area in which the merchandise may be resold, or that affect the value of the merchandise substantially.
2. The sale of, or the price actually paid or payable, for the imported merchandise is not subject to any condition or consideration for which a value cannot be determined.
3. No part of the proceeds of any subsequent resale, disposal, or use of the imported merchandise by the buyer will accrue directly or indirectly to the seller, unless an appropriate adjustment to the transaction value can be made for those proceeds.
4. The buyer and seller are not related, or the buyer and seller are related, but the transaction value is acceptable.

These four conditions may not seem like much the first time you read them, but a careful study reveals that Customs' restrictions on transaction value forces many otherwise-permissible import transactions into a more complex appraisement methodology. Take, for example, the fourth restriction, in which the buyer and seller are not related, or *the buyer and seller are related, but the transaction value is acceptable.* Many large, multinational companies have nearly all of their international transactions structured between related parties. There are only two ways that the transaction value between a related buyer and seller is acceptable. First, if an examination of the circumstances of sale indicates that the relationship did not influence the price actually paid or payable, that is, even though the buyer and the seller are related, they operate at an "arms length" or as if they were not related for their international transactions.

The only other way that the transaction value between a related buyer and seller is acceptable is if the transaction value of the imported merchandise closely approximates (1) the transaction value of identical merchandise, or of similar merchandise, in sales to unrelated buyers in the U.S.; (2) the deductive value or computed value of identical merchandise, or of similar merchandise; and (3) each value (from 1 or 2) that is used for comparison relates to merchandise that was exported to the U.S. at or about the same time as the imported merchandise. All this means is that the use of transaction value can often be easier said than done.

Oh, CRAPP!

If we continue with our original analogy of paying your federal income taxes, you know that your taxable income is not necessarily what you bring home in your paycheck. Investment income, tips, interest earned, and gambling earnings are all taxable — to name a few. The same premise holds true with Customs valuation. If you thought you had transaction value down, think once again. You have to also include the CRAPP: Commissions, Royalties, Assists, Proceeds, and Packing costs.

Selling commissions incurred by the buyer (any commission paid to the seller's agent) who is related to or controlled by, or works for or on behalf of, the manufacturer or the seller are dutiable and must be added to the transaction value of the merchandise. Royalties or license fees that the buyer is required to pay as a condition of sale are also dutiable and must be added to the transaction value of the merchandise.

Assists may be the most complex part of Customs valuation and certainly merit some detailed explanation. The following is a list of what an assist can be if supplied directly or indirectly, and free of charge or at reduced cost, by the buyer of imported merchandise for use in connection with the production or the sale for export to the U.S. of the merchandise:

1. Materials, components, parts, and similar items incorporated in the imported merchandise
2. Tools, dies, molds, and similar items used in the production of the imported merchandise
3. Merchandise consumed in the production of the imported merchandise
4. Engineering, development, artwork, design work, and plans and sketches that are undertaken in a country other than the U.S. and are necessary for the production of the imported merchandise

Any of these items described as an assist would be dutiable, meaning that the duty rate will also be calculated against the "assists value" in addition to the value of the merchandise. However, there are areas in which an assist would not apply, including when the service or work (1) is performed by an individual domiciled within the U.S., (2) is performed by that individual while acting as an employee or agent of the buyer of the imported merchandise, or (3) is incidental to other engineering, development, artwork, design work, or plans or sketches that are undertaken within the U.S. If you find that you have a dutiable assist, you will need to determine how much that assist is worth for Customs purposes. The value of an assist is the cost to acquire or produce the assist. The value of an assist always includes the transportation costs to the place of production. If the assist were leased, the value would be the cost of the lease (still including transportation costs).

To close out our CRAPP acronym, "proceeds" accruing to the seller from the resale, disposal, or use of the imported merchandise are also dutiable and must be added to the transaction value. Finally, "packing costs" are always dutiable and must be added to the transaction value if not already included. A company's internal Import or Compliance Department can provide guidance on valuation. If such a department does not exist in a company, Customs or a qualified broker may also provide assistance.

What About Deductions?

If we return to our income tax analogy, we all know that there are several items we can deduct from our income before we determine our basis for taxation. For example, medical expenses, charitable contributions, state and local taxes, and IRA contributions are all tax deductible. Having told you about all the things you must add to your Customs value, let us now focus on those items you can deduct to "*save*" duty and fees. Customs does provide U.S. importers some breaks, one of which is with reasonable costs or charges that are incurred for construction, erection, assembly, maintenance of, or the technical assistance provided for, the merchandise after importation. These are all nondutiable costs and may be deducted from your transaction value to determine your Customs appraised value.

The transportation (including forwarder and broker fees) and insurance costs of the imported merchandise and any Customs duties and taxes are also nondutiable and may be deducted if identified separately from the price paid or payable. It is important to understand where deductions can be made when negotiating a final price on your imported product. If the foreign supplier has "offered" to take ownership of the clearances, it is important for any buyer to understand where the supplier's import costs can be decreased. The more knowledgeable a buyer is on international costs and deductions, the less chance of being deceived. A simple caveat is to know what the supplier is paying.

"First Sale" — Nissho Iwai American Corp. v. United States (Fed. Cir. 1992)

In Chapter 6, we introduced the transfer pricing concept of Triangulation. Generally, Customs presumes that the transaction value (that is, the amount on which duties are calculated) is based on the price actually paid by the importer. The "first sale" rule, which was judicially approved in 1992 in the Nissho Iwai case, allows the importer to request that duties be calculated based on the price paid by a middleman to the manufacturer. The IRS has also ruled that the U.S. importer's taxable basis in the imported merchandise would not be limited to the dutiable value of the merchandise, as Section 1059A of the Internal Revenue Code would suggest, but may instead be adjusted upward to reflect additional markups charged by the "middleman"/parent that were not included in dutiable value.

There are four basic requirements in order for an international transaction to be eligible for the benefits of "first sale": (1) goods must be clearly destined for the country of import, (2) a "bona fide" sale occurred in the first sale transaction, (3) the first sale was conducted at an arm's length price, and (4) there must be a clear and complete documentary trail of the first sale transaction.

Using the first sale premise, multinational companies may be able to reap both duty and tax savings. Companies should consult with their tax, customs, and legal experts before initiating a first sale customs valuation program, but with careful planning, first sale benefits can save an enormous amount of money.

Transaction Value of Identical or Similar Merchandise

If the transaction value of your imported merchandise cannot be determined or if the use of transaction value is not permitted for your transaction, then the next method of appraisement to consider is the value of identical merchandise, immediately followed by the value of similar merchandise. "Identical merchandise" refers to merchandise identical in all respects to, and produced in the same country and by the same person as, the merchandise being appraised. "Similar merchandise" means merchandise produced in the same country and by the same person as the merchandise being appraised and is like the merchandise being appraised in characteristics and component materials, that is, commercially interchangeable. In order to use transaction value of identical or similar merchandise, the identical or similar merchandise must have been sold for export to the U.S. and exported at about the same time as the merchandise being appraised. If two or more transaction values for identical merchandise are discovered, the lower should be used.

Deductive Value

If transaction value of similar merchandise cannot be used, then deductive value becomes the next method of appraisement to consider. Deductive value can be defined as the resale price in the U.S. minus (1) commissions paid or agreed to be paid, (2) profit and general expenses (in connection with U.S. sales, must be consistent with those of the usual profits in the U.S. of the same kind of merchandise), (3) costs of insurance and transportation from the country of export to the U.S. (includes brokerage costs), (4) costs of insurance and transportation from the place of importation in the U.S. to the delivery destination (includes brokerage costs), (5) Customs' duties and other federal taxes, and (6) processing of the merchandise after importation (only deducted if greatest aggregate quantity is used).

The price used for deductive value depends on when and in what condition the merchandise is sold in the U.S.:

1. If the merchandise is sold in the condition as imported, at or about the date of importation of the merchandise being appraised, the price is the unit price at which the merchandise concerned is sold in the greatest aggregate quantity at or about such date.

   Example: Merchandise is sold to an unrelated person from a price list that grants favorable unit prices for purchases made in larger quantities:

Sale Quantity	Unit Price	Number of Sales	Total Quantity Sold at Each Price
1–10 units	$100	10 sales of 5 units	65
		5 sales of 3 units	
11–25 units	$95	5 sales of 11 units	55
Over 25 units	$90	1 sale of 30 units	80
		1 sale of 50 units	

   The greatest number of units sold at a price is 80, therefore, the unit price in the greatest aggregate quantity is $90.

2. If the merchandise concerned is sold in the condition as imported, but not sold at or about the date of importation of the merchandise being appraised, the price is the unit price at which the merchandise concerned is sold in the greatest aggregate quantity after the date of importation of the merchandise being appraised, but before the close of the ninetieth day after the date of such importation.

3. If the merchandise concerned was not sold in the condition as imported and not sold before the close of the ninetieth day after the date of importation of the merchandise being appraised, the price is the unit price at which the merchandise being appraised, after further processing, is sold in the greatest aggregate quantity before the 180th day after the date of such importation. This provision will apply to appraisement of merchandise only if the importer so elects at the time of filing the entry summary.

Computed Value

If deductive value cannot be used, then computed value becomes your appraisement methodology by default. You still may have options available if computed value will not work, but you are quickly running out of options. Computed value is defined as the sum of (1) the cost or value of the materials and the fabrication and other processing of any kind employed in the production of the imported merchandise, including labor; (2) an amount for profit and general expenses, including overhead; (3) any assist value; and (4) packing costs. Computed value is not easy to use if you are dealing with an unrelated vendor because it basically forces the vendor to disclose all of its costs and profit. If you have been forced into using computed value because your relationship with a party keeps you from being allowed to use transaction value, then you may experience difficulty with getting your related vendor to provide its costs and profits.

Other Reasonable Method or Derived Value

If you have gone through the above four methods and are still coming up short of finding an ideal appraisement methodology, Customs will accept another reasonable method. If you use this method, it must be based on one of the earlier four methods. Customs will not accept any of the following as methods of appraisement:

1. Selling price in the U.S. of merchandise produced in the U.S.
2. A system that provides for the appraisement of imported merchandise at the higher of two alternative values
3. The price of merchandise in the domestic market of the country of exportation
4. A cost of production, other than a value determined under Customs regulation § 152.106 for merchandise that is identical or similar merchandise to the merchandise being appraised
5. The price of merchandise for export to a country other than the U.S.
6. Minimum values for appraisement
7. Arbitrary or fictitious values

Classification

Classification of imported merchandise must be done in accordance with the Harmonized Tariff Schedule of the United States (HTSUS, often simply HTS) as mentioned in Chapter 1. In the U.S., the International Trade Commission's Office of Tariff Affairs and Trade Agreements is responsible for publishing and maintaining the HTS. The HTS carries the weight of law and can only be amended by executive order or act of Congress. To further educate you in the classification arena, we will go into the classification level of detail for which a Classification Specialist would be responsible. Each classification has a duty rate.

The HTS is a classification system that assigns a ten-digit number to every imported product, from soup to nuts and everything in between. The HTS is divided into ninety-seven chapters, twenty-one sections, and contains more than 5,000 provisions. The ten-digit number is broken down by: Chapter, 12; Heading, 1234; Subheading, 1234.56; Tariff Subheading, 1234.56.78; and finally, by statistical breakout, 1234.56.7890. As you can see, the ten-digit number is separated by decimals between the fourth and fifth digits and between the sixth and seventh digits. The "H" in HTS stands for harmonized. The classification system is harmonized at the six-digit level throughout the world, at least across the World Customs Organization's (WCO) member countries (196 countries worldwide). What that means is that no matter where you are importing, that country's tariff classification should start with the same six digits as those you will use to import the product. The remaining portion of the tariff classification code is left to the discretion of individual nations. Some countries only have eight-digit codes, while others have eleven. In the U.S., you will need to assign a ten-digit commodity code.

This precise ten-digit number not only tells Customs what it is that you are importing, it also tells both you and Customs how much duty you will owe when you import, as was discussed in Chapter 2. There are four possibilities for duty: duty free, *ad valorem,* specific, or compound. Duty-free goods are simply those that have no duty assessed on their import into the U.S. (for example, see Bamboo shoots under item 0710.80.1500 in the example tariff schedule shown in Figure 7.1). *Ad valorem* is a Latin term meaning based on the value. The majority of provisions in the tariff schedule today carry *ad valorem* duty rates (see Sweet Corn at 14% under item 0710.40.0000 in Figure 7.1). It is 14 percent of the Customs value based on one of the approved appraisement methods discussed above, less any allowable deductions.

A specific duty rate is one based on weight, quantity, volume, or some other unit of measurement, rather than the value (see Chickpeas [garbanzos] under item 0710.29.0500 at 1¢/kg in Figure 7.1). Specific duty rates are common across the agricultural and petroleum imports into the U.S. Finally, if you are really lucky, you will have a compound duty rate. This simply means that you must pay both an *ad valorem* and a specific duty rate on your imported merchandise (see Mushrooms under item 0710.80.2000 at 5.7¢/kg + 8% in Figure 7.1).

Heading/ Subheading	Stat/ Suff	Article Description	Unit of Quantity	Rates of Duty 1 General	Rates of Duty 1 Special	Rates of Duty 2
0710 (con.)	00	Vegetables (uncooked or cooked by steaming or boiling in water), frozen (con.): Leguminous vegetables, shelled or unshelled (con.): Other:				
0710.29 0710.29.05	00 00	Chickpeas (garbanzos)	kg -----	1¢/kg	Free (A,CA,CL,E, IL,J,JO,MX,SG)	4.4¢/kg
0710.29.15	00	Lentils	kg -----	0.1¢/kg	Free (A,CA,CL,E, IL,J,JO,MX,SG)	1.1¢/kg
0710.29.25	00	Pigeon peas: If entered during the period from July 1 to September 30, inclusive, in any year	kg -----	Free		8.6¢/kg
0710.29.30	00	Other	kg -----	0.8¢/kg	Free (A*,CA,CL,E, IL,J ,JO,MX,SG)	8.6¢/kg
0710.29.40	00	Other	kg -----	3.5¢/kg	Free (A+,CA,CL,D, E,IL,J,JO,MX,SG)	7.7¢/kg
0710.30.00	00	Spinach, New Zealand spinach and orache spinach (garden spinach)	kg -----	14%	Free (A+,CA,D,E, IL,J,JO,MX) 12.2% (CL,SG)	35%
0710.40.00	00	Sweet corn	kg -----	14%	Free (A+,CA,D,E, IL,J,MX) 2.8% (JO) 12.2% (CL,SG)	35%
0710.80 0710.80.15	00 00	Other vegetables: Bamboo shoots and water chestnuts, other than Chinese water chestnuts	kg -----	Free		35%
0710.80.20	00	Mushrooms	kg -----	5.7¢/kg 8%	Free (A+,CA,D,E, IL,J,JO,MX) 4.9¢/kg +	22¢/kg + 45%

Figure 7.1. Snapshot of a classification page. (Compliments of www.cbp.gov.)

Much like valuation, there are complex rules for classification. All classification is based on the General Rules of Interpretation (GRIs) (www.usitc.gov). There are six GRIs that serve as the governing principles for all classification:

1. The table of contents, alphabetical index, and titles of sections, chapters and sub-chapters are provided for ease of reference only; for legal purposes, classification shall be determined according to the terms of the headings and any relative section or chapter notes and, provided such headings or notes do not otherwise require, according to the following provisions:

2. (a) reference in a heading to an article shall be taken to include a reference to that article incomplete or unfinished, provided that, as entered; the incomplete or unfinished article has the essential character of the complete or finished article. It shall also include a reference to that article complete or finished (or failing to be classified as complete or finished by virtue of this rule), entered unassembled or disassembled.

2. (b) Any reference in a heading to a material or substance shall be taken to include a reference to mixtures or combinations of that material or substance with other materials or substances. Any reference to goods of a given material or substance shall be taken to include a reference to goods consisting wholly or partly of such material or substance. The classification of goods consisting of more than one material or substance shall be according to the principles of rule 3.

3. When, by application of rule 2(b) or for any other reason, goods are, *prima facie*, classifiable under two or more headings, classification shall be affected as follows:

(a) The heading which provides the most specific description shall be preferred to headings providing a more general description. However, when two or more headings each refer to only part of the materials or substances contained in mixed or composite goods, or to only part of the items in a set put up for retail sale, those headings are to be regarded as equally specific in relation to those goods, even if one of them gives a more complete or precise description of the goods.

(b) Mixtures, composite goods consisting of different materials or made up of different components, and goods put up in sets for retail sale, which cannot be classified by reference to 3(a), shall be classified as if they consisted of the material or component which gives them their essential character, insofar as this criterion is applicable.

(c) When goods cannot be classified by reference to 3(a) or 3(b), they shall be classified under the heading, which occurs last in numerical order among those which equally merit consideration.

4. Goods which cannot be classified in accordance with the above rules shall be classified under the heading appropriate to the goods to which they are most akin.

5. In addition to the foregoing provisions, the following rules shall apply in respect to the goods referred to therein:

(a) Camera cases, musical instrument cases, gun cases, drawing instrument cases, necklace cases and similar containers, specially shaped or fitted to contain a specific article or set of articles, suitable for long-term use and entered with the articles for which they are intended, shall be classified with such articles when of a kind normally sold therewith. This rule does not, however, apply to containers which give the whole its essential character;

(b) Subject to the provisions of rule 5(a) above, packing materials and packing containers entered with the goods therein shall be classified with the goods if they are of a kind normally used for packing such goods. However, this provision is not binding when such packing materials or packing containers are clearly suitable for repetitive use.

6. For legal purposes, the classification of goods in the subheadings of a heading shall be determined according to the terms of those subheadings and any related subheading notes and, *mutatis mutandis*, to the above rules, on the understanding that only subheadings at the same level are comparable. For the purposes of this rule, the relative section, chapter and subchapter notes also apply, unless the context otherwise requires.

In addition to the GRIs, there are General Notes, Section Notes, and Chapter Notes, each of which carry the weight of law and must be complied with when classifying your imported merchandise. A snapshot of a classification page is provided in Figure 7.1.

The rules surrounding classification are complex to say the least. If you are dealing with a technical product, this becomes even more the case. At the root of Customs' enforcement of the import regulations is the assurance that they have received all money due. Because a product's duty rate is directly tied to the tariff classification, it becomes very critical to your Customs compliance group to have this little ten-digit code correct. For this reason, we recommend that you have a technical expert involved in your classification process. For example, if you are importing chemicals, a chemist is a logical choice for your classification specialist. If you are importing electronic components for satellites, you should consider having an electrical engineer involved in the classification process.

Classification Decision Tree Tool as a Best Practice

An importer should also strive for consistency with classifications. You would not want different business units or divisions within your company to be importing the same product under totally different classifications. For this reason, we recommend that tariff classifications be performed as a centralized function. A company that assigns responsibility for classifying imported product to multiple individuals runs the risk of these individuals arriving at different classifications as a result of varied opinions or lack of experience/expertise. You should always import the same product the same way each time you import it, unless some new information has changed your opinion of the correct classification. A best practice for ensuring consistent classifications is to implement a classification database or to tie the classification to the imported product's part number and data within your import order processing system.

A final point on consistent classifications can be provided from the automotive industry. If you are an importer of automotive parts, for example, you will be dealing in thousands of products. Many of these products will be similar, based on the type of product; for example, brake pads or bumpers. You may also need to source the same parts from a dozen different vendors worldwide, who all assign their own product number. A company in this situation would be well served to create a classification decision tree that would assist the importer. This would ensure that products with similar or identical properties and characteristics were classified the same way and that identical parts from different vendors were always classified the same way. The classification decision tree should be developed as a best practice tool for the company's most common products. The decision tree should have simple questions that help guide the classification of a product down a clear and consistent path. The questions in the decision tree are also based on the breakouts in the HTS, the section and chapter notes, and any relevant U.S. Customs rulings.

Binding Rulings

What if I am just not comfortable with the classification or I am torn between two numbers that seem equally correct? If you are not sure, Customs will provide you with the classification that they determine to be correct if you request a binding ruling to assist with future imports, as briefly discussed in Chapter 2. As a result of a binding ruling process, the classification will be reviewed, determined, and will serve to eliminate questionability from Customs on future clearances. There are a few pros and cons to binding rulings. Probably the biggest negative of the Customs binding ruling process is that it is extremely time consuming.

Only in 2004 did Customs make any effort to automate the ruling request process by introducing an e-mail–based ruling request system called e-Ruling. Even with this enhancement, it will still take an importer twenty-five to thirty-five days from the date of request to receive the ruling. If you are urgently awaiting the launch of a new product, this wait may not fit into your supply chain. The whole process is simply too cumbersome to make it practical for a company dealing with hundreds or thousands of products. Another negative is cost. If you are granted a binding ruling, this agreement of the classification and its corresponding duty rate is final for the duration. So, if you are going to obtain a ruling, it is wise to advocate for the classification with the most advantageous tariff when you request your ruling.

In order to do this, you will often want to solicit the advice of a trade attorney, consultant, or technical expert to help you make legal and technical argument in support of the lowest-duty classification. With the best trade attorneys currently charging in excess of $500 per hour, you may need to perform a cost-benefit analysis to determine how much you are willing to invest on the classification. Because a binding ruling lasts forever, a victorious duty-free classification could save you a significant amount of money over the life of the product. On the pro side, if you have a binding ruling for your product, Customs can never come back at a later date and assert that you have improperly classified your merchandise, resulting in the underpayment of duties. If you have a ruling, you take the risk of having to pay additional duties as a result of an audit or a Customs request for information out of the picture. Also, if you are importing many similar products, it may be wise to obtain a ruling on one of those products that can serve as a nice basis for classifying other similar products. The cons may outweigh the pros when it comes to binding rulings. Nonetheless, rulings have their place and can be a valuable tool to establish classification basis for your core products and to minimize risk of being assessed future duties on your key products.

Country of Origin

Like valuation and classification, origin is not white or black. The country of origin is not simply the country from which you imported the goods. Rather, Customs defines country of origin as the country in which (1) the good is wholly obtained or produced, (2) the good is produced exclusively from domestic materials, or (3) each foreign material incorporated in that good undergoes an applicable change in tariff classification; that is, the finished product's tariff classifications must likely be different from that of the component or raw materials in order for a new country of origin to be created for Customs purposes. Customs requires that further work or material added to an article in another country must affect a "substantial transformation" in order to render such other country the country of origin.

In recent years, the U.S. has experienced a proliferation of bilateral and regional free trade agreements, such as the North American Free Trade Agreement (NAFTA). To make things even more complicated, each new free trade agreement that the U.S. enters into has slightly different rules of origin. What this means is that the rules of origin for determining whether a product qualifies for preferential tariff treatment under the NAFTA may be different, for example, from the rules for the U.S.-Chile FTA and both may differ from the U.S.-Singapore FTA.

If you are sourcing material from a country that is eligible for one of the U.S. preferential trade agreements, you want to ensure that your supplier can certify, without a doubt, that the products you are seeking to import are indeed considered to be from the country of origin that merits the preferential tariff. If the products were made in Chile, but for one reason are not considered Chilean origin under the U.S.-Chile FTA's rules of origin, the product will be subject to a duty. Importers should also be conscious of what an imported raw material can do to the country of origin of any finished good that will be exported to one of the U.S.' preferential trading partners. For example, if you have a large customer base in Mexico that is accustomed to importing your finished goods duty free under the NAFTA, they may be extremely distraught if, by your switching to a raw material from a foreign supplier, your product no longer qualifies as NAFTA origin and they must now pay an 18 percent tariff on the previously duty-free product. Who would have ever thought you could lose a customer over country of origin?

Marking

Marking is the last of the four Customs compliance principles and hopefully the most simple. Customs requires that unless excepted by law, every article of foreign origin (or its container) imported into the U.S. shall be marked in a conspicuous place as legibly, indelibly, and permanently as the nature of the article (or container) will permit, in such manner as to indicate to an ultimate purchaser in the U.S. the English name of the country of origin of the article, at the time of importation into the Customs territory of the U.S. Containers of articles excepted from marking shall be marked with the name of the country of origin for the article unless the container is also excepted from marking. The simple requirement is that if you are importing foreign merchandise, most likely that merchandise must be marked with the country of origin.

The only area where this requirement begins to get complex derives from the fact that there are exceptions. Probably the most common marking exceptions are found on Customs' "J-list." The J-list is provided for in 19 CFR § 134.33 and includes things like beads, ball bearings, eggs, feathers, and bamboo shoots. The items on the J-list are excepted from marking, but the outermost container in which the J-list item reaches the ultimate purchaser is required to be marked to indicate the origin of its contents. 19 CFR § 134.32 also provides some general exceptions to the marking requirements. Examples of these general exceptions include articles that were produced more than twenty years prior to their importation into the U.S., articles that cannot be marked prior to shipment to the U.S. except at an expense economically prohibitive of its importation, articles that are incapable of being marked, articles imported for use by the importer and not intended for sale in their imported or any other form, and products of possessions of the U.S.

Marking penalties are among some of Customs' most severe. In addition to monetary penalties, Customs can demand that merchandise that they have deemed to be marked improperly be redelivered to the port of origin. If the product that must be redelivered has already been sold to customers and cannot be redelivered, Customs can assess a fine equal to the value of the merchandise for failure to redeliver. We strongly caution importers not to rely on a marking exception unless your product unequivocally qualifies for one of the exceptions. When in doubt, make your supplier clearly mark the delivery.

MY COMPANY DOES NOT HAVE A COMPLIANCE PROGRAM — WHERE DO I START?

If you are sourcing goods globally in the post 9/11 era, sooner or later your company will need to address the "compliance" issue. Otherwise, the newly created inbound supply chain operation may face major delays, fines, penalties, and/or bad press. Any company should strive to be a "reasonable care" importer and take the necessary steps to ensure the security and safety of its inbound freight to the U.S. If your company does not have any compliance program or lacks an informal program, we advocate that your company create or formalize a Customs compliance program. There are ten elements that are crucial to a successful compliance program. These elements are listed below with a brief narrative provided for each.

1. Senior Management Support

Management commitment and support, or lack thereof, may well be the single biggest key to the success or failure of a company's compliance program. In order for the compliance program to be successful, the company's highest management must fully support compliance. Compliance should be interwoven into the company's vision, values, and code of conduct. A company's CEO should be ultimately responsible for the compliance of the company. A company's compliance policies should be ratified by the board of directors and signed by the CEO. A company's management should also commit to compliance by providing adequate resources to ensure the success of the program.

2. Written Policies and Procedures

A successful compliance program must be one based on internal controls. Today, a company may be 100 percent compliant for its international business, however, if internal controls are nonexistent (such as written policies and procedures), a company could easily commit an expensive violation the next time the "import guy" is on vacation. The bottom line for global procurement has been affected. To avoid major problems, companies should adopt a Customs Compliance Manual (CCM), as well as set formal company policy for import and Customs compliance. The CCM is the procedure manual that supports the policies at the operational level. The policies should be regularly reviewed, signed again by the CEO, and communicated company-wide on an annual basis. The CCM should be considered a fluid document, updated regularly as regulations change or if procedures are determined to be inefficient or ineffective. The CCM procedures should be drafted on the quality concept of "we say what we do and we do what we say."

3. A "Center of Expertise"

Activities affecting compliance can occur far and wide across a company, including some hard-to-find places. The rules and regulations involved in global sourcing and logistics are vast to say the least, and they can impact personnel in almost every department of the company. A research scientist, inventory planner, or accountant should not be expected to know this vast number of rules, nonetheless, they should have a contact available who does. Companies should create a centralized Compliance Department headed by at least a director-level manager to serve as the company's "center of expertise" on compliance matters.

The Compliance group should be comprised of an experienced and knowledgeable staff and should receive sufficient resources to ensure that the group remains a center of expertise. The Compliance staff should regularly attend seminars and training in order to stay abreast of the latest compliance developments. The staff would arrange face-to-face meetings with government agencies to understand their roles, positions, and requirements. They would then supply this information to a supply chain operation. This center of expertise should also be recognized company-wide as the voice of the company organization on all applicable compliance matters when dealing with any government agency; that is, communication with the government should only occur through this group, presenting "one face" to the government agencies.

4. Responsible Compliance Personnel

Another key to a successful compliance program is to have a network of personnel responsible for varying aspects of compliance at multiple levels throughout the company. As mentioned previously, the CEO should be ultimately responsible for the company's compliance. Any government agency will look favorably on commitment to compliance from the top of the organization.

A company should create a Compliance Control Unit (CCU), reporting to the CEO for compliance purposes. The CCU's administrator should be the head of the company's compliance center of expertise, the Compliance Director, who is charged with handling the day-to-day activities of the CCU. The CCU should be comprised of senior management representing each of the key stakeholders for the Compliance Department. For example, the CCU contributing members may be the heads of supply chain or sales/marketing for each of the company's divisions or business units. The CCU should also include a legal representative, ideally an attorney from the General Counsel's office who is charged with responsibilities for trade compliance. The Compliance Director should identify the proper CCU members and the CEO should formally invite them to serve in that capacity.

The CCU should meet at least quarterly to discuss compliance matters and should set the company's compliance procedures by consensus. By creating a CCU that consists of the key stakeholders, the compliance procedures can be written in such a way that business processes are not hindered and business processes can be developed that do not compromise compliance.

Reporting to the CCU should be the next line of compliance personnel, those at the operational level. Wherever shipments are processed globally (for example, site, divisional, or centralized), Control Officers (CO) should be established, such as Import Control Officers (ICO), Foreign Trade Zone (FTZ) Administrators, etc. These officers are the personnel with operational responsibility for shipments and should be empowered to determine whether any given shipment can occur (see Figure 7.2). The CO must be well trained on compliance matters, as he/she will be the person most intimately involved with the

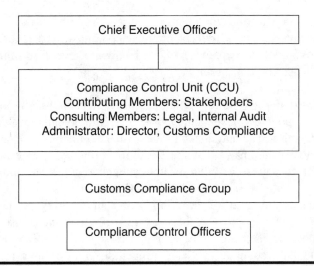

Figure 7.2.   Tier structure of Compliance group.

actual shipments. The Compliance group would provide the necessary training and guidance as well as audit the function. A CO should report to the CCU for compliance responsibility. The CCU will set certain compliance goals and objectives for the CO. The CO's supervisors should be required to seek the input of the Compliance Director when preparing their performance reviews.

5. Accountability

A compliance program without accountability is like a tiger without teeth. All company compliance personnel should have incentives for ensuring compliance. For example, the CO should have certain compliance objectives. If the CO exceeds expectations on compliance objectives, he/she should be proportionally rewarded during the next performance review. On the other hand, a company should also include disincentives for noncompliance. A company's compliance policies should include disciplinary action for noncompliance up to and including termination for a willful or grossly negligent action.

6. Training Programs

A company can have all the compliance procedures in the world, but if no investment is made in training, the compliance program will surely fail. As mentioned previously, compliance matters are far-reaching. Personnel in virtually every department of the company can encounter an issue that requires some knowledge of the Customs compliance program. Any one of these individuals could add unnecessary costs, delays, or create compliance issues for a company if they lack compliance awareness. Listed below are several recommendations for a compliance training program.

a. **Policy training** — Every employee should receive training on the compliance policies on an annual basis. A recommendation would be to conduct this in an automated fashion, such as either on-line or via e-mail. We also recommend that the Customs compliance policy training be combined with some other existing annual compliance training, such as business ethics, Sarbanes-Oxley, and antitrust.

b. **Target training to job function** — For any employees either directly or indirectly involved in the import distribution and logistics process, training modules should be established based on job function. For example, an accountant can have a much different training program than a logistics representative. Repetitive training is recommended for any employee directly involved in the import distribution and logistics process. Any such employee should receive a refresher course at least biennially.

c. **Automated training** — Based on our experiences, face-to-face or otherwise facilitated training sessions for a large audience have proven ineffective in a large company. The biggest weakness that has been identified with facilitated training sessions is low attendance. Simply put, in a large company, there is always something more important to do than to commit to one to two hours of compliance training. A company should automate its compliance training by offering the training modules online. Employees can take the required courses at their leisure and start and stop as they please.

d. **Required competency (testing)** — Training may be a worthless effort if no one learns or gains anything from it. For this reason, a company should include competency testing as part of its training programs. This is especially critical if the training is automated as described above. Employees required to take the training should also be required to obtain a passing grade on an automated test that immediately follows the training session. If a passing grade is not achieved, the employee should be required to retake the session. This technique encourages the employee to apply him- or herself better to the training at hand.

e. **Compliance Council** — For those most intimately involved with compliance activities throughout the company, a Compliance Council should be established that meets at least three times a year. The COs are the targeted members of the Compliance Council. The Council meetings are to be hosted by the Customs Compliance group and will provide the CO with pertinent updates to regulations and company procedures. Ideally, Council meetings will feature guest speakers from pertinent government agencies, supply chain operations, suppliers, regulatory groups, forwarders/brokers, law firms, and even a company in a similar industry to benchmark your activities and processes.

7. Auditing

A world-class compliance program must include an element of monitoring or verification of the effectiveness of the compliance internal controls. A compliance program should include annual auditing of each shipping/receiving location. Once a sufficient number of audits have been conducted to assess risk properly, certain sites may be audited less frequently, for example, biennially. A company's auditing process should be based on quality principles, with a documented and public audit process; that is, the audited site should fully expect and understand what the auditor will be seeking. The audits must be designed to verify the effectiveness of the company's procedures as well as to identify any areas of systemic noncompliance. Any nonconformity should undergo a root cause analysis followed by a formal corrective action process.

8. Communication

The success of any program depends on good communication. This is especially the case for a compliance program. The Customs Compliance group should be charged with providing regulatory updates to both those directly and indirectly involved in import distribution and logistics. An example of these updates is a *Federal Register* notice with a summary of the regulation change and its impact to the company. The Customs Compliance group must also form a communication network of individuals who support the company's overall compliance. For example, regular communication and interaction with the Law and RA Departments will be a critical avenue for driving the compliance program's success forward. It is also essential to have open communication between internal departments within a supply chain that markets imported products. If the compliance requirements are not secured, this will have a direct effect on the distribution of an imported product.

9. Authority

If the Customs Compliance group is not given ample authority to enforce the company's compliance policy and procedures, the program can be weakened or even fail. For this reason, a Compliance group must be considered a governance body, charged with not only setting (through the buy-in of the CCU), but also enforcing, the company's compliance policies and procedures.

10. An Automated System

If all of the above nine elements are present, any company will prosper in a strong, well-organized compliance program. If the compliance program is to be global in nature, it cannot reach the status of "world class" unless the company implements an automated compliance system. There are numerous software products currently available (such as Vastera, Open Harbor, NextLinx, OCR Services, and TradeBeam) that allow a company to automate its compliance screens and integrate them into the order-processing and logistics systems. Many of these products are capable of integrating multiple country requirements and all provide a systematic method of blocking noncompliant shipments. A company should evaluate the automated compliance products currently available and implement the one that is best suited to the company's products, processes, and order-processing system. The global implementation cost of such a product can easily run into seven figures. However, cost evaluations must include the impact of expensive penalties resulting from noncompliance issues and the risks that can be eliminated as a result of automation.

A VISION FOR YOUR COMPANY'S CUSTOMS COMPLIANCE GROUP

Any Customs Compliance group should be a world-class compliance organization and on the leading edge within its industry. Internal customers will value the services and will consider the company group as partners in their business processes. The government agencies with which the group interacts will have a certain level of respect and trust for the company because of the top performance and trust partnership with them. They will view your company as a responsible company. This vision will be recognized through performance in internal and external audits and through participation in compliance industry programs. For example, this vision can be fulfilled and the company will have gained further recognition when asked to present its successes at popular compliance seminars such as the American Association of Exporters and Importers' (AAEI) annual update. The CBP recently published "Best Practices for Compliant Companies" in conjunction with their Importer Self Assessment (ISA) program. They are provided verbatim below and can be found on the Customs website (www.cbp.gov).

1. **Have management's commitment.** — *(Control Environment)*
   Demonstrate management's commitment to compliance.
   - Establish a statement of corporate policy that addresses Customs and Border Protection (CBP) matters.
   - Solicit a statement from the Board of Directors that assigns authority and responsibility to the customs group.
2. **State compliance and cost goals.** — *(Risk Assessment)*
   Identify and analyze relevant risk and develop internal goals to manage the risk.
   - Conduct post-entry reviews and compare these against established goals.
   - Determine how risk areas should be managed.
   - Resolve control weaknesses in a timely manner.
3. **Develop formal policies.** — *(Control Activities)*
   Develop, implement and/or modify formal policies and procedures to ensure that management's goals and objectives are met.
   - Verify the accuracy of the Internal Control Manual to ensure processes and procedures achieve prescribed goals and objectives.
   - Modify controls that are ineffective or inefficient and report to management.
   - Define accountability and controls in job descriptions.
4. **Establish training programs.** — *(Information & Communication)*
   Ensure that employees receive appropriate training and guidance to effectively discharge their responsibilities.
   - Convey pertinent information to the right people at the appropriate time.
   - Disseminate CBP information via company's communication system (i.e. intranet, bulletin board, mail).
5. **Conduct internal control reviews.** — *(Monitoring)*
   Conduct periodic process reviews to assess the performance quality of the internal controls.
   - Use external or internal audit to periodically review each business unit to confirm that corporate policies are implemented and mandate corrective action when necessary.
   - Adjust testing in response to changing risk.
6. **Create compliance group.** — *(Information & Communication)*
   Establish a customs group.
   - Foster open communication channels between all departments that may be involved in the CBP processes.

- Establish control activities and self-testing processes to verify the accuracy of the company's internal control system since the quality of the information generated affects the ability of management to make decisions.

7. **Access executives for needed resources.** — *(Control Environment)* Raises the importance of the Customs group and provides adequate authority for the group to interact with other departments as needed.

- Organize the customs group so that it is visible to top-level management (e.g. attaching to tax or legal department/division).
- Provide an awareness of supply chain structure. Many executives know their sales figures but do they know their key import statistics and suppliers?

8. **Develop compliance requirements for suppliers.** — *(Control Activities)*
Develop contract language on purchase agreements.

- Develop and implement controls to help ensure that CBP transactions are valid, properly authorized and accurately processed.
- Request suppliers provide regulatory reporting information when applicable (NAFTA, GSP, etc.).
- Exercise reasonable care over operations performed by service providers.

9. **Establish a record-keeping program.** — *(Control Activities)*
Establish a record-keeping program.

- Maintain a record keeping system that forms an audit trail from production control through payment to CBP entry.
- Provide supporting documentation for CBP transactions in a timely manner.

10. **Partner with Customs & Border Protection** *(Information & Communication)*
Enhance partnership by:

- Participate in voluntary CBP programs such as: C-TPAT, CSI, ISA, FAST, ACE and etc.

The ten elements for a successful Customs compliance program proposed in this chapter are designed to fulfill Customs' best practice standards. If a company were to implement the ten elements outlined above under strong leadership, the company would enjoy a world-class compliance program for years to come. Any corporation can rise to the challenge to transform their compliance program or develop one from the ground up.

CONCLUSION

This chapter was intended to provide another level of detail to the four main elements of focus for Customs: Classification, Valuation, Country of Origin, and Marking. In order to ensure internal controls for providing accurate clearance information for any imported product, a compliance tier structure is vital and would reflect the company positively to Customs. Creating a Compliance Department will provide numerous perks, including a central area of expertise on government requirements, fielding compliance issues for new product launches, and providing one face to the government agencies. Focus Assessments and other audits by Customs and the government agencies can be subjected on any importer at any given time. Customs has been known to conduct an unexpected, impromptu spot visit. It is imperative that the right compliance structure be in place to disseminate the essential information needed to those involved within the inbound supply chain arena. The next chapter will address trade optimization in which readers will sharpen their sourcing skills to gain further savings. The government offers many duty-free options to importers. We advise you to learn what they are and take full advantage of them.

8

TRADE OPTIMIZATION: PROGRAMS THAT CONTRIBUTE TO A COMPANY'S BOTTOM LINE

Much of this book has been devoted to explaining new requirements of U.S. Customs and other government agencies pertaining to the importation of goods in the post 9/11 era. While these new requirements have been designed to protect the U.S. and its citizens, they undoubtedly introduce new cost elements into the import supply chain. This chapter is devoted to trade optimization programs that can help you deliver savings to your company's bottom line in the form of minimized tariffs. With the myriad post 9/11 requirements and their corresponding costs, an importing company will need to take advantage of every opportunity for savings if it is to remain competitive.

FREE TRADE AGREEMENTS

As discussed in Chapter 7, the country of origin of an imported product may have an impact on the duty rate of that product when you import it, as the U.S. has clearly shifted its trade policy over the course of recent years. Previously, the U.S. was content to promote trade through participation in the World Trade Organization (WTO). The WTO's progress is slow and deliberate due to the

huge number of countries participating in negotiations to eliminate trade barriers. The U.S. tariffs are already among the lowest in the world, so in WTO
negotiations, the U.S. may not have much to bring to the table compared to
developing countries with average tariffs of 35 percent. Beginning with the
Clinton administration and expanding into the Bush era, the U.S. set forth on
a path towards eliminating barriers with its trading partners. The U.S. continues
to play an active role in the WTO; however, to balance the slow progression
of the WTO, the U.S. has begun to negotiate bilateral and regional trade agreements at unprecedented levels.

North American Free Trade Agreement

An early change in U.S. policy was probably first realized with the passing of
the NAFTA on January 1, 1994, which implemented a trilateral trade agreement
between the U.S., Canada, and Mexico. You may recall NAFTA opponent H.
Ross Perot speaking about the "sucking noise" of NAFTA taking away U.S.
jobs. A savvy importer can prove Mr. Perot wrong or at least prove that U.S.
companies and their employees can benefit from the NAFTA. If you can find
a supplier of your product in Canada or Mexico with pricing that is competitive
with suppliers in Asia or Europe, your landed cost of goods will likely be less
if the goods you import from the NAFTA region qualify for preferential tariff
treatment.* For example, in the 2004 U.S. tariff schedule, glass votive
candleholders from Japan carried a 6.6 percent tariff, while those same votive
candleholders are duty free from Mexico when qualifying for the NAFTA.
Imagine what bringing 6.6 percent to the bottom line of a low-margin product
could do to your business.

The Generalized System of Preferences

The GSP is a multilateral agreement in which the U.S. participates. In simple
terms, some of the rich countries of the world offer duty-free entry of goods
to poor and developing countries in an effort to stimulate the economies of those
developing nations. If a product qualifies for GSP, it is always duty free for
import into the U.S. GSP probably offers the simplest rules of origin of any of
the preferential trade agreements. In order for a product to qualify for GSP, the
value or cost of materials plus direct costs of processing must be 35 percent
or more of the appraised value of the goods at the time of entry into the U.S.
In order for imported merchandise to qualify for GSP, the merchandise must

---

* Refer to Chapter 7 for rules of origin. Just because goods are sourced from Canada or
  Mexico does not mean that they necessarily qualify for preferential tariff treatment under
  the NAFTA. Simply put, there are special rules of origin for each free trade agreement.

also ship directly from the GSP-eligible country. A current list of GSP-eligible countries is provided on the Customs website (www.cbp.gov). If the product you need to source is available from one of these countries, you may realize a tremendous duty savings when compared to sourcing the same product from a more developed country.

Other Free Trade Agreements

The U.S. has seen a proliferation of bilateral and regional free trade agreements under the Bush administration. By the end of 2004, free trade agreements had been implemented with Jordan, Singapore, and Chile and new trade agreements either signed or initiated with Australia, Bahrain, Morocco, Panama, the South African Customs Union (SACU), the Central American countries (CAFTA), and the Free Trade Area of the Americas (FTAA), which would span most of North and South America. Each of these free trade agreements will have its own set of specific rules of origin. In order to ensure that you have the most current information available to you at the time you are making a decision about purchasing an imported product, we recommend that you review the latest information available about U.S. preferential trade agreements by visiting the U.S. Trade Representative's (USTR) website (www.ustr.gov) and the U.S. International Trade Commission's (USITC) website (www.usitc.gov).

Getting in on the Negotiations:
How Can You Make an Impact?

If you are looking to play an active role in how the U.S. trade policy is set, you may be able to make an impact. By regularly reviewing the USTR and USITC websites and monitoring the *Federal Register* notices from both of those agencies, you may quickly find an opportunity to influence U.S. trade policy in your favor. For example, you may currently import tweezers from Bahrain that are subject to a 4 percent tariff. As part of the negotiations between the U.S. and Bahrain, a ten-year phase out of duty on tweezers is proposed. You make your voice heard by providing written comments on the benefits of an immediate phase-out of Bahrain tweezers. If you are lucky and neither country receives any opposition to your suggestion, you may be importing those tweezers duty free ten years sooner.

TARIFF SUSPENSIONS

Why pay duty if you do not need to? A tariff suspension is one avenue to pursue temporarily to avoid paying duty on products that are not produced in the U.S.

When they were first introduced, tariffs were the primary source of revenue for the U.S. government. Now they are only a minimal source of revenue, but are used to protect certain segments of U.S. businesses from foreign competition. If there are no domestic producers of a given commodity, the U.S. government does not have any objections to eliminating the import tariffs from the product. As discussed in Chapter 7, the Harmonized Tariff Schedule (HTS) carries the weight of law. Accordingly, it requires an act of Congress to amend the HTS. This means the process to suspend the duty on your product requires the introduction of a bill in Congress.

There are really only two requirements for the U.S. government to consider suspending the duty on a product. First, it must be noncontroversial; that is, there can be no U.S. producers of the product and eliminating the duty must have no negative impact on U.S. jobs or economy. Second, eliminating the duty on the product cannot reduce the revenue of the U.S. government by more than $500,000 per year. If the revenue reduction would exceed $500,000 per year, you may also consider a tariff reduction (taking you to the cap amount) rather than a full tariff suspension.

All legislation affecting the revenue of the U.S. must be initiated in the House of Representatives, so we recommend that you seek out the congressional representative from the district most impacted by eliminating the duty on your product. If your firm has a Washington, D.C. office, that would be the ideal resource to use to reach out to your selected representative. If your firm does not have a Washington office, this solicitation can be done on your own or through a paid consultant or lobbyist. Before you ever initiate this visit, you will want to create an informational portfolio that outlines why eliminating the duty on this product is good for the U.S. and how it will benefit your representative's district. You will also need to estimate how much duty will be saved per year for the next four years. Ideally, your product will be totally unique with no domestic producers or competition. If your product is unique, but also has domestically made products that compete with it, you will need to outline carefully how your product is different from those products made in the U.S. Ideally, you will be able to explain humanitarian or economic benefits to the U.S. from your product.

It may take a little convincing, but as long as your product meets the two criteria discussed earlier, you should be able to find a representative to introduce a bill to suspend the duty on your product temporarily. While it is not necessary, you may also find it beneficial to find a senator to introduce a companion bill in the U.S. Senate. The whole process is driven by the House Ways and Means Committee, which reviews all individual bills to ensure that they are indeed noncontroversial and within the $500,000 per year revenue limit. The USITC conducts the actual review of the individual tariff suspension bills. The USITC will verify the revenue impact based on trade statistics and forecasts provided by the importers and will also contact any companies potentially impacted by the duty suspension to ensure that the bill will not have a negative impact on U.S. jobs or the economy.

All individual bills that pass the review of the USITC and House Ways and Means are eventually bundled into a larger piece of legislation that may also include other miscellaneous tariff and Customs provisions. During the 106th and 107th Congresses, this legislation of bundled tariff suspensions was known as the Miscellaneous Tariff Bill (MTB). Historically, MTBs are passed as one of the last actions during a session of Congress. The 106th Congress failed to pass the MTB and the 107th Congress agreed to carry over the MTB from the 106th rather than forcing all new individual bills to be introduced, reviewed, and bundled. The MTB passed by unanimous consent during a lame-duck session in late November 2004 of the 107th Congress and then only by the invoking of cloture by Senate majority leader, Senator Frist.

To summarize, the tariff suspension process is a relatively simple process whereby an importer can save a significant amount of duty provided a few criteria can be met. The tariff suspension process cannot be characterized as a quick fix, but rather a long and deliberate process. There are no guarantees that your bill will ever pass as you are totally at the mercy of the U.S. political system. While tariff suspensions are not supposed to be controversial or partisan, the 106th and 107th Congresses have proven otherwise.

DUTY DRAWBACK

Duty drawback is probably one of the most underutilized methods of getting money back from the U.S. government. If you export any amount of the products that you import, or use your imports to make new products that are later exported, you are probably eligible for some type of duty drawback. Actual duty drawback refunds are calculated at 99 percent of the original import duty paid.

Duty drawback is divided into four major types based on two characterizations:

1. Unused versus manufacturing: Will you export the merchandise that you imported in an unused condition or will you manufacture something else from it? There are a few things that you can do to your imported products without losing their status as unused for drawback purposes. These include some incidental operations such as cleaning, inspecting, and testing.
2. Will you directly identify the imported merchandise that is exported or will you substitute commercially interchangeable merchandise? The former is described as Direct Identification drawback, while the latter is

Table 8.1. Options for Duty Drawback.

Characterization	Substitution	Direct Identification
Unused	X	X
Manufacturing	X	X

Substitution drawback. You must combine one selection from each characterization, which leaves importers with four options for duty drawback (see Table 8.1).

The four options offer unique benefits to the importer and each has its own set of requirements and regulations for compliance.

Substitution Manufacturing: 1313(b) Drawback

The combination with the most flexible benefits is Substitution Manufacturing, which is provided for by 19 USC § 1313(b). Substitution Manufacturing drawback allows duty to be refunded on designated imports based on exports of finished articles that were made with raw materials that are commercially interchangeable with the designated imported merchandise. Note that the exports used in Substitution Manufacturing drawback do not actually need to be made with/from imported merchandise, provided the raw materials are commercially interchangeable with the imported merchandise for which you are claiming the duty drawback.

For example, a U.S. television manufacturer makes its Model AR22 with a specific transistor that historically has been made in a U.S. plant. Due to some production problems at the U.S. transistor plant, the TV manufacturer imports several shipments of the same transistors from its sister plant in Japan. When imported from Japan, the TV manufacturer pays a 6.2 percent tariff. The TV manufacturer can claim Substitution Manufacturing drawback on exports of its Model AR22 televisions, even when they have been produced with the U.S. transistors. This is the "substitution" concept in its simplest terms.

You can see the opportunities that Substitution Manufacturing drawback can offer. There are also some guidelines that must be followed. First, you can only make Substitution Manufacturing drawback claims pursuant to a Customs ruling. Customs offers a few general manufacturing rulings (see 19 CFR § 191), but in most cases, you will need to have obtained a specific manufacturing ruling from Customs before you can begin claiming drawback based on your manufacturing process. There is a specific format that must be followed when applying for a drawback ruling that can be found in the appendix to the Custom

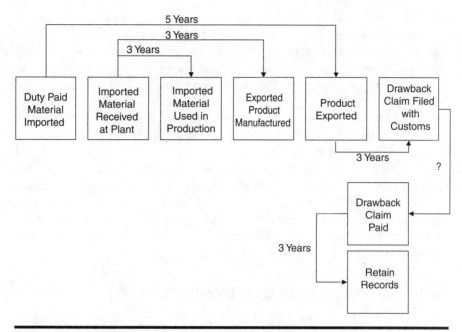

Figure 8.1. Substitution Manufacturing drawback 1313(b).

regulations pertaining to duty drawback located at 19 CFR § 191. Be aware that Customs can take up to ninety days from the receipt of your application to approve your ruling and that ninety-day clock starts all over again if Customs must request additional information.

The second requirement of Substitution Manufacturing drawback that can create hurdles is the time frame. The imported merchandise must be used in manufacturing within three years from the date of receipt. The exported articles must be produced within three years from the date of receipt of the imported merchandise and must be exported within five years of the date of importation of the designated imported merchandise. Finally, drawback claims must be filed within three years of the date of export (see Figure 8.1). If your import to production to export process fits these time frames, you should be eligible to recoup duty via Substitution Manufacturing drawback.

NAFTA Rules

Substitution Manufacturing has an interesting and unfortunate intersection with the NAFTA. Under the NAFTA, some exports to Canada and Mexico are either not eligible for drawback or are limited by what is referred to as the "lesser of the two" rule. To determine whether exports to the NAFTA countries are eligible for Substitution Manufacturing drawback, you must know the U.S. duty paid on the imported merchandise and the Canadian or Mexican duty rate on the finished exported product. Drawback may be claimed on the lesser of the amount due to the two countries (the U.S. versus the export destination of either Canada or Mexico). If the exported product that was made in the U.S. qualifies for NAFTA, the "lesser of the two" will almost definitely be zero, meaning no drawback is available on that export.

For example, a U.S. film manufacturer uses a special chemical, with a 6.5 percent tariff from Japan, in its production. The film is exported to Canada. However, it qualifies for the NAFTA and is duty free when imported into Canada. In this case, the export to Canada is not eligible for drawback. Each type of drawback has slightly different NAFTA restrictions or eligibilities that will be pointed out as each is discussed.

Substitution Unused: 1313(j)(2) Drawback

Substitution Unused drawback applies the substitution principles described for Substitution Manufacturing drawback simply without manufacturing. Substitution Unused drawback can be useful when an importer also has a U.S. plant that makes the same product as a foreign plant or when a company switches production from a foreign location to a U.S. plant that also supplies other parts of the world.

19 USC § 1313(j)(2) provides for drawback on merchandise that is commercially interchangeable with imported merchandise if the commercially interchangeable merchandise is exported or destroyed under Customs supervision within three years of the date of importation of the imported merchandise. The commercially interchangeable merchandise cannot be used in the U.S. before the exportation or destruction occurs and must be in the possession of the drawback claimant.

One example of a Substitution Unused drawback scenario would be a commodity-type chemical such as benzene. A company may need to produce benzene at numerous plants throughout the world and may need to supply plant sites throughout the world from these plants. Because of supply and demand, pricing volatility, and production capacity, the company may now need to export benzene from a country where it needed to import benzene several months ago. This scenario provides a good opportunity for Substitution Unused drawback.

It should be noted that the Substitution Unused drawback is not currently eligible on exports to Canada or Mexico.

Direct Identification Unused: 1313(j)(1) Drawback

Direct Identification Unused drawback is provided for by 19 USC § 1313(j)(1). As implied by the name, the merchandise for which drawback is claimed must be exported without having been used. The time frames for Direct Identification Unused drawback are the same as for Substitution Unused, however, the merchandise that is either exported or destroyed under Customs supervision must be the same exact material that was imported and on which duty was paid (that is, direct identification). In order to use this type of drawback, the claimant must be able to directly tie the import to the export and must be able to document the path from import to export through inventory records that can directly identify the merchandise for which drawback is being claimed.

Many companies use the U.S. as a warehousing location to supply all of North America. If this scenario includes the warehousing and distribution of imported goods throughout Canada and Mexico, Direct Identification Unused drawback becomes an avenue to recoup the duties paid in the U.S. on merchandise that is ultimately sold into Canada or Mexico. For example, a U.S. firm imports pipe cutters from China and then sells those pipe cutters into the U.S., Canada, and Mexico. Any of the pipe cutters exported to Canada and Mexico are eligible for Direct Identification Unused drawback. Exports to Canada and Mexico are eligible for Direct Identification Unused drawback without special consideration.

Direct Identification Manufacturing: 1313(a) Drawback

Direct Identification Manufacturing drawback is provided for by 19 USC § 1313(a). Direct Identification Manufacturing drawback offers the least flexibility of the four types of drawbacks discussed in this chapter and is the hardest to maintain. This type of drawback combines the premises of manufacturing (the imported merchandise is used to produce something else that is later exported) and direct identification (you must be able to directly account for and identify the imported merchandise in the exported product and through every step in between). There are only a few occasions where Substitution Manufacturing drawback is not a better option, so discussion will be limited to this introductory paragraph.

Key Drawback Benefits: Accelerated Payment Privileges and Waiver of Prior Notification of Intent to Export

If you have a duty drawback program, one benefit that the Customs regulations provide is sure to catch your attention. Without the benefit of "Accelerated Payment Privileges," a drawback claimant only receives the drawback refunds when Customs liquidates the drawback claim. This may not sound so bad at first, but Customs can take several years to liquidate drawback claims.

A drawback claimant can apply to Customs for accelerated payment privileges. When claims are filed under accelerated payment, Customs will pay you within thirty days. In order to receive these benefits, a drawback claimant must apply to Customs in accordance with the drawback regulations. As part of the application, the drawback claimant must make certain commitments to Customs and provide details of the claimant's drawback program and record keeping procedures. Customs can take up to ninety days to approve this application and if it is returned as incomplete, the ninety-day clock begins anew. The only potential negative aspect of accelerated payment is that Customs will typically hold a large number of claims or a large dollar amount of drawback as unliquidated until Customs can send a team of auditors to verify the accuracy of those claims that were paid under accelerated payment. This can leave drawback records open to audit for an extended period of time, a nightmare that equals an IRS audit.

The second drawback benefit of "Waiver of Prior Notification of Intent to Export," (WPN) applies only to Substitution Unused and Direct Identification Unused drawback. Under both types of unused drawback, the exporter must notify Customs prior to the export of goods that will be used in a future drawback claim. Customs then has the right to inspect the merchandise prior to export. With WPN privileges, the requirement to notify Customs is waived. In order to receive WPN privileges, the drawback claimant must again make a detailed application to Customs, which includes a series of commitments to Customs by the claimant. WPN privileges are definitely beneficial if your drawback program will include any type of unused drawback.

Certificates of Delivery and Manufacture

Certificates of Delivery (CD) and Certificates of Manufacture (CM) are two ways that another company can transfer the right to claim drawback on duty that they paid to you. If you buy a product that another U.S. company has imported, you can request a CD and then become eligible to claim drawback on any duty that your domestic supplier may have paid. In essence, you can create your own price reduction by negotiating CDs into your purchase agreement. Also, the CD you receive will reveal the amount of duty paid per unit of measure. Assuming you can figure out the classification and duty rate of the product, you will be able to determine your supplier's cost for the product from their supplier. This may serve to enlighten you to negotiate a better price with them or to look to purchase the product directly from a foreign supplier.

The CM is merely an expansion of the CD principle. With a CM, your supplier can use an imported raw material to produce a new product that they sell to you. With a CM, they are able to transfer the duty applicable to the imported content of the product you purchase.

FOREIGN TRADE ZONES AND BONDED WAREHOUSES

Foreign trade zones (FTZ) are areas within the U.S. that the government considers outside of the U.S. Customs territory. Certain types of merchandise can be imported into an FTZ without going through formal Customs entry procedures or paying import duties. Some of the benefits of operating within an FTZ are obvious; for example, an FTZ can help you defer paying duties. The National Association of Foreign Trade Zones provides the following list of ten benefits derived from operating an FTZ.

1. Imports may be admitted and held in an FTZ without paying U.S. Customs duties.
2. FTZ users can pay the duty rate on component material or merchandise produced from component material, whichever is lower.
3. Customs duties are never paid on merchandise exported from a zone.
4. Duties are reduced or eliminated on materials subject to defect, damage, obsolescence, waste, or scrap.
5. Merchandise may be exported and returned to an FTZ without duty payment.
6. Spare parts may be stored, returned, or destroyed without duty payment.
7. Delays in Customs clearances and duty drawback are eliminated.
8. Duties are not owed on labor, overhead, or profit attributed to FTZ production operations.
9. Quality control inspections can identify substandard goods to be destroyed or returned without duty payment.
10. No duty is owed on in-bond, zone-to-zone transfer of FTZ merchandise.

FTZs that can provide the largest financial impact are those developed around an inverted tariff arrangement. In an FTZ approved for manufacturing, the users can pay the duty rate on component material or merchandise produced from component material, whichever is lower. When component materials have a higher tariff than the finished good, this creates an inverted tariff situation. A dramatic example of an inverted tariff opportunity can be found in the pharmaceutical industry where active drug ingredients are currently 6.5 percent as organic compounds (when not found in the Pharmaceutical Appendix of the HTS). Pharmaceuticals in dosage forms such as tablets or capsules are always duty free, so a pharmaceutical company can import an active drug ingredient from Japan or Europe and avoid paying duty by performing the tablet-making process within an FTZ. Active drug ingredients are normally very expensive, so an FTZ can allow a drug company to avoid enormous amounts of duty.

FTZs offer a wide array of benefits. If you are intrigued by the ten benefits offered above, we recommend that you check the National Association of Foreign Trade Zones' website (www.naftz.org).

FTZs also have some problems. First, they are not simple to establish or maintain. The FTZ application process is both long and detailed. To provide a conservative estimate, count on a year for an FTZ application to be approved from start to finish. FTZs do not exist without cost. Just to apply for an FTZ can easily exceed $100,000, if outside counsel or consultants are required. Depending on the size and scope of the FTZ, at least some portion of a person's job will need to be devoted to the running of the FTZ and handling the required documentation and record keeping. In a large and complex FTZ, the operations may require several persons to be devoted solely to the operation and mainte-nance of the FTZ.

Finally, FTZs inherently add an additional level of liability to the company in terms of increased Customs compliance requirements and scrutiny. FTZs can be audited by Customs as a separate audit from any other normal Customs audit. So a company operating an FTZ could receive an import audit and an FTZ audit within the same year. Despite these complications, FTZs offer the potential for enormous financial savings for an importer and should not be overlooked by a company seeking to optimize its international supply chain and reduce import costs.

TARIFF OPTIMIZATION

The term "tariff optimization" encompasses all of the concepts in this chapter. If an importer is going to be successful in today's competitive international arena, it will need to consider each and every program described in this chapter each time a prospective import purchase is contemplated. A key to success with tariff optimization is to review transactions while they are still in the planning stages. If you wait until containers are already arriving at the port, you will most likely have lost your opportunity to remain competitive. When procuring goods in the international arena, you need to evaluate which trade programs are ap-plicable to your transaction and ask: What countries can you source the product from? Are any of the countries eligible for preferential trade agreements with the U.S.? Is our product unique and eligible for a tariff suspension? Are there any opportunities to take advantage of duty drawback, an FTZ, or a bonded warehouse? The savvy procurer will evaluate all of these trade programs before determining the true landed cost and before deciding where to buy the product. Now, read on to Chapter 9 to learn how the trade industry must adhere to new post 9/11 security requirements to ensure a continuous import privilege.

9

THE EFFECTS OF HEIGHTENED SECURITY ON THE INBOUND SUPPLY CHAIN

The events of 9/11 have forever changed the way that business will be conducted both in the U.S. and abroad. There once was a time when we moved materials globally and were only concerned about meeting requirements that were, for most purposes, harmless. There was also a time when the government believed that it was in full control of the inbound and outbound movements in the U.S. It was during those times that U.S. Customs believed it could focus most of its effort on revenue collection through duties, harbor maintenance fees, and merchandise processing fees. Findings of the dreaded Customs audit usually resulted in monetary penalties for unpaid duties and inherent flaws in procedures.

September 11 became the catalyst that drove the government to re-evaluate its priorities with regard to the areas it was targeting for enforcement (revenues). In the process of reconstructing the way we import, however, Customs realized there was no way that it could attack terrorism on its own. Support would need to come from beyond the government. An unimaginable shift in the relationship between the government and industry was introduced. This shift has forced supply chains to restructure global business procurement processes to ensure the security of their purchased product from its origin until it is received into inventory. Security is now a vital component of the goals of any supply chain. The fairest price, quickest delivery turnaround, ensured compliance, and secured heightened security are the essential characteristics of a responsible global procurement practice.

From another aspect, 9/11 impacted more than the U.S Customs Service. It was the unpalatable truth that the U.S. was not invincible that led to the creation of the Department of Homeland Security (DHS). In an effort to focus on the security of our nation, the government combined the U.S. Customs Service and Immigration to form Customs and Border Protection (CBP). This combination was the first step in the establishment of a more secure border through the concept of "one face at the border," which meant that people and cargo would be screened by a unified body. It also increased the awareness of officers through open communication and combined goals. Although this reorganization was a quick and clean decision, the government could not afford to staff CBP with the number of agents needed. Therefore, in November 2001, the DHS introduced the Customs-Trade Partnership Against Terrorism Program (C-TPAT). Two months after the tragedy of 9/11, the U.S. Customs Service had positioned itself to begin the war against terrorism. As the government realized it could not do the job alone, it turned to industry for help, in the form of C-TPAT (see Figure 9.1).

Figure 9.1. This is why Customs knows that homeland security is so important. (Courtesy of the www.cbp.gov photo gallery.)

CUSTOMS-TRADE PARTNERSHIP AGAINST TERRORISM

The purpose of C-TPAT was to challenge both Customs and the trade community to design a new approach to supply chain security that would secure U.S. borders from threats, while continuing to allow legitimate business to flow through. The program is currently available to importers, carriers, brokers, and other industry sectors. If used effectively by responsible company supply chains, C-TPAT can improve delivery turnaround without increasing bottom-line expenditures. The goal of this program is to take a set of fundamental guidelines that have been established by CBP and then build on them. That is, Customs has laid the foundation of the program through the development of a Supply Chain Security Profile that outlines criteria for a company to compare itself to and measure the similarities or differences. Figure 9.2 reflects the pattern of global terrorism.

In its initial rollout of C-TPAT, it was not the intention of Customs to eliminate or disqualify a potential member because of the submission of an inadequate profile. The goal was to work in partnership with industry to recognize the companies that are operating securely, and work with companies that are not, through the sharing of best practices learned by Customs from certified members. This was an enormous breakthrough for Customs since its typical role is to police industry and apply penalties for infractions. Since its inception, more than 9,200 C-TPAT members have participated in the international trade community at the time this book was drafted. Read on below to learn how Customs has changed the C-TPAT program since its inception.

ELIGIBILITY

C-TPAT is designed to address the security procedures of all components of the global supply chain: production, transportation, storage, importation, and distribution. Customs has opened the program to a number of partners in a broad spectrum of industries:

- Importers
- Licensed customs brokers
- Air carriers
- Sea carriers
- Rail carriers
- Air freight consolidators/ocean transport intermediaries and nonvessel operating common carriers (NVOCCs)
- U.S./Canada border highway carriers
- U.S. Marine port authority/terminal operators

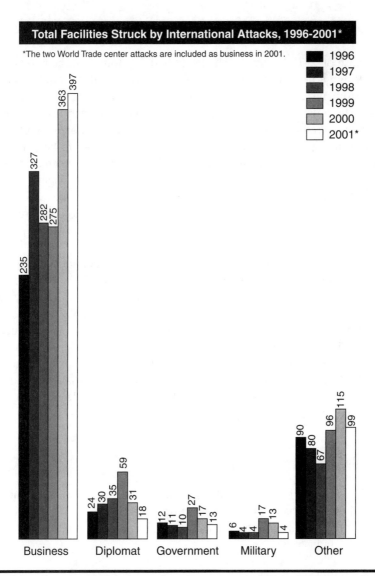

Figure 9.2. Patterns of global terrorism, Department of State 2002 (www.cbp.gov).

Since the majority of terrorist attacks have been on businesses, the main objectives of C-TPAT are to protect our borders and the businesses that operate within those borders. It is clear that international business impacts our national security. Therefore, it is the goal of C-TPAT to enhance the efficiency of business operations indirectly by incorporating the principles of supply chain management together with an enhanced awareness of security needs within those principles. For example, information is an integral part of a supply chain function that can improve efficiency, but if important data are placed in the wrong hands, the results could be detrimental to your operations. Therefore, C-TPAT looks at the business to evaluate its supply chain elements from a security perspective. This evaluation not only bolsters the relationship with Customs and the safety of our borders, but also adds certain efficiencies to the supply chain.

MEMORANDUM OF UNDERSTANDING

The Memorandum of Understanding (MOU) (see www.cbp.gov) is the first step in the C-TPAT certification process that initiates your organization's intent to participate in the program voluntarily. The MOU outlines the purpose of the program and the commitments for both the applicant and Customs. Since this program is voluntary, the MOU contains language that expresses the ability of either party to withdraw from the partnership at any time. Since the foundation of this program was built on the intention to develop partnerships, it was important for Customs to stress that this was a voluntary partnership and either party could terminate at any time. It is also important to note that being a C-TPAT–certified partner does not grant you any exemption from your compliance duties under reasonable care and Customs will still enforce violations against a certified C-TPAT partner.

This may seem like an awkward relationship, since the same organization that will be your "partner" can also penalize you for noncompliance. Consequently, it is important to realize that Customs is your partner in all efforts to secure our borders and they have drawn a line between these activities. The Supply Chain Security Profile and validation processes are what Customs uses to evaluate your activities regarding C-TPAT. Customs has reportedly used the C-TPAT validation process to provide importers with recommendations for improvement and to share security best practices. However, if Customs determines that you have not been forthcoming with your security profile or are not following through on your side of the MOU agreements, it will draw the line and either revoke your C-TPAT privileges or require you to institute corrective action measures.

THE SUPPLY CHAIN SECURITY PROFILE QUESTIONNAIRE

The Supply Chain Security Profile Questionnaire ("profile") is the second part in the certification process and must be submitted within sixty days of the MOU. The profile is what Customs uses to determine your initial certification.

In its initial version, importers were required to address their security program including facilities security, theft prevention, shipping and receiving controls, information security controls, internal controls, personnel security, and service provider requirements. Customs provided the following general recommendations that were to be followed on a case-by-case basis depending on the company's size and structure and may not be applicable to all. Clearly, these were guidelines and not mandatory elements.

- **Procedural security** — Procedures should be in place to protect against unmanifested material being introduced into the supply chain. Security controls should include the supervised introduction/removal of cargo; the proper marking, weighing, counting, and documenting of cargo/cargo equipment verified against manifest documents; the detecting/reporting of shortages/overages; and procedures for verifying seals on containers, trailers, and railcars. The movement of incoming/outgoing goods should be monitored. Random, unannounced security assessments of areas under your company's control within the supply chain should be conducted. Procedures for notifying Customs and other law enforcement agencies in cases where anomalies or illegal activities are detected, or suspected, by the company should also be in place.
- **Physical security** — All buildings and rail yards should be constructed of materials that resist unlawful entry and protect against outside intrusion. Physical security should include perimeter fences; locking devices on external and internal doors, windows, gates, and fences; adequate lighting inside and outside the facility; and the segregation and marking of international, domestic, high-value, and dangerous-goods cargo within the warehouse by a safe, caged, or otherwise fenced-in area.
- **Access controls** — Unauthorized access to facilities and conveyances should be prohibited. Controls should include positive identification of all employees, visitors, and vendors. Procedures should also include challenging unauthorized/unidentified persons.
- **Personnel security** — Companies should conduct employment screening and interviewing of prospective employees to include periodic background checks and application verifications.
- **Education and training awareness** — A security awareness program should be provided to employees including the recognition of internal conspiracies, maintaining cargo integrity, and determining and addressing unauthorized access. These programs should offer incentives for active employee participation in security controls.
- **Manifest procedures** — Companies should ensure that manifests are complete, legible, accurate, and submitted in a timely manner to Customs.

- **Conveyance security** — Conveyance integrity should be maintained to protect against the introduction of unauthorized personnel and material. Security should include the physical search of all readily accessible areas, the securing of internal/external compartments and panels, and procedures for reporting cases in which unauthorized personnel, unmanifested materials, or signs of tampering are discovered.

On March 25, 2005, Customs forever changed the C-TPAT program by introducing new minimum-security criteria for importer C-TPAT participation. Although the minimum criteria were only introduced for importers at the time of publication of this book, we believe that Customs will introduce minimum criteria for all groups eligible to participate in C-TPAT (for example, carriers, brokers, etc.). When Customs introduced the March 25 criteria, they also instituted an on-line C-TPAT application process for importers. We expect rapid changes in this arena and therefore recommend that you consult the C-TPAT postings available at www.cbp.gov to ensure that you are receiving the most current and correct program details.

At the time of publication, Customs had recently posted the following requirements for the importer's C-TPAT application process:

1. Active U.S. importer or nonresident Canadian importer into the U.S.
2. Have a business office staffed in the U.S. or Canada
3. Have active U.S. Importer of Record ID(s) in either of the following formats:
   - U.S. Social Security Number
   - U.S. Internal Revenue Service–assigned ID(s)
   - CBP-assigned Importer ID
4. Possess a valid continuous import bond registered with CBP
5. Have a designated company officer that will be the primary cargo security officer responsible for C-TPAT
6. Commit to maintaining CBP C-TPAT supply chain security criteria as outlined in the C-TPAT importer agreement
7. Create and provide CBP with a C-TPAT supply chain security profile, which identifies how the importer will meet, maintain, and enhance internal policy to meet the C-TPAT importer security criteria

The most current application process at the time of this writing is provided verbatim below from the Customs website. Note that incorporated into the application instructions are the new March 25, 2005 minimum criteria. While not totally evident at its initial reading, Customs has confirmed to the trade that the new minimum criteria are indeed risk based and may be addressed by the importer accordingly.

APPLICATION INSTRUCTIONS

Step 1. Prepare a C-TPAT Supply Chain Security Profile

Importers are required to complete and submit to CBP a *Supply Chain Security Profile* that addresses each item in the C-TPAT Security Criteria for Importers. The security profile should summarize the importer's commitment to ensuring adherence to the following C-TPAT security criteria for importers:

C-TPAT SECURITY CRITERIA FOR IMPORTERS

Importers must conduct a comprehensive assessment of their international supply chains based upon the following C-TPAT security criteria. Where an importer outsources or contracts elements of their supply chain, such as a foreign facility, conveyance, domestic warehouse, or other elements, the importer must work with these business partners to ensure that pertinent security measures are in place and adhered to throughout their supply chain. The supply chain for C-TPAT purposes is defined from point of origin (manufacturer/supplier/vendor) through to point of distribution and recognizes the diverse business models C-TPAT members employ.

C-TPAT recognizes the complexity of international supply chains and endorses the application and implementation of security measures based upon risk analysis. Therefore, the program allows for flexibility and the customization of security plans based on the member's business model.

Appropriate security measures, as listed throughout this document, must be implemented and maintained throughout the importer's supply chains, based on risk.

Business Partner Requirements

Importers must have written and verifiable processes for the selection of business partners including manufacturers, product suppliers, and vendors.

Security Procedures

For those business partners eligible for C-TPAT certification (carriers, U.S. ports, terminals, brokers, consolidators, etc.), the importer must have documentation (e.g., C-TPAT certificate, SVI number, etc.) indicating whether these business partners are or are not C-TPAT certified.

For those business partners not eligible for C-TPAT certification, importers must require business partners to demonstrate that they are meeting C-TPAT security criteria via written/electronic confirmation (e.g., contractual obligations via a letter from a senior business partner officer attesting to compliance; a written statement from the business partner demonstrating their compliance with C-TPAT security criteria or an equivalent WCO accredited security program administered by a foreign customs authority; or by providing a completed importer security questionnaire). Based upon a documented risk assessment process, non-C-TPAT eligible business partners must be subject to verification of compliance with C-TPAT security criteria by the importer.

Point of Origin
Importers must ensure business partners develop security processes and procedures consistent with the C-TPAT security criteria to enhance the integrity of the shipment at point of origin. Periodic reviews of business partners' processes and facilities should be conducted based on risk, and should maintain the security standards required by the importer.

Participation/Certification in Foreign Customs Administration's Supply Chain Security Programs
Current or prospective business partners who have obtained a certification in a supply chain security program being administered by foreign Customs administration should be required to indicate their status of participation to the importer.

Other Internal Criteria for Selection
Internal requirements, such as financial soundness, capability of meeting contractual security requirements, and the ability to identify and correct security deficiencies as needed, should be addressed by the importer. Internal requirements should be assessed against a risk-based process as determined by an internal management team.

Container Security
Container integrity must be maintained to protect against the introduction of unauthorized material and/or persons. At point of stuffing, procedures must be in place to properly seal and maintain the integrity of the shipping containers. A high-security seal must be affixed to all loaded containers bound for the United States. All seals must meet or exceed the current PAS ISO 17712 standards for high-security seals.

Container Inspection

Procedures must be in place to verify the physical integrity of the container structure prior to stuffing, to include the reliability of the locking mechanisms of the doors. A 7-point inspection process is recommended for all containers:

- Front wall
- Left side
- Right side
- Floor
- Ceiling/roof
- Inside/outside doors
- Outside/undercarriage

Container Seals

Written procedures must stipulate how seals are to be controlled and affixed to loaded containers, to include procedures for recognizing and reporting compromised seals and/or containers to CBP or the appropriate foreign authority. Only designated employees should distribute container seals for integrity purposes.

Container Storage

Containers must be stored in a secure area to prevent unauthorized access and/or manipulation. Procedures must be in place for reporting and neutralizing unauthorized entry into containers or container storage areas.

Physical Access Controls

Access controls prevent unauthorized entry to facilities, maintain control of employees and visitors, and protect company assets. Access controls must include the positive identification of all employees, visitors, and vendors at all points of entry.

Employees

An employee identification system must be in place for positive identification and access control purposes. Employees should only be given access to those secure areas needed for the performance of their duties. Company management or security personnel must adequately control the issuance and removal of employee, visitor, and vendor identification badges. Procedures for the issuance, removal, and changing of access devices (e.g., keys, key cards, etc.) must be documented.

Visitor Controls
Visitors must present photo identification for documentation purposes upon arrival. All visitors should be escorted and visibly display temporary identification.

Deliveries (Including Mail)
Proper vendor identification (ID) and/or photo identification must be presented for documentation purposes upon arrival by all vendors. Arriving packages and mail should be periodically screened before being disseminated.

Challenging and Removing Unauthorized Persons
Procedures must be in place to identify, challenge, and address unauthorized/unidentified persons.

Personnel Security
Processes must be in place to screen prospective employees and to periodically check current employees.

Pre-Employment Verification
Application information, such as employment history and references, must be verified prior to employment.

Background Checks/Investigations
Consistent with foreign, federal, state, and local regulations, background checks and investigations should be conducted for prospective employees. Once employed, periodic checks and reinvestigations should be performed based on cause and/or the sensitivity of the employee's position.

Personnel Termination Procedures
Companies must have procedures in place to remove identification, facility, and system access for terminated employees.

Procedural Security
Security measures must be in place to ensure the integrity and security of processes relevant to the transportation, handling, and storage of cargo in the supply chain.

Documentation Processing
Procedures must be in place to ensure that all information used in the clearing of merchandise/cargo is legible, complete, accurate, and

protected against the exchange, loss, or introduction of erroneous information. Documentation control must include safeguarding computer access and information.

Manifesting Procedures
To help ensure the integrity of cargo received from abroad, procedures must be in place to ensure that information received from business partners is reported accurately and in a timely manner.

Shipping and Receiving
Arriving cargo should be reconciled against information on the cargo manifest. The cargo should be described accurately and the weights, labels, marks, and piece count indicated and verified. Departing cargo should be verified against purchase or delivery orders. Drivers delivering or receiving cargo must be positively identified before cargo is received or released.

Cargo Discrepancies
All shortages, overages, and other significant discrepancies or anomalies must be resolved and/or investigated appropriately. CBP and/or other appropriate law enforcement agencies must be notified if illegal or suspicious activities are detected, as appropriate.

Security Training and Threat Awareness
A threat awareness program should be established and maintained by security personnel to recognize and foster awareness of the threat posed by terrorists at each point in the supply chain. Employees must be made aware of the procedures the company has in place to address a situation and how to report it. Additional training should be provided to employees in the shipping and receiving areas, as well as those receiving and opening mail.

Additionally, specific training should be offered to assist employees in maintaining cargo integrity, recognizing internal conspiracies, and protecting access controls. These programs should offer incentives for active employee participation.

Physical Security
Cargo handling and storage facilities in domestic and foreign locations must have physical barriers and deterrents that guard against unauthorized access. Importers should incorporate the following C-TPAT physical security criteria throughout their supply chains as applicable.

Fencing
Perimeter fencing should enclose the areas around cargo handling and storage facilities. Interior fencing within a cargo handling structure should be used to segregate domestic, international, high-value, and hazardous cargo. All fencing must be regularly inspected for integrity and damage.

Gates and Gate Houses
Gates through which vehicles and/or personnel enter or exit must be manned and/or monitored. The number of gates should be kept to the minimum necessary for proper access and safety.

Parking
Private passenger vehicles should be prohibited from parking in or adjacent to cargo handling and storage areas.

Building Structure
Buildings must be constructed of materials that resist unlawful entry. The integrity of structures must be maintained by periodic inspection and repair.

Locking Devices and Key Controls
All external and internal windows, gates, and fences must be secured with locking devices. Management or security personnel must control the issuance of all locks and keys.

Lighting
Adequate lighting must be provided inside and outside the facility including the following areas: entrances and exits, cargo handling and storage areas, fence lines, and parking areas.

Alarm Systems and Video Surveillance Cameras
Alarm systems and video surveillance cameras should be utilized to monitor premises and prevent unauthorized access to cargo handling and storage areas.

Information Technology Security
Password Protection
Automated systems must use individually assigned accounts that require a periodic change of password. Information technology (IT) security policies, procedures, and standards must be in place and provided to employees in the form of training.

Accountability

A system must be in place to identify the abuse of information technology (IT) including improper access, tampering, or the altering of business data. All system violators must be subject to appropriate disciplinary actions for abuse.

Step 2. Submission of Your Application

Submit your C-TPAT application and other required supplemental information via the C-TPAT Online Application submission process, located at the application web link provided (C-TPAT Online Application: https://apps.cbp.gov/ctpat/).

Step 3. After Entering Your Online Application

Applicants will be directed to **upload** your *Supply Chain Security Profile*. The **only** acceptable file formats are limited to: .doc, .rtf, .pdf, and .txt files.

IMPORTANT: You must be ready to UPLOAD your *Supply Chain Security Profile* IMMEDIATELY on completion of the online application.

Step 4. On Receipt

CBP will review the importer's completed *Supply Chain Security Profile*. After CBP completes the profile review, the importer will receive feedback on their *Supply Chain Security Profile* within sixty days.

Recommendations for Completing Your Profile

Although the process for completing the profile is fairly straightforward, there are some areas worth researching and documenting. Depending on the size of your organization, you may already have many of these procedures in place through various departments within your company. For example:

- Your HR Department might already have policies and procedures in place for screening employees.
- Your plant sites may have facility-specific security policies in place.
- If your organization is involved with a trade organization like the American Chemistry Council (ACC), you may already have security guidelines in place required for membership in the trade organization. The ACC's Responsible Care® has stringent transportation security guidelines that participating organizations must follow to maintain

membership. You may be able to work with your Traffic Department to identify how to incorporate these policies and procedures in your profile.

In addition to identifying policies and procedures that may already exist within your organization, there are other areas that you can research in order to evaluate the level of risk your organization carries. For example;

- You should research all of your points of origin and establish what percentage of your shipments originates in Container Security Initiative (CSI) ports. As you will read later in this chapter, CSI ports have U.S. Customs officials on site who inspect shipments prior to their loading onto U.S.-bound vessels. If a majority of your shipments depart from one of these ports, you have an added level of security.
- You should evaluate the steamship lines that carry your shipments as well as the brokers that clear them. These two providers play a critical role in your inbound supply chain and if they have obtained C-TPAT certification, they have added another level of security to your supply chain.
- You will need to evaluate all of the vendors that supply your U.S. operation and unless they are affiliated with your organization, you will need to inform them of your intent to participate in the C-TPAT program and they will need to confirm their support. The level of detail you go into on vendor evaluation will depend largely on their location, organization, and the relationship they have with your company. For example, if you are a subsidiary of a large European organization and you buy the majority of your materials from other subsidiaries around the world, you may want to obtain global support from Headquarters, which will (in turn) drive your affiliates to support your efforts. Furthermore, there is somewhat less of a threat of contaminating your supply chain if you are purchasing from a sister company.
- Some companies that have vendors throughout Africa and Asia may need to visit these vendor sites and try to drive change in these businesses, and in certain cases, companies may need to stop purchasing from certain businesses that cannot or will not make the necessary changes to secure their supply chain at the origin.

THE BENEFITS OF PARTICIPATING IN C-TPAT

C-TPAT offers businesses a patriotic opportunity to play an active role in the war against terrorism. By participating in this worldwide supply chain security initiative, companies will ensure a more secure supply chain for their employees, suppliers, and customers. Beyond these essential security benefits, Customs will offer potential benefits to C-TPAT members, including:

- A reduced number of inspections (reduced border times).
- An assigned account manager (if one is not already assigned).
- Eligibility for account-based processes (for example, bimonthly/monthly payments).
- An emphasis on self-policing, not Customs verifications.
- In the event of another breach of our nation's security, C-TPAT members are more likely to have their supply chain moving quicker than those who are not participating in the program.

Following the introduction of the March 25, 2005 minimum criteria, CBP Commissioner Bonner introduced a new three-tier system of benefits. Tier 1 represented C-TPAT members who met the new criteria, Tier 2 represented those C-TPAT members who had been validated by Customs and passed, and Tier 3 represented those validated C-TPAT importers who had demonstrated best practices. The higher an importer's tier, the higher their benefits would be. Due to the rapid changes in C-TPAT, we again recommend consulting www.cbp.gov for the latest details.

C-TPAT VALIDATION PROCESS

The C-TPAT Validation Process was established by Customs to ensure that companies that had received C-TPAT certification were, in fact, enforcing the policies and procedures outlined in their profile. Since Customs bases their decision to expedite the release of cargo and/or reduce the number of examinations on the profile that a company submits, they developed the validation process to authenticate the profiles. Although it may seem quite threatening, the validation process is not an audit. It is more of a forum for Customs to evaluate the participant's actual processes and procedures compared to those documented in the profile. Customs intends to utilize these validations as an opportunity to share best practices and guide the participant in the right direction. The validation process takes about ten days and, depending on the findings, the participant will either have their certification confirmed or their C-TPAT privileges suspended until corrective actions have been completed. Customs has established that validation will occur within the first three years of certification and they select companies based on a number of factors including risk, volume, etc.

Customs will use the validation process to ensure that importer members are meeting the new minimum criteria.

C-TPAT REQUIREMENTS FOR BROKERS, FORWARDERS, AIR CARRIERS, ETC.

C-TPAT also has requirements for partners in a supply chain system.

Brokers

Develop and implement a sound plan to enhance security procedures. These are general recommendations that should be followed on a case-by-case basis depending on the company's size and structure and may not be applicable to all firms.

- **Procedural security** — Companies should notify Customs and other law enforcement agencies whenever anomalies or illegal activities related to security issues are detected or suspected by the company.
- **Documentation processing** — Brokers should make their best efforts to ensure that all information provided by the importer/exporter, freight forwarder, etc., and used in the clearing of merchandise/cargo, is legible and protected against the exchange, loss, or introduction of erroneous information. Documentation controls should include, where applicable, procedures for:
  - ☐ Maintaining the accuracy of information received, including the shipper and consignee name and address, first and second notify parties, description, weight, quantity, and unit of measure (such as boxes, cartons, etc.) of the cargo being cleared.
  - ☐ Recording, reporting, and/or investigating shortages and overages of merchandise/cargo.
  - ☐ Safeguarding computer access and information.
- **Personnel security** — Consistent with federal, state, and local regulations and statutes, companies should establish an internal process to screen prospective employees and verify employment applications. Such an internal process could include background checks and other tests depending on the particular employee function involved.
- **Education and training awareness** — A security awareness program should include notification being provided to Customs and other law enforcement agencies whenever anomalies or illegal activities related to security are detected or suspected. These programs should provide:

☐ Recognition for active employee participation in security controls.

☐ Training in documentation fraud and computer security controls.

Manufacturers

Develop and implement a sound plan to enhance security procedures. These are general recommendations that should be followed on a case-by-case basis depending on the company's size and structure and may not be applicable to all firms. The company should have a written security procedure plan in place that addresses the following:

- **Physical security** — All buildings should be constructed of materials that resist unlawful entry and protect against outside intrusion. Physical security should include:
  ☐ Adequate locking devices for external and internal doors, windows, gates, and fences.
  ☐ Segregation and marking of international, domestic, high-value, and dangerous-goods cargo within the warehouse by a safe, caged, or otherwise fenced-in area.
  ☐ Adequate lighting provided inside and outside the facility to include parking areas.
  ☐ Separate parking area for private vehicles separate from the shipping, loading dock, and cargo areas.
  ☐ Having internal/external communications systems in place to contact internal security personnel or local law enforcement police.
- **Access controls** — Unauthorized access to the shipping, loading dock, and cargo areas should be prohibited. Controls should include:
  ☐ The positive identification of all employees, visitors, and vendors.
  ☐ Procedures for challenging unauthorized/unidentified persons.
- **Procedural security** — Measures for the handling of incoming and outgoing goods should include protection against the introduction, exchange, or loss of any legal or illegal material. Security controls should include:
  ☐ Having a designated security representative to supervise the introduction/removal of cargo.
  ☐ Properly marked, weighed, counted, and documented products.
  ☐ Procedures for verifying seals on containers, trailers, and railcars.
  ☐ Procedures for detecting and reporting shortages and overages.
  ☐ Procedures for tracking the timely movement of incoming and outgoing goods.
  ☐ Proper storage of empty and full containers to prevent unauthorized access.

- ☐ Procedures to notify Customs and other law enforcement agencies in cases where anomalies or illegal activities are detected or suspected by the company.
- **Personnel security** — Companies should conduct employment screening and interviewing of prospective employees to include periodic background checks and application verifications.
- **Education and training awareness** — A security awareness program should be provided to employees including recognizing internal conspiracies, maintaining product integrity, and determining and addressing unauthorized access. These programs should encourage active employee participation in security controls.

Warehouses

Develop and implement a sound plan to enhance security procedures. These are general recommendations that should be followed on a case-by-case basis depending on the company's size and structure and may not be applicable to all firms. As defined in this guideline, warehouses are facilities that are used to store and stage both Customs bonded and nonbonded cargo. The company should have a written security procedure plan in place addressing the following:

- **Physical security** — All buildings should be constructed of materials that resist unlawful entry and protect against outside intrusion. Physical security should include:
  - ☐ Adequate locking devices for external and internal doors, windows, gates, and fences.
  - ☐ Adequate lighting provided inside and outside the facility to include parking areas.
  - ☐ Segregation and marking of international, domestic, high-value, and dangerous-goods cargo within the warehouse by a safe, caged, or otherwise fenced-in area.
  - ☐ Separate parking area for private vehicles separate from the shipping, loading dock, and cargo areas.
  - ☐ Having internal/external communications systems in place to contact internal security personnel or local law enforcement police.
- **Access controls** — Unauthorized access to facilities should be prohibited. Controls should include:
  - ☐ The positive identification of all employees, visitors, and vendors.
  - ☐ Procedures for challenging unauthorized/unidentified persons.
- **Procedural security** — Procedures should be in place to protect against unmanifested material being introduced into the warehouse. Security controls should include:

- ☐ Having a designated security representative to supervise the introduction/removal of cargo.
- ☐ Properly marked, weighed, counted, and documented cargo/cargo equipment verified against manifest documents.
- ☐ Procedures for verifying seal on containers, trailers, and railcars.
- ☐ Procedures for detecting and reporting shortages and overages.
- ☐ Procedures to notify Customs and other law enforcement agencies in cases where anomalies or illegal activities are detected or suspected by the company.
- ☐ Proper storage of empty and full containers to prevent unauthorized access.
- **Personnel security** — Companies should conduct employment screening and interviewing of prospective employees to include periodic background checks and application verifications.
- **Education and training awareness** — A security awareness program should be provided to employees including recognizing internal conspiracies, maintaining cargo integrity, and determining and addressing unauthorized access. These programs should encourage active employee participation in security controls.

Air Carriers

Develop and implement a sound plan to enhance security procedures. These are general recommendations that should be followed on a case-by-case basis depending on the company's size and structure and may not be applicable to all firms.

- **Conveyance security** — Aircraft integrity should be maintained to protect against the introduction of unauthorized personnel and material. Conveyance security procedures should include:
  - ☐ The physical search of all readily accessible areas.
  - ☐ Securing all internal/external compartments and panels.
  - ☐ Procedures for reporting cases in which unmanifested materials or signs of tampering are discovered.
- **Access controls** — Unauthorized access to the aircraft should be prohibited. Controls should include:
  - ☐ The positive identification of all employees, visitors, and vendors.
  - ☐ Procedures for challenging unauthorized/unidentified persons.
- **Procedural security** — Procedures should be in place to protect against unmanifested material being introduced aboard the aircraft. Security controls should include:

- ☐ Having complete, accurate, and advanced lists of international passengers, crews, and cargo.
- ☐ Having a positive-baggage-match identification system providing for the constant security of all baggage.
- ☐ Properly marked, weighed, counted, and documented cargo/cargo equipment under the supervision of a designated security representative.
- ☐ Procedures for recording, reporting, and/or investigating shortages and overages.
- ☐ Procedures to notify Customs and other law enforcement agencies in cases where anomalies or illegal activities are detected or suspected by the carrier.
- ■ **Manifest procedures** — Companies should ensure that manifests are complete, legible, accurate, and submitted in a timely manner to Customs.
- ■ **Personnel security** — Employment screening, application verifications, the interviewing of prospective employees, and periodic background checks should be conducted.
- ■ **Education and training awareness** — A security awareness program should be provided to employees including recognizing internal conspiracies, maintaining cargo integrity, and determining and addressing unauthorized access. These programs should encourage active employee participation in security controls.
- ■ **Physical security** — The carrier's buildings, warehouses, and on/off ramp facilities should be constructed of materials that resist unlawful entry and protect against outside intrusion. Physical security should include:
  - ☐ Adequate locking devices for external and internal doors, windows, gates, and fences. Perimeter fencing should also be provided.
  - ☐ Adequate lighting inside and outside the facility, including parking areas.
  - ☐ Segregation and marking of international, domestic, high-value, and dangerous-goods cargo within the warehouse by means of a safe, caged, or otherwise fenced-in area.

Sea Carriers

Develop and implement a sound plan to enhance security procedures. These are general recommendations that should be followed on a case-by-case basis depending on the company's size and structure and may not be applicable to all firms.

- ■ **Conveyance security** — Vessel integrity should be maintained to protect against the introduction of unauthorized personnel and material. Conveyance security should include:

☐ The physical search of all readily accessible areas.

☐ Securing all internal/external compartments and panels as appropriate.

☐ Procedures for reporting cases in which unmanifested materials or signs of tampering are discovered.

■ **Access controls** — Unauthorized access to the vessel should be prohibited. Controls should include:

☐ The positive identification of all employees, visitors, and vendors.

☐ Procedures for challenging unauthorized/unidentified persons.

■ **Procedural security** — Procedures should be in place to protect against unmanifested material being introduced aboard the vessel. Security controls should include:

☐ Having complete, accurate, and advanced lists of crews and passengers.

☐ Having a designated security representative to supervise that cargo is loaded and discharged in a secure manner.

☐ Procedures for reporting shortages/overages appropriately.

☐ Procedures for notifying Customs and other law enforcement agencies in cases where anomalies or illegal activities are detected or suspected by the company.

■ **Manifest procedures** — Manifests should be complete, legible, accurate, and submitted in a timely manner pursuant to Customs regulations.

■ **Personnel security** — Employment screening, application verifications, the interviewing of prospective employees, and periodic background checks should be conducted.

■ **Education and training awareness** — A security awareness program should be provided to employees including recognizing internal conspiracies, maintaining cargo integrity, and determining and addressing unauthorized access. These programs should encourage active employee participation in security controls.

■ **Physical security** — The carrier's buildings should be constructed of materials that resist unlawful entry and protect against outside intrusion. Physical security should include adequate perimeter fencing, lighting inside and outside the facility, and locking devices on external and internal doors, windows, gates, and fences.

Land Carriers

Develop and implement a sound plan to enhance security procedures. These are general recommendations that should be followed on a case-by-case basis depending on the company's size and structure and may not be applicable to all firms.

- **Conveyance security** — Integrity should be maintained to protect against the introduction of unauthorized personnel and material. Conveyance security procedures should include:
  - ☐ The physical search of all readily accessible areas.
  - ☐ Securing all internal/external compartments and panels.
  - ☐ Procedures for reporting cases in which unmanifested materials or signs of tampering are discovered.
- **Physical security** — All carrier buildings and rail yards should be constructed of materials that resist unlawful entry and protect against outside intrusion. Physical security should include:
  - ☐ Adequate locking devices for external and internal doors, windows, gates, and fences. Perimeter fencing should be addressed.
  - ☐ Adequate lighting inside and outside the facility, including parking areas.
  - ☐ Segregation and marking of international, domestic, high-value, and dangerous-goods cargo within the warehouse by means of a safe, caged, or otherwise fenced-in area.
- **Access controls** — Unauthorized access to facilities and conveyances should be prohibited. Controls should include the positive identification of all employees, visitors, and vendors as well as procedures for challenging unauthorized/unidentified persons.
- **Procedural security** — Procedures should be in place to protect against unmanifested material being introduced aboard the conveyance. Security controls should include:
  - ☐ Proper marking, weighing, counting, and documenting of cargo/ cargo equipment under the supervision of a designated security representative.
  - ☐ Procedures for verifying seals on containers, trailers, and railcars.
  - ☐ Procedures for detecting and reporting shortages and overages.
  - ☐ Tracking the timely movement of incoming and outgoing goods.
  - ☐ Procedures to notify Customs and other law enforcement agencies in cases where anomalies or illegal activities are detected or suspected by the company.
- **Manifest procedures** — Companies should ensure that manifests are complete, legible, accurate, and submitted in a timely manner to Customs.
- **Personnel security** — Companies should conduct employment screening and interviewing of prospective employees to include periodic background checks and application verifications.
- **Education and training awareness** — A security awareness program should be provided to employees including recognizing internal conspiracies, maintaining cargo integrity, and determining and addressing

unauthorized access. These programs should encourage active employee participation in security controls.

Air Freight Consolidators/Ocean Transportation Intermediaries, and NVOCCs

Develop and implement a sound plan to enhance security procedures. These are general recommendations that should be followed on a case-by-case basis depending on the company's size and structure and may not be applicable to all firms.

- **Procedural security** — Companies should notify Customs and other law enforcement agencies whenever anomalies or illegal activities related to security issues are detected or suspected by the company.
- **Documentation processing** — Consolidators should make their best efforts to ensure that all information provided by the importer/exporter, freight forwarder, etc., and used in the clearing of merchandise/cargo, is legible and protected against the exchange, loss, or introduction of erroneous information. Documentation controls should include, where applicable, procedures for:
  - ☐ Maintaining the accuracy of information received, including the shipper and consignee name and address, first and second notify parties, description, weight, quantity, and unit of measure (such as boxes, cartons, etc.) of the cargo being cleared.
  - ☐ Recording, reporting, and/or investigating shortages and overages of merchandise/cargo.
  - ☐ Tracking the movement of incoming and outgoing cargo.
  - ☐ Safeguarding computer access and information.
- **Manifest procedures** — Companies should participate in the Automated Manifest System (AMS) and all data submissions should be complete, legible, accurate, and submitted in a timely manner pursuant to Customs regulations.
- **Personnel security** — Consistent with federal, state, and local regulations and statutes, companies should establish an internal process to screen prospective employees, and verify applications. Such an internal process could include background checks and other tests depending on the particular employee function involved.
- **Education and training awareness** — A security awareness program should include notification being provided to Customs and other law enforcement agencies whenever anomalies or illegal activities related to security are detected or suspected. These programs should provide:

   ☐ Recognition for active employee participation in security controls.
   ☐ Training in documentation fraud and computer security controls.

OTHER POST 9/11 CUSTOMS' SECURITY PROGRAMS: 24-HOUR RULE

To continue with the discussion of new security requirements, on December 2, 2002, Customs implemented another measure to protect our borders and secure our inbound supply chain. This measure came in the form of the 24-Hour Manifest Rule, also known as the Advance Manifest System (AMS) Ruling (not to be confused with the Automated Manifest System [AMS] discussed earlier), which requires that all vessel operating carriers and automated nonvessel operating common carriers (NVOCCs) submit a cargo declaration twenty-four hours before any cargo is loaded aboard a vessel bound for the U.S. The AMS 24-Hour Ruling also applies to air, truck, and rail movements and was rolled out by Customs in various stages by mode of transport. The burden of responsibility for providing accurate information resides with the shipper. The shipper needs to provide carriers with more complete information sufficiently in advance of shipment to facilitate the carriers' preparation of the required declaration. The following is information for which Customs requires advanced notification:

1. Shipper's and consignee's complete names and addresses
2. Detailed cargo information, exact description, weights, and pieces
3. Port of loading
4. Last foreign port where the vessel will stop en route to the U.S.
5. Vessel name, number, country of documentation, Standard Carrier Alpha Code (SCAC), and voyage number
6. Scheduled arrival date at first U.S. port of call
7. First foreign port where carrier takes possession of the cargo
8. Hazardous material code
9. Container number
10. Container seal number, serial number of the last seal applied when the container was loaded

Noncompliance under the AMS 24-Hour Ruling may result in fines and penalties up to $10,000 per incident. Importers and consignees are not directly subject to the rules' requirements, but may suffer consequences of noncompliance. It is recommended that supply chains validate the handling of their shipments moved by various logistics providers to ensure compliance.

Historically, carriers utilized the AMS to transmit cargo information to U.S. Customs approximately forty-eight hours before arrival into U.S. ports. The new AMS 24-Hour Ruling requires earlier transmittal of cargo information. The time frame for transmitting to Customs by the service provider depends on the mode of transportation. The AMS Ruling is intended to give officials time to inspect suspicious cargo in the foreign port of loading. The carriers are required to notify Customs regarding the contents and recipients of international cargo either before it is loaded at a foreign port or before it reaches the U.S., as opposed to already being en route. Cargo information is transmitted to the "foreign" Customs agent in lieu of the U.S. Customs agent.

If notice obligations are not fulfilled, carriers risk denial to enter the U.S. port. Noncompliance actions may be raised against the carrier as well as potential penalties and claims for liquidated damages against the carrier. As noted in Chapter 3, a Purchasing Agent must be leery of carriers/service providers charging assessorial fees for the new AMS 24-Hour Ruling requirements. If AMS Ruling fees are being added to your transportation or brokerage costs, a debate should be conducted of specifically how much added work the carrier, forwarder, broker, or shipper took on. It should be understood that the AMS 24-Hour Ruling is a new requirement for those in the business of transporting freight to the U.S. Any additional costs, if any, subjected to the transportation industry (carriers) (such as automation), should be absorbed by the carriers and/or service provider and not passed on to their customers. No fee should justifiably be passed on to importers as this is a need to remain current with the requirements of the transportation industry. The time frame of hours before cargo is laden aboard the vessel, aircraft, rail, or truck at a foreign port are noted below:

- **Ocean** — Twenty-four hours PRIOR to loading. Information filed by carriers only.
- **Air** — Four hours PRIOR to the arrival of the aircraft at the first port of arrival in the U.S. Information filed by carrier or entity identified by carrier such as a Customs broker.
- **Truck** — Thirty minutes to one hour PRIOR to the carrier's arrival at a U.S. port of entry, depending on the specific Customs-approved system employed in transmitting the required data. Information filed by inbound truck carrier may also be filed by U.S. importer.
- **Rail** — Two hours PRIOR to the arrival of the cargo at the U.S. port of entry. Information filed by rail carrier.

Carriers may either utilize a service center or port authority to transmit data on their behalf or they may elect to develop a direct interface between their carrier company and Customs. A list of those entities that have developed a Sea AMS interface can be found under the heading of Sea AMS Data Processing Services at http://www.customs.treas.gov/xp/cgov/import/operations_support/automated_systems/ams/.

Carriers that do not have access to the Automated Manifest System (Non-AMS) are required to submit a paper cargo declaration twenty-four hours prior to loading at the foreign port. NVOCCs that are not automated will be required to submit their cargo declarations to the carrier for input into AMS, twenty-four hours prior to loading at the foreign port.

The automated system does have its benefits and can improve clearance and delivery turnaround. Consideration should be put forth on utilizing a carrier that is already participating in the AMS.

FREE AND SECURE TRADE

FAST is the first completely paperless cargo release mechanism to be put into place by U.S. Customs. The paperless processing is achieved through electronic data transmissions and transponder technology. FAST is automated and allows for the expedited release of highly compliant cargo from major importers, thus reducing congestion at our land borders. This program allows U.S./Canada and U.S./Mexico partnering importers to increase the integrity of supply chain security by offering expedited clearance to carriers and importers enrolled in C-TPAT or Canada's Partners in Protection (PIP), which is basically Canada's version of C-TPAT.

It is designed to streamline and integrate registration processes for drivers, carriers, and importers; minimizing paperwork and ensuring that only **"low-risk"** participants are enrolled as members. The initiative seeks to expedite the clearance of transborder shipments of compliant partners by reducing Customs information requirements, dedicating lanes at major crossings to FAST participants, using common technology, and physically examining cargo transported by these low-risk clients with minimal frequency. The program is a catalyst for both Customs administrations to participate in the enhanced technologies by using transponders, which would make it easier to clear low-risk shipments and would mitigate the cost of program participation for FAST partners. Any truck using FAST lane processing must be a C-TPAT–approved carrier, carrying qualifying goods from a C-TPAT–approved importer, and the driver must possess a valid FAST-Commercial Driver Card. FAST processing is based on advanced electronic transmission of information. FAST membership may ultimately expedite Customs clearance and cargo crossing at both northern and southern borders. FAST-approved highway carriers will benefit from:

- Dedicated lanes (where available) for greater speed and efficiency in the clearance of FAST transborder shipments
- Reduced number of examinations for continued compliance with Customs FAST requirements
- A strong and ongoing partnership with the Canadian (PIP) and U.S. Customs (C-TPAT) administrations
- Enhanced supply chain security and safety while protecting the economic prosperity of both countries
- The knowledge that they are carrying shipments for a C-TPAT-approved importer
- A head start for the upcoming modifications to FAST that will expand eligible electronic cargo release methods

The FAST processing of Pre-Arrival Processing System (PAPS) shipments is currently in use and will commence at expanded locations along the northern border during the remainder of 2005. The PAPS is a Customs Automated Commercial System (ACS) border cargo-release mechanism that utilizes bar-code technology to expedite the release of commercial shipments while processing each shipment through Border Cargo Selectivity (BCS) and the Automated Targeting System (ATS). Importer, carriers, commercial drivers, and manufacturers are required to register with Customs in order to participate.

CONTAINER SECURITY INITIATIVE

In an effort to secure the U.S. post 9/11, Customs developed yet another program that is specifically designed to protect our borders from future attacks. Entitled the Container Security Initiative (CSI) and briefly addressed in Chapter 3, it was designed to push our borders out. That is, Customs identified the twenty-five major seaports that account for approximately 80 percent of all container traffic into the U.S. and deployed Customs officers to those ports. Once deployed, the CBP officials work with their host-nation counterparts to target for high-risk cargo containers, which are examined and/or inspected, helping to protect containerized shipping from exploitation by terrorists. Within the DHS, Customs' main principle behind this program is that the U.S. will be the last line of defense rather than the first point of attack. According to Customs, CSI consists of the following four core elements:

1. Using intelligence and automated information to identify and target containers that pose a risk for terrorism

2. Prescreening those containers that pose a risk at the port of departure before they arrive at U.S. ports
3. Using detection technology to prescreen containers that pose a risk quickly
4. Using smarter, tamper-evident containers

Customs provides a list on their website of the ports that are actively participating in CSI and have U.S. Customs officials on the ground examining any containers that may pose a threat prior to departure. Containerized shipping is a critical component of global trade since 90 percent of international trade moves or is transported in containers. When the host country determines that a container, indicated as high-risk by its CSI team, will be screened (for example, "X-rayed" using noninvasive inspection equipment) and/or opened and physically inspected, the host country determines who will pay for those direct costs. In the U.S., the importer pays the costs associated with moving, screening, unloading, and inspecting containers (see Figure 9.3).

FINAL NOTE

The programs described were all developed since 9/11, whether for security purposes or to improve delivery turnaround of trade, and they all require the participation of C-TPAT. Eventually, participation in C-TPAT will be required in order to excel in the global trade industry with continued supply chain efficiency. Selected new security programs for importing will be extended to the export arena and the U.S. will have an equal obligation to secure U.S. product for its foreign customers. Importers should know the depths of their position of responsibility to their company and to the trade community. Procuring product from multiple vendors, importing various types of materials that may be targets for terrorism, or dealing with a high-risk country all require reasonable-care efforts. It is essential that supply chain managers are familiar with all the security programs. The payoff is a seamless transition of product without detention or risk to the U.S. Continue on to Chapter 10 to acquire more knowledge on other ambient factors impacting the global supply chain and what global e-sourcing has to offer.

As explained earlier, since the drafting of this book, CBP has released new C-TPAT requirements that must be met in order to either maintain C-TPAT status or obtain first-time certification. For companies that are already C-TPAT members, CBP has set forth a gradual, phased implementation that began with the hardening of the physical supply chain which had to have occurred by May 25, 2005. The phases gradually shift from a physical focus to a foreign focus

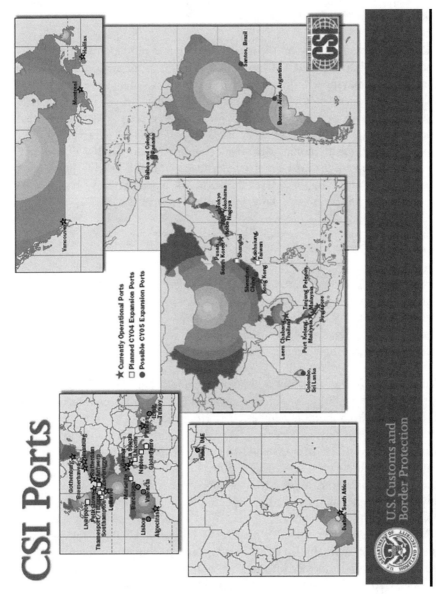

Figure 9.3.   CSI ports (www.cbp.gov).

in the third and final phase. That is, by September 25, 2005, C-TPAT members must have written and verifiable processes for the selection of business partners. Essentially, CBP is looking for its members to look beyond our borders to our suppliers to reduce the risk of someone introducing contraband into our supply chain at the early stages.

As for new applicants, there will be no phased program. Any new applicant will be required to meet the new requirements before being accepted into the program.

This move by CBP elevates our expectations that C-TPAT is here to stay and that CBP takes it very seriously. For more information, go to www.cbp.gov and click on C-TPAT.

10

IMPACT ON GLOBAL SUPPLY CHAINS

September 11, 2001 gave us a whole new insight into how unsafe our borders are and Chapter 9 covered the government's steps to secure our borders. These events definitely added to the complexity of expanding our borders to source materials overseas. The nature of outsourcing and the current strength of the Euro do not allow much opportunity to find lower-cost materials in first-world countries, therefore, our focus tends to be on third-world countries, which often experience instability, corruption, and risk of failure. However, in the right situation, these countries could provide us with the costs savings to drive competitive advantage, boost revenues, and sustain a positive income.

It is this gamble that procurement professionals deal with every day, finding further savings while controlling risk. For those who have worked in the field of global sourcing prior to 9/11, we know that those events tightened things up within our borders, but many of the threats actually existed before that fateful day. This chapter will guide you through the basics of strategic sourcing and go through a step-by-step process for determining your true landed cost, thus allowing you to make a sound and educated business decision as to whether or not to push your activities beyond the domestic arena.

AN OVERVIEW OF STRATEGIC SOURCING

To better assist in understanding strategic sourcing, Nathan Kelley, Senior e-Procurement Specialist for a global professional services and logistics procurement company, draws on his expertise in this field and provides insight into this arena. Kelley begins by explaining, "Strategic sourcing is a process by which the goods, materials, and services needed to run a business are obtained at the lowest possible total cost of ownership. The total cost of ownership is certainly made up of real costs like price and shipping costs, but also of less-tangible costs like quality, reliability of delivery, and payment terms. It is also important to note that, while individual costs of these goods, materials, and services is important, it is really reducing the total cost of all things sourced which is the ultimate goal." Kelley continues by explaining the following essential processes.

Identifying Opportunities

Identification of sourcing opportunities seems as if it should be the easiest step of the process and yet it is often one of the biggest roadblocks. These roadblocks come in many forms: long-term contracts or relationships, lack of knowledge that the product is needed, insignificant spend to catch any attention, or not enough time/personnel to devote to the product. Kelley addresses each of these in turn.

- Long-term relationships with suppliers can impede the sourcing process across every step, but during the first step, it is usually manifested as a blind spot in the vision of the person seeking sourcing opportunities. Remember that relationships are important to vendors because they prevent you from looking elsewhere for their products or services. They should be important to the buyer too, but for different reasons, namely reliability and easy redress of problems. It is important that the sourcing professional does not allow that relationship to overshadow common sense sourcing decisions.

- Lack of knowledge of needs is another issue that drives poor sourcing decisions. As enterprise resource planning (ERP) systems and spend analysis tools help to drive spend visibility, it will become apparent just how much opportunity has been missed over the years. Companies are living, breathing entities. They constantly change size and shape, acquiring and disposing of pieces of their business. Each new acquisition generally comes with a new, usually disparate data system and it takes time to capture these data in some unified package.

- Sometimes the "spend" on some groups of products or services simply is not significant enough to catch anyone's attention. Often, these are areas where companies are most likely to overpay. Even on relatively smaller spends, savings of 50 to 70 percent are likely to be significant and, therefore, should not be ignored.

Gathering Data

This is probably the most crucial step and usually the one that is most often inadequately completed. There are really two types of data that must be gathered: product data and market data.

Product data are primarily viewed as forecast usage, but in order to effectively source a product or service, and prevent problems down the road, much more information is required. Historical pricing provides a baseline for negotiating a new price and allows a later calculation of cost reduction. Specifications are perhaps even more important than forecast usage in sourcing a product or service. Specifications must be as complete as possible. The buyer must establish not only what exactly must be sourced, but also how it must be delivered, requirements for packaging, and any additional special requirements.

This type of information is sometimes only available from those who deal directly with the product or service. Other times, the best way to obtain this information is by conducting an internal survey of the direct users of the product. It is important to meet the required specifications, but it is also important to remember that one of the chief barriers to sourcing a product or service is that the specifications have been set too tight so as to restrict the business to certain suppliers. While there are real requirements that must be heeded, a sourcing professional must push people to examine stretching the requirements when costs can be significantly reduced. Never go outside of specifications, though, without at least a commitment to make the new specification work.

It is also important to acknowledge that, while one can never have too much data in sourcing, one can take too much time to gather these data. Those too concerned about obtaining accurate data can miss opportunities. Sometimes, the required data will take too long to obtain or simply does not exist. When this is the case, reasonable assumptions must be made. Remember that every detail not defined or any incorrect assumption made will lengthen the sourcing process, particularly in the award implementation phase, and potentially jeopardize the success of the sourcing project.

The second important type of data, which must be gathered, is market data. That is, who sells this product, in which specifications; what are the manufacturing and sales capacities of the various vendors; what is the market situation for components of this product; what are potential alternatives to this product or service that can be used as leverage in negotiations? A sourcing professional must research the products or services he/she buys. A great deal of information is available on the Internet through various search engines or Lexus/Nexus services. There are also a number of publications available that list suppliers for various products and services, as well as publications specific to individual products or services.

Kelley closes by remarking, "As globalization becomes more than just a buzzword, more effort must be focused on suppliers that exist beyond our borders."

SOURCING BEYOND OUR BORDERS

Today's fast-paced and ever-changing business world has created so much turmoil that we find ourselves struggling to find steady ground. The economy continues to fluctuate and every executive is trying to come up with a strategy that is going to generate positive returns and "clot the bleeding." Procurement is no stranger to this turmoil, with purchasing executives being held accountable for increased prices in raw material and natural resources that have been well beyond their control. There are very few procurement professionals who have not had to write to their vendors and plead for lower costs through these troubling times. Fortunately, there are strategies that may offer some help.

Many of us look beyond our borders for the answers to our problems; initially, we looked to countries like China, India, and many other Eastern nations to provide us with cheaper raw materials. We were even willing to sacrifice some levels of quality in order to meet prescribed cost reductions that were handed down to us. When once it seemed like we exhausted all sources of materials, we decided that we could actually outsource people too, which led us to the increased importation of cheaper visible and invisible trade. Although these strategies can be very fruitful, there are many factors that were overlooked or unknown, which impacted the true results of our procurement efforts. This chapter is going to look at a number of factors that impact global sourcing and identify areas that can have a positive effect on the procurement professional and the bottom line.

THE CULTURES

Clearly, the difference in cultures is a topic that has been covered in almost every business book, seminar, and classroom. The field of global procurement has evolved to a level where the focus is no longer on understanding based solely on the cultures and logistics, but on the impacts of recent events on our actions and our movements. One of the most difficult hurdles to overcome in global procurement is the distance between our vendors and ourselves. There are many companies that have been burned on transactions that resulted in material that did not ship, which saw some recourse in the form of a Letter of Credit. Then we had instances where substandard material was shipped and this was met with preshipment samples or inspections, but this never guaranteed that the sample would be an accurate representation of the shipment. There are dozens of books that have addressed these issues, yet the recent developments of the world have made these instances seem somewhat trivial.

Many recent events have changed the rules for those of us who have worked in organizations where we had the luxury of traveling to our vendor's countries to negotiate and develop relationships. Typically, the companies that many source from are located in third-world countries and these nations sometimes have suffered political unrest and may have different beliefs than the U.S. This is especially prevalent in situations between East, Middle East, and West. Such events have forced us to pay more attention to both our relationships and our movements. When and if we must travel to these countries, it is critical that the proper precautions be taken. There are travel advisories posted on the State Department's website that identify the areas of risk and, in some cases, implement a travel ban. If it is absolutely necessary to travel to the source country, depending on the source country, your company's financial position, and the size of the deal, you may want to consider the following;

1. If your budget is limited, you may ask your vendor/potential vendor to meet you in a neutral country that is close to his location.
2. If your vendor is located in a rural area, you may make arrangements to meet in a major city. For example, many Chinese plants are located in rural areas, but vendors are often willing to meet in Beijing or Shanghai.
3. There are a number of organizations that offer executive protection during your visits to hostile countries. Triple Canopy (http://www.triplecanopy.com) is an organization that offers armed protection for executives and diplomats in the most challenging environments. Obviously, this is the most expensive of the options and should only be considered for high-value deals that demand your presence at any cost.

If you, in fact, do decide to travel to a source country that may be risky (most third-world countries), many of these vendors will arrange for you to be picked up at the airport. Do not even think of public transportation or taxis as an option. It would also be wise to contact the American embassy or consulate in the destination country before your trip and discuss the current climate in that country. In fact, it is often a good idea to register with the embassy on your arrival. A list of U.S. embassies and consulates can be found at http://usembassy.state.gov.

It is also important to ensure that you check if a visa is required to travel to the vendor country. Countries like the People's Republic of China will require that you have documentation inviting you to their country before issuing a visa. Therefore, you may need to receive documents for your trip prior to applying for your visa. In the event that you need assistance in obtaining your passport, visas, etc., there are companies that will assist and even expedite whenever necessary (an example of such a company can be found at http://www.abriggs.com).

At this point, it should be very clear that the decision to venture overseas requires a lot more than a couple of phone calls, e-mails, or possibly a day trip on a commuter jet. Understanding the culture, environment, and regulations is a critical step in the right direction towards a successful international venture. In addition to the websites mentioned above, the State Department provides a lot of useful information at http://www.state.gov/travel/. This site contains valuable information on cultures, health conditions, visas, and many other critical and useful topics to ensure your safe and well-researched travel.

Now that we have covered a critical area of "know before you go," we can move on to understanding what you must know to evaluate successfully the total cost of ownership of the materials you intend to import. Defining and understanding the true landed cost of your purchase may be the difference between a smart successful venture into outsourcing or a complete financial catastrophe. Quite often, we are so determined to cut costs that we jump at offers that seem too good to be true. The next section will take you through the steps involved to understand your true landed cost.

UNDERSTANDING AND CONTROLLING YOUR TRUE LANDED COST

Once we decide to look beyond our borders to source materials, we expect to find significant cost savings and we often neglect to define/understand the real cost of our purchases. There are several outcomes that we may be faced with, which are as follows:

1. We obtain favorable pricing and freight for the material, but find out about the many potential ancillary costs once it is too late.
2. We may have the material arrive and enjoy a significant cost savings temporarily, until our sales division tries to sell the product to a customer in a country that is a partner in a free trade agreement (NAFTA, for example). Depending on the circumstances, our material may be less competitive than a domestic manufacturer.
3. An organization may very possibly import a material and overlook certain regulations that are not caught by the government initially. We need to

remember that it is possible for violations to be detected and penalties imposed for up to five years after the time of entry.

Understanding the true cost of our transactions is a critical factor in gaining a competitive advantage and sustaining profits. However, if we neglect to re-search every angle of the transaction thoroughly, we will find ourselves at a loss. Once you decide to go beyond your borders, it is important to realize that you have stepped into the realm of rules, regulations, processes, and procedures, and every decision that you make from the purchasing agreement through to resale of the imported good or finished good that was made from the imported material must be analyzed and reviewed. This chapter and this book can be used as guide to what to look out for and what to remember when evaluating and executing these transactions.

There are many programs and opportunities available to the purchasing professional and, ultimately, the driving force when evaluating opportunities is the total landed cost back in the U.S. For example, many of us are quoted prices so low that we automatically assume that the landed cost will be cheaper than the domestic prices. Unfortunately, it is not that simple. Even if we include freight costs, we still may not have captured the entire scenario.

There are several touch points that are important for you to evaluate once you have selected a vendor. Obviously, first and foremost is the total cost of ownership, which is developed through the following steps:

- **Step One** in the new procurement process is to establish our base price on which the rest of our landed cost will be based. It is important to understand the Incoterms that are selected for the transaction(s). Which-ever Incoterm you select will establish the level of responsibility and risk in the transaction. A common Incoterm that is used in transactions with Asia is Free On Board (FOB). The FOB term ultimately transfers the responsibility and risk over to the buyer once the shipments pass from the ships and rail in the originating country. In doing this, the buyer is responsible for the ocean freight, insurance, and clearance in the destination country (including all duties, taxes, charges, drayage, etc.). It is important to remember that once you accept these terms, you will also be the Importer of Record (IOR) in the U.S. Being the IOR means that you are responsible for correctly classifying and declaring the correct information to U.S. Customs and they may audit this import for a period of up to five years after the date of entry into the U.S. This chapter will only touch on some of the implications and responsibilities of being the IOR.

- **Step Two** is to evaluate the freight and insurance involved in shipping the material to its ultimate destination. Your organization may have contracts with steamship lines or NVOCCs, which would make this a simpler process. However, if you have no experience in this field, you can contact any forwarding and/or brokerage organization and they can assist you in establishing the cost of freight and insurance right to your door (including all formalities at the port, such as Customs clearance, payment of duties, etc.). Forwarders/brokers have offices throughout the world, which can be helpful when you are purchasing from a country where you have no representation. Furthermore, they negotiate annual contracts with the steamship lines and insurance carriers based on their total volume. Therefore, the smaller importer that does not have the volume to negotiate favorable rates directly with the steamship lines and insurance companies can benefit from these contracts.

- **Step Three** involves classifying your material. This can be a complicated process and should not be taken lightly. Incorrectly classifying a material for importation could have significant legal and financial implications. It is also important to note that you may arbitrarily classify a product and Customs may accept that classification at the time of entry. However, they (Customs) have up to five years to review your entry and if there are any errors, you may have to pay fines and penalties in addition to the payment of unpaid duty plus interest on the misclassified product. The temptation is always there to try to classify your product in a way that makes it duty free. This temptation must be avoided at all costs. As the IOR, you are responsible for correctly classifying your material and you will be held completely accountable for any errors due to ignorance or negligence. Depending on the material you are importing, it may be best to have a Licensed Customs Broker or classification expert assist you in the classification of the material. There is always the additional option of obtaining a Binding Ruling (see Chapter 2).

- **Step Four:** Once you have established the classification of the material, it is then important to determine if there are any quota restrictions, import license requirements, antidumping, or countervailing duties that will need to be taken into consideration. As the world changes size, we become exposed to increased competition and increased visibility. This situation results in a reaction from the government, which attempts to tighten the reins and protect the local economy. The U.S. is very active in the protection of its domestic operations and the following are some of the measures the government will use to protect domestic industry.

As you begin to deal with potential vendors overseas, there is also a certain level of risk management that must be performed as you evaluate the opportunity.

Examples of these measures are steps that the government/World Trade Organization take to protect domestic economies from unfair competition. For example, there were antidumping duties imposed on steel products being imported into the U.S. in an effort to protect the domestic producers' business from lower-cost imports. This resulted in a duty being applied to certain commodity codes in an effort to raise the import value of the material to be more competitive with domestic prices. Chapter 8 covered these topics in more detail, but it is important to remember not to overlook those areas that could drastically impair a deal that appears to be unbeatable at face value.

At this point, we have touched on some of the important factors that will impact you as the IOR. Depending on your comfort level with these areas, it may be possible that the company that you are dealing with has representation in the U.S. and you may investigate the possibility of buying from its U.S. counterpart and avoiding the responsibility of being the IOR, or you could negotiate different Incoterms with the vendor (for example, DDP [delivered duty paid]) and the seller handles everything to your door. The next steps will discuss important factors to consider that will impact you after you have taken ownership of the goods.

- **Step Five** is concerned with the impact of exchange rates on your potential purchase. Currency hedging allows a company to mitigate or neutralize the effect of changes in currency valuation in the future. It is possible for a company to gear its purchasing strategy in order to hedge currency contracts so as to almost completely eliminate short-term currency valuation risk.

Nate Kelley explains this strategy as follows: "Currency devaluation relative to the dollar in a market country has a negative effect on sales revenue in U.S. dollars. However, this negative effect can be counteracted by short sale of currency contracts in the amount of the forecasted sales revenue in the market country's currency. These currency contracts will decrease in value by an amount equal to the change in valuation of the currency contracts from the current period forward price to the next period spot price. The company will then receive this amount upon settlement, exactly offsetting the negative effect of the currency devaluation on sales revenue, provided revenue forecasts were accurate."

"Similarly," Kelley continues, "when currency in a production country increases in value relative to the dollar, this has a negative effect on costs in U.S. dollars. A purchase of contracts in the production country's currency in the amount of forecast production costs will exactly offset the increased costs in U.S. dollars due to the increased currency value."

"A simple summary of this strategy is that contracts are sold in the market countries in the amount of the anticipated sales revenues and purchased in the production countries in the amount of the production costs. In countries that are both market countries and production countries, purchases should equal costs minus revenues. If this number is negative, the amount should be short sold."

"It must be remembered, however, that this hedging strategy will also eliminate any beneficial changes in currency valuation by requiring a payment when currency value increases in a market country or decreases in a production country."

The strategy detailed above will completely eliminate currency risk for one quarter ahead. It does not affect the risk of long-term trends in currency valuation. It does, however, allow the company to eliminate uncertainty in currency valuation for the next quarter forecasts of costs, revenues, and income. Because of the importance of forecasting in hedging policy, it is essential that sales and production cost forecasts are as accurate as possible. Poor forecasting brings currency valuation uncertainty back into the calculation of costs, revenues, and net income. Thus, in addition to the errors directly introduced by poor forecasting, there will be additional errors due to currency fluctuations.

Forecast revenues and production costs are used in hedging decisions. In order to determine the effectiveness of these hedges, the forecasts must be compared to actual costs and revenues. Kelley finishes his tutorial by providing a comparison between forecast and actual sales revenue in each overseas market by quarter which are viewed in Tables 10.1, 10.2, and 10.3 for a sample company. To simplify the example, hedging and settlements are done quarterly in the example.

- **Step Six** answers the question: What do you intend to do with the material once it has been received in the U.S.? Many companies are importing raw materials into the U.S. that are used in a domestic manufacturing process. Others import merchandise into the U.S. and distribute it domestically and in many cases, re-export to Canada and Latin America. It is especially important to determine if you intend to ship your imported merchandise to any country that has a free trade agreement with the U.S. The NAFTA is probably the most well-known free trade agreement, but there are many more, both in place and on the horizon (see Chapter 8). Materials that qualify for the NAFTA can enjoy

Table 10.1. 2004 International Sales Revenue by Quarter.

	Japan		Mexico		China		U.K.		Germany	
	Forecast	Actual	Forecast	Actual	Forecast	Actual	Forecast	Actual	Forecast	Actual
Q1	487,913,300	395,455,550	33,247,555	31,252,235	15,438,822	15,529,748	1,546,974	1,463,676	1,932,894	1,885,949
Q2	414,000,000	400,500,000	32,170,000	30,798,930	15,255,800	15,892,660	1,586,000	1,478,432	1,836,985	2,131,882
Q3	417,630,000	398,790,690	31,184,000	30,954,362	16,600,000	16,992,810	1,536,500	1,468,400	2,211,700	2,050,225
Q4	384,250,000	399,823,450	31,490,000	31,127,537	15,294,000	15,077,022	1,461,800	1,456,031	2,032,050	2,015,568
	1,703,793,300	1,594,569,690	128,091,555	124,133,064	62,588,622	63,492,240	6,131,274	5,866,539	8,013,629	8,083,624

Table 10.2. International Production Costs by Quarter.

	Shanghai, China		Tijuana, Mexico	
	Forecast	Actual	Forecast	Actual
Q1 2004	47,560,842	46,771,985	45,301,943	45,301,943
Q2 2004	37,099,755	38,247,170	50,701,970	49,490,217
Q3 2004	42,590,764	42,423,454	53,392,744	51,437,733
Q4 2004	53,081,876	52,916,146	55,099,180	54,862,286
	180,333,237	**180,358,755**	**204,495,837**	**201,092,179**

duty-free treatment when shipped from within the NAFTA region (U.S., Canada, and Mexico), but must first undergo a stringent qualification process.

Many organizations neglect to take into consideration the impact of sourcing material from a nonoriginating country and end up paying significant duties into Canada and Mexico. The impact can be even more significant in an organization that actively participates in the NAFTA. For example, a purchasing department may discover that they can source a feedstock cheaper overseas than its domestic equivalent. However, if they are not communicating with the persons handling the NAFTA process, they may introduce nonqualifying material into their production process, thus potentially disqualifying the once-qualified material. The impact of this can be costly since once the material has been produced, there is no way to revert the process and you will be faced with covering significant non-NAFTA duties (especially into Mexico). Furthermore, in the event of an audit, your company could face severe penalties and repayments of duties, which can go back five years. Therefore, it is imperative that all decisions to change the source of raw materials be communicated throughout the organization to maintain compliance and continue the duty avoidance.

It has become blatantly obvious that we must look beyond our borders in order to compete. It has also become painfully clear that what lies beyond our borders has the potential of providing huge rewards, but the risks are also high. We must ensure that when we do look overseas, we evaluate the personal risk (terrorism, etc.) as well as the quality and accuracy of the potential material. This chapter should have given some insight as to what to look out for, while ensuring the lowest cost of ownership. It is critical to remember to watch who you are buying from, where they are located, what they are providing, what is the true landed cost, and what you intend to do with the shipment once it is here. What lies beyond our borders holds the potential to really boost our

Table 10.3. 2004 International Currency Futures Contract Exposures.

Trans. #	Contract Financial Institution	Trade Date	Transaction Type	Period of Futures Contract	Total No. of Contracts	Currency	Currency Forward Price ($)	Position Total Cost ($)	Contract Settle or Cash Date	Settle or Cashout Unit Price ($)	Cashout Total Value ($)	Settlement Position Gains ($)	Settlement Position Losses ($)
JPYQ104A	Lamont	12/30/03	Short	Q1 2004	(487.91)	JPY	129.00	(3,782,274)	3/31/04	121.00	(4,032,341)	—	250,068
JPYQ204A	Lamont	3/31/04	Short	Q2 2004	(414.00)	JPY	130.00	(3,184,615)	6/30/04	129.00	(3,209,302)	—	24,687
JPYQ304A	Lamont	6/30/04	Short	Q3 2004	(417.63)	JPY	131.00	(3,188,015)	9/30/04	129.00	(3,237,442)	—	49,427
JPYQ404A	Lamont	9/30/04	Short	Q4 2004	(416.60)	JPY	129.00	(3,229,457)	12/31/04	129.00	(3,229,457)	—	—
MXNQ104A	Lamont	12/30/03	Long	Q1 2004	14.69	MXN	9.50	1,546,137	3/31/04	9.50	1,546,137	—	—
MXNQ204A	Lamont	3/31/04	Long	Q2 2004	20.82	MX	9.40	2,215,282	6/30/04	9.30	2,239,102	23,820	—
MXNQ304A	Lamont	6/30/04	Long	Q3 2004	23.35	MXN	9.00	2,593,895	9/30/04	9.00	2,593,895	—	—
MXNQ404A	Lamont	9/30/04	Long	Q4 2004	27.25	MXN	9.00	3,028,323	12/31/04	9.00	3,028,323	—	—
CNYQ104A	Lamont	12/30/03	Long	Q1 2004	30.50	CNY	9.50	3,210,947	3/31/04	9.70	3,144,742	—	66,205
CNYQ204A	Lamont	3/31/04	Long	Q2 2004	22.83	CNY	10.00	2,282,868	6/30/04	10.00	2,282,868	—	—
CNYQ304A	Lamont	6/30/04	Long	Q3 2004	25.82	CNY	10.00	2,582,345	9/30/04	10.00	2,582,345	—	—
CNYQ404A	Lamont	9/30/04	Long	Q4 2004	36.19	CNY	10.00	3,618,514	12/31/04	10.00	3,618,514	—	—
GBPQ104A	Lamont	12/30/03	Short	Q1 2004	(1.55)	GBP	0.70	(2,209,963)	3/31/04	0.70	(2,209,963)	—	—
GBPQ204A	Lamont	3/31/04	Short	Q2 2004	(1.59)	GBP	0.70	(2,265,714)	6/30/04	0.70	(2,265,714)	—	—
GBPQ304A	Lamont	6/30/04	Short	Q3 2004	(1.54)	GBP	0.70	(2,195,000)	9/30/04	0.70	(2,195,000)	—	—
GBPQ404A	Lamont	9/30/04	Short	Q4 2004	(1.49)	GBP	0.70	(2,123,086)	12/31/04	0.70	(2,123,086)	—	—
EURQ104A	Lamont	12/30/03	Short	Q1 2004	(1.93)	EUR	0.93	(2,078,381)	3/31/04	0.92	(2,100,972)	—	22,591
EURQ204A	Lamont	3/31/04	Short	Q2 2004	(1.84)	EUR	0.97	(1,893,799)	6/30/04	0.97	(1,893,799)	—	—
EURQ304A	Lamont	6/30/04	Short	Q3 2004	(2.21)	EUR	0.97	(2,280,103)	9/30/04	1.00	(2,211,700)	68,403	—
EURQ404A	Lamont	9/30/04	Short	Q4 2004	(2.07)	EUR	1.00	(2,065,532)	12/31/04	1.00	(2,065,532)	—	—
												92,223	412,977
											Net 2004 position		$(320,754)

This company's net position for 2004 from currency hedging was unfavorable by $320,754. This means that currency has generally moved in a direction favorable to the company.

business, but we need not get greedy and jump at what seems like the deal of a lifetime.

Remember, if it seems too good to be true, it usually is, but the steps in this chapter should help you to determine what you need to know to make a fair assessment of the cost. Continue to enhance your education by reading on to Chapter 11, where you will enjoy an adventure into the new millennium by exploring the new world of trading products and global supply chain planning via new technology.

NEW TECHNOLOGY

When asked to write about new technology, it is obvious that the information will be outdated by the time it hits the press. Therefore, the goal should be geared more towards the types of tools that are available and the scope of their utility. Today's successful software providers can become "has beens" overnight, so we must focus on the elements of technology that are beneficial and lasting. In the field of procurement, there are processes that are timeless and although the technology changes at a tremendous rate, certain fundamental concepts remain the same.

As companies around the world pressure their procurement people to cut costs every year and define measurable reductions, the bottom line becomes "pricing can only go so low." However, management does not want to hear that what you have is the "lowest possible price." They want to see metrics defining more cost savings. Therefore, today's procurement professional must look to technology, processes, and other tools that will allow him or her to identify other areas for savings and continue to improve the "bottom line." In the last few years, we have seen a large increase in technological advancements for domestic procurements. These advancements have come in the shape of reverse auctions and e-business techniques, and they have made a significant impact on U.S. businesses. However, as our domestic options dwindle, everyone has been looking beyond our borders to find new technology and electronic data that allow us to reduce costs, understand our markets, and gain competitive advantage.

CHANGING STRATEGIES IN A CHANGING TECHNOLOGICAL MARKETPLACE

In Chapter 10, Nathan Kelley provided an overview of strategic sourcing. Kelley now defines the changing strategies in the ever-evolving technological marketplace. "Sourcing processes throughout industry," Kelley begins, "are gradually incorporating more technology, as helpful tools are developed to meet the needs of sourcing professionals. A company may today be a leader in the industry in taking advantage of these technologies in its sourcing processes, yet that company must continue to stay ahead of the curve, as new innovations are made available to procurement organizations. As quickly as the technology is improving, a company can quickly find itself at a competitive disadvantage if it fails to heed this advice." Kelley continues by defining the following elements.

History

e-Sourcing as a concept began in the 1990s with companies like Freemarkets, which ran full-service reverse auctions and on-line bidding sites like Chemconnect and Chemmatch. Reverse auctions were run in various areas of procurement and were found to be extremely successful in some areas, while less so in others. At a time when anything with an e- or a dot-com was gold, many companies began to experiment with these types of tools, with varying degrees of success.

Opportunities

As technology improved, many companies began to re-examine their e-procurement strategy to take advantage of new trends and new technology in the marketplace. Until this point, the focus in e-sourcing had been primarily on the reverse auction and the cost reductions associated with it. It became apparent, however, that there is new technology available in the marketplace that makes the sourcing team's job easier throughout the sourcing process, even if a reverse auction is not appropriate for the particular sourcing project.

While procurement personnel have been trained in strategic sourcing in most leading companies, the degree to which the established sourcing process is adhered to varies and the documentation of that process in each sourcing project fluctuates widely among groups and sourcing projects. Additionally, buyers keep records of sourcing projects in different ways. With older technology tools, bids that are run on-line can be accessed by management or by other procurement people within the company, but this is a very small percentage of the total number of bids run in a typical procurement organization and really only captures the bid itself. To remedy this situation, many companies have developed or purchased some stand-alone procurement tools, which are often helpful in documenting the results of sourcing projects, but these tools usually have limited capability in tracking the process itself. If all sourcing projects were run through the use of an integrated sourcing suite, all would be captured in a common space for purposes of audit, lessons learned, experience exchange, and best practices. Additionally, it would eliminate the need for file cabinets full of data that are currently inaccessible to most buyers.

What Is an Integrated Sourcing Suite?

An integrated sourcing suite is a grouping of tools, much like the MS Office suite, to help procurement people do their jobs. Also like MS Office, it is designed to be relatively transparent to its users. It consists of several different interconnected tools that help the procurement professional do the following:

- Assemble teams for sourcing projects and communicate within the team
- Gather and store sourcing information
- Keep a time line of events and responsibilities in the procurement process
- Find appropriate vendors to participate in the process
- Build RFIs, RFPs, RFQs or reverse auctions, as appropriate
- Assemble and analyze responses
- Organize and optimize the decision process
- Create contracts from award decisions and standard templates
- Negotiate contract terms and conditions
- Create searchable contract profiles for easy access by other concerned parties
- Store scanned, executed documents
- Track contract compliance

See Figure 11.1.

Project Management: Audit Proofing Your Sourcing Project

We have all been through internal audits and know how unpleasant they can be. The integrated sourcing suite can be a very useful tool in preparing for these audits. In particular, the project management piece of the integrated sourcing suite provides a time line of the entire sourcing process and becomes the dashboard to guide a buyer, manager, or auditor to all details surrounding a sourcing event. This tool also helps to keep sourcing projects on schedule and prevents a team from missing steps in the procurement process.

e-RFx: Making the "e" Invisible

The common perception is that the e-RFx is just a broader version of a reverse auction. It makes more sense to set the term aside and just say RFP, RFQ, or RFI. This is simply a tool that helps you to create, manage, and analyze the

Figure 11.1. Sourcing suite, sample functions included.

results of a bid. It replaces the function that word processors and spreadsheets have had in creating a bid and allows the team to look at responses in an organized fashion. It also allows use of some other bidding functionality like reverse auction and optimization, where applicable.

Reverse Auction

If you have used the reverse auction in the past and liked it, you should be very impressed by the look of the latest generation of tools on the market. The operation, security, user-friendliness, and data extracts are superior to tools in the recent past. These allow a more transparent and efficient process. If you have not used reverse auctions for various reasons, or have had a bad experience with a reverse auction, it would be worth it to you to take a second look. The technology has improved to allow a real-time quantification of some of the creative solutions, which can be brought into a proposal. The result is that the vendor feels total value is being taken into account, rather than just price. This is a real improvement over earlier technology that should meet the concerns of suppliers who have been reluctant to participate in reverse auctions in the past.

Optimization

As stated earlier, optimization tools help buyers to make award decisions. In the past, award decisions for complex bid packages were often made by "gut feel." The tools required to do quantitative optimization were simply not available, largely due to insufficient computing power. The increased computer performance available today has finally made award optimization through modeling of complex business constraint scenarios possible. The capabilities of these tools and the time required to analyze data improves constantly. This allows quantitative analysis of various business decisions, instead of gut feel. The savings generated through the use of these tools have been impressive, but, nearly as important, is the added ability to make educated business decisions.

Contract Management

Many companies have developed internal tools and processes for contract development and management. Included in the typical integrated sourcing suite is a tool that allows contracts to be generated directly from an award decision, based on previously generated and approved templates. The tool can then be used to negotiate the contract language among the buyer, seller, and legal departments of each firm. It can be a repository for both searchable contract profiles and scanned versions of the final executed documents. Lastly, the tool can be used to notify owners of an important date milestone and, when linked with a spend visibility tool, monitor contract compliance and notify owners of usage milestones.

Kelley concludes his analysis by remarking, "As procurement organizations continue to improve, they must also continue to be leaders in technological innovation. The implementation of this new technology requires a commitment from the procurement organization to training its personnel to use these new tools. Time is certainly a commodity these days, but the time invested will be rewarded in time saved many times over. The cost reductions and efficiency achieved will mean real improvement to a company's bottom line, which will far outweigh the investment."

In addition to these tools discussed, there are also software packages available that can assist in understanding true landed costs as well as the technological advancements of U.S. Customs that have an impact on the field of global sourcing. The chapter will continue on to discuss these areas.

UTILIZING TECHNOLOGY TO UNDERSTAND TRUE LANDED COSTS

Earlier, we discussed the importance of understanding the true landed cost of your purchased materials. There are many areas to consider when calculating true landed cost (import duties, tariff suspensions, etc.) and today we have tools that allow us to capture many of the factors that impact these costs. For example, a Rockville, Maryland software provider (NextLinx) provides a suite of international trade and compliance software and their Internet solution provides an excellent landed cost calculator. Real-time visibility into all associated costs of transporting goods across borders is essential to creating a cost- and time-efficient global supply chain. Unknown to most buyers and sellers, the total "landed cost" of a shipment, beyond the initial price of the goods, includes transportation and insurance fees, customs duties, unique taxes such as excise tax, value-added tax, as well as other origin and destination charges.

Capturing all of these data can be a daunting task. With the **NextLinx Landed Cost Calculator**, *all* costs associated with delivering goods door to door *from* any country *to* any other country in the world are accounted for, providing a comprehensive and extremely valuable tool for any global corporation.

Market Challenge

Global manufacturers and distributors cannot afford to be surprised by a significant difference in "expected" versus the "actual" cost of goods on arrival in the country of import, and with thousands of suppliers and customers, managing cross-border transaction costs can be a challenging task. Specific costs can vary significantly based on the source country, destination country, mode of transport, the parties involved, and the type of goods being shipped. Therefore, total landed cost calculations must be determined efficiently and accurately in order to improve and maintain profitability in the global marketplace.

Solution

A software-based, landed cost calculator enables companies to:

- Optimize procurement decisions
- Provide real-time total cost quotes
- Determine ideal source and distribution locations

Total Landed Cost Benefits

The qualitative and quantitative benefits realized by utilizing a landed cost calculator include:

- Cost savings based on improved visibility in the costs of conducting international trade
- Reduced duty payments by taking advantage of preferential trade agreements
- Reduced postsale customer service costs by delivering goods at expected prices

- Decreased operational expenses by eliminating manual tasks and costly mistakes
- Optimized profits through proper pricing strategies
- Increased top-line revenues by enabling global sales
- Improved customer satisfaction

Value-Add Features

A landed cost calculator makes cross-border transactions easy by providing the following key functional components for global trade:

- **In-depth content** — Supports *every* critical cost detail for *every* product, which includes duty rates, taxes, regulatory content, country-specific business rules, and preferential trade agreements for all the leading trade nations.
- **Integrated compliance** — Determines all regulatory compliance for all landed costs that may include embargoes, official denied party lists, along with many other import and export regulations that may prohibit certain transactions and shipments from occurring.
- **Transportation and insurance** — Incorporates transportation rates from existing systems or computes rates based on contracts with logistics service providers. Transportation and insurance charges are identified by leg (inland origin, international, or inland destination) and are then apportioned among the shipment line items to arrive at proper FOB and CIF values for duty and tax calculations.
- **Unique taxes** — Calculates duties, excise tax, value-added tax, provincial taxes, profit taxes, statistical taxes, customs fees, port charges, and all other import taxes.
- **Preferential trade agreements** — Identifies the country-specific trade agreements to ensure that the lowest-possible duty rate will be applied no matter where a product is shipped. Transshipment rules, rules of origin, and other critical details are also maintained.
- **Units of measure** — Determines the appropriate unit of measure of goods and automatically converts one unit of measure to another in order to calculate duties and taxes accurately that generally differ by country.
- **Basis of valuation** — Incorporates the Incoterm used in each transaction along with the valuation method chosen by the specific Customs agency for every landed cost calculation.
- **Currency converter** — Computes landed costs in the currency specified by the user and applies up-to-date exchange rates as defined by the

destination country's Customs authority. This feature is especially critical in calculations where different currencies must be considered for different taxes.

TECHNOLOGY AND U.S. CUSTOMS

The Customs modernization effort began in 2001 with the Automated Commercial Environment (ACE) and the International Trade Data System (ITDS) programs focusing on cargo import and export operations. The ACE and ITDS formed one system providing a "single screen" for the international business community to interact with Customs and all government agencies on import/export requirements. In the future, Customs modernization will include passenger processing, investigative and intelligence support, human resources, and financial management programs. Customs' new technology foundation, referred to as the Enterprise Architecture, is established to support all field activities and align information technology with the strategic objectives of Customs and all agencies. As a result, the ACE will revolutionize how Customs processes goods imported into the U.S. by providing an integrated, fully automated, information system to enable the efficient collection, processing, and analysis of commercial import and export data. This change will be critical to the visibility of your import records to Customs, allowing (you and Customs) real-time access to your import data through the availability of powerful reporting capabilities that can be used for both business and compliance activities.

The ACE will simplify dealings between Customs and the trade community by automating time-consuming and labor-intensive transactions and moving goods through the ports and into markets faster and at lower cost. It provides national processing and views as Customs moves away from port-by-port processing. By providing the right information, tools, and foresight, ACE will also be a critical element for trade enforcement and in preventing cargo from becoming an instrument of terrorism.

ACE benefits include:

- Enhanced border security
- Increased access to data
- Reduced paper handling
- Over sixty downloadable reports
- Increased flow of trade
- Simplified and expedited cargo release
- Periodic monthly statements
- On-line access to data

The cutting-edge technology in ACE will increase capabilities, streamline processes, and generate billions of dollars in benefits to the government and the trade community. It is being designed to be flexible and adaptable so it can change as business needs change and/or as new technologies become available.

The modernization effort has gained momentum since the systems integration contractor began work on ACE in August 2001. The ACE is a large-scale, complex project that will be the foundation of Customs-wide modernization and critical work has already been accomplished to help ensure success. Currently, the ACE Secure Data Portal, the on-line access point to ACE, is accessible to more than 1,000 CBP and trade community users. The ACE capabilities will be expanded approximately every six months as the project continues.

The ACE Secure Portal

The ACE Secure Portal is a web-based interface that will allow you to have almost "live" access to your import data. The ACE Secure Portal allows importers to see the same data that Customs sees at almost the same time. Access to these data allows an importer to spot costly broker mistakes before they require postentry corrections (prior to ten days from the date of entry). The data will reveal if any brokers are making entry without your authorization or proper Power of Attorney. Finally, the data will allow the importer to analyze where costs are entering the supply chain and answer a variety of important questions. What countries have the most duty for your products? What HTS numbers are you importing the most? Is there any way to consolidate suppliers? Could you minimize the impact of duties by utilizing one of the trade optimization programs discussed in Chapter 8?

Customs is carefully preparing for the transition from the current systems to ACE. A transitional architecture will be in place temporarily to support dual operations and facilitate the transfer of data. Official record systems and data will be migrated to ACE and dependence on older systems will diminish. By employing this transition strategy, Customs will steadily modernize its systems and processes to provide significantly more reliable and efficient operations for its users.

USING TECHNOLOGY FOR MARKET INTELLIGENCE

Today, when we are forced to drive prices down and look beyond our borders for raw materials and finished goods to get us that competitive advantage, there are a number of tools available that can help an international procurement professional. Did you know that unless you specifically request confidentiality, your import manifests and bill of lading data are publicly available? In many cases, it is possible to see all the details of an import's shipment right down to the lot numbers. The new laws eliminating the ability to use the "said to contain" statements on bills of lading have broadened confidentiality concerns even more.

There are two things we are now going to do: (1) tell you how to request confidentiality for your import shipments and (2) show you some resources that can be used to gain market intelligence about your competition.

Subsection (c)(I) of section 431, Tariff Act of 1930, as amended (19 USC 1431), provides that specified information contained on an arriving vessel manifest is available for public disclosure. Pursuant to section 103.31(d), Customs Regulations (19 CFR 103.31(d)), the following are the data elements on an import manifest that would not be made available for public disclosure when confidentiality has been requested:

Shipper name	Consignee name	Notify party name
Shipper address	Consignee address	Notify party address

Pursuant to T.D. 88-38, relating to the Automated Manifest System, the following data elements that comprise the automated vessel manifest are available for public disclosure (items with an asterisk will not be disclosed if confidentiality is requested):

Carrier code	Weight unit
Vessel country	Shipper name*
Vessel name	Shipper address*
Voyage number	Consignee name
District/port of unloading	Consignee address*
Estimated arrival date	Notify party name*
Bill of lading number	Notify party address*
Foreign port of loading	Piece count
Manifest quantity	Description of goods
Manifest units	Container number
Weight	Seal number

There are a lot of data about your shipment that are readily available to anyone who knows where to find them. Do you want to protect your data? Section 103.31(d), Customs Regulations (19 CFR 103.31(d)) states the following:

(d) *Confidential treatment—*(1) *Inward manifest.* An importer or consignee may request confidential treatment of its name and address contained in inward manifests, to include identifying marks and numbers. In addition, an importer or consignee may request confidential treatment of the name and address of the shipper or shippers to such importer or consignee by using the following procedure: (i) An importer or consignee, or authorized employee, attorney or official of the importer or consignee, must submit a certification (as described in paragraph (d)(1)(ii) of this section) claiming confidential treatment of its name and address. The name and address of an importer or consignee includes marks and numbers, which reveal the name and address of the importer or consignee. An importer or consignee may file a certification requesting confidentiality for all its shippers. (ii) There is no prescribed format for a certification. However, the certification shall include the importer's or consignee's Internal Revenue Service Employer Number, if available. There is no requirement to provide sufficient facts to support the conclusion that the disclosure of the names and addresses would likely cause substantial harm to the competitive position of the importer or consignee. (iii) The certification must be submitted to the

> Disclosure Law Officer,
> Headquarters,
> U.S. Customs Service,
> 1300 Pennsylvania Avenue, NW.,
> Washington, DC 20229.

(iv) Each initial certification will be valid for a period of two years from the date of receipt. Renewal certifications should be submitted to the Disclosure Law Officer at least 60 days prior to the expiration of the current certification. Information so certified may be copied, but not published, by the press during the effective period of the certification. An importer or consignee shall be given written notification by Customs of the receipt of its certification of confidentiality.

FINDING OTHER VALUABLE INFORMATION

Now that we have discussed how to protect yourself, let us talk about how you can find information about your competition. The most popular source for obtaining data on inbound shipments would be a company called PIERS. PIERS offers detailed data that are gathered from the ships' manifests and bills of lading documenting import/export activity at all ports in the U.S. and Puerto

Rico. PIERS verifies, enhances, and organizes these data to create comprehensive intelligence about exporters, importers, cargoes, waterborne trade, and regional markets. Businesses use PIERS to track the players in their industry and to find and qualify global trading partners. The most relevant PIERS product might be the PIERS U.S. Waterborne Import Data, which provides comprehensive information on all U.S. waterborne imports. The following is a brief description of the product:

1. **Features:**
   - ☐ Choose your **preferred medium** — CD-ROM or TradeIntelligence @PIERS.com.
   - ☐ Choose your **areas of interest** — Focus on product categories or trade lanes or trading parties.
   - ☐ Drill down to the **transaction detail** you need — including country, commodity, product category, or company — with powerful query capabilities.
   - ☐ Select from more than **twenty different standard reports,** designed to aid analysis from all angles — including importers, suppliers, commodities, market share, and more.
   - ☐ **Download or export** your data to spreadsheets, business model, decision-support, marketing, or other database **application software.**
2. **Data fields include**:
   - ☐ **Who** — Bill of lading number, carrier, consignee name and address, in-bond code, manifest number, notify parties' names and addresses, precarrier, shipper name and address, vessel, vessel registry, voyage number.
   - ☐ **What** — AMS detailed commodity description, container number, harmonized tariff code, marks and numbers, and PIERS commodity description. Cargo quantity/unit of measure; cargo weight and volume; container size, twenty-foot equivalent unit (TEU) count*; estimated value*.
   - ☐ **When** — Arrival date, departure date, loading date.
   - ☐ **Where** — Coastal region, country of origin, foreign destination, foreign port name and code, U.S. final destination, U.S. port name and code.
   *These data fields are print only. All other data fields are available for printing and downloading.
3. **Use these data to**:
   - ☐ **Identify and qualify new suppliers** — Search by harmonized tariff code, commodity description, geographic location; sort by volume, estimated value, level of activity.

☐ **Find new customers** — Look up consignees, shippers, notify parties; search by commodity, product, brand; follow purchasing patterns.

☐ **Measure market share** — Rank sellers by activity, volumes, estimated values; identify buyers' mainstay suppliers.

☐ **Keep track of the competition** — Identify your competitors, their key markets, customers, products, sales volumes.

☐ **Oversee long-distance business relationships** — Monitor compliance with supply contracts, detect parallel imports, dumping, gray market diversions, trademark piracy, counterfeiting.

As you can see, there are a lot of data available that can provide the opportunity to be more competitive and to better understand markets and competition. With the right knowledge of available technology, it is possible to protect you and your company as well as position yourself to become more knowledgeable and put your company on the offensive in the battle for market share. As they say "knowledge is power," and these few tools can give you:

■ The knowledge needed to avoid making costly mistakes by not understanding your true landed costs

■ Access to the same information that Customs sees, allowing you to analyze your own imports accurately and discover/correct any errors that could cost your company if found in an audit

■ The data to examine your competition's import activities, determine new opportunities, and gain the upper hand in your market

DISTRIBUTION STRATEGIES USING DATABASES AND DATA WAREHOUSES INSTEAD OF SHOPPING CARTS: WHERE PRODUCT IS MANUFACTURED AND DISTRIBUTED HAS VASTLY BROADENED

A foreign manufacturer can maintain inventory in the U.S. or in another country as discussed in Chapter 6. Controlling the time factor in which the product can be received is a Purchasing Department's first concern. How fast and by which avenue can you procure the product? In the fast-paced, global industry, purchasing agents need to have a powerful repository of information that is easy to use and access and for which suppliers have connecting technology; so powerful that an entire supply chain operation database can be built. Electronic Database Interchange (EDI) was on the forefront. Let us look to where technology has taken us. Providing a basic scenario, consumers physically utilize shopping carts to shop. Other consumers utilize the Internet to shop, which requires minimal physical movement. Using just the computer's mouse, the Internet is accessible and easy to utilize. Purchasing agents and inventory managers can utilize the Internet — build a database warehouse and have a visual to product information by units, by dollars, by a single store, by season, and by region, all within a few seconds; automation that permits a visual to all distribution activities until final delivery to customers. A supplier can quickly identify if they need to make an increase or reduction in inventory. Within seconds, inventory can be adjusted. A purchasing agent can establish a blanket agreement and electronically issue releases directly into the supplier's inventory, setting up all the terms and conditions of the sale that include all country compliance-clearance requirements.

BAR CODING TAKEN TO A NEW LEVEL

Another new technology that is rolling out is the bar-coding concept taken to the next level. Bar coding is discussed in Chapter 5 for hospitals and patients of biological and over-the-counter products. Bar coding has been around for quite a long time, but has now had its own upgrade known as radio frequency identification (RFID). This tiny little gadget is reinventing the process of receiving inventory and keeping track of what is coming in and going out. Products with RFID tags are being placed on storage shelves around the world. Foreign suppliers have begun rolling out an RFID network to track shipments from central distribution centers to superstores.

In an effort to cooperate with the retailer's secure supply chain initiative, the manufacturer will attach RFID tags to its own shipping trays and pallets at its own national distribution center before being loaded and sent through its supply chain to retail stores. When shopping, consumers want desired items to be available and on the shelves. By extending the use of radio bar codes through secure supply chain initiatives, suppliers are be able to improve on-shelf availability while reducing shrinkage.

The RFID tags and supporting system does not come cheap. Currently, radio bar codes are being used on high-value goods with future plans to expand across entire supply chains over the next few years. Diane Lewandowski, Manager Export and Distribution Compliance of a major U.S.-based health-care corporation, has witnessed the growing trend of RFID and offers insight into the new RFID technology rage. Lewandowski begins by explaining, "A variety of bar-code systems have been used for tracking inventory for decades. In the retail world, consumers witness bar-code tracking as their purchases pass across the checkout counter scanner. Bar coding is not mandatory, but may as well be, since large retailers expect the items they order to carry bar codes. The goal at checkout is accuracy and efficiency, aided by scanning with very little necessity for keying."

Lewandowski continues, "The vast majority of bar coding has been the familiar black parallel lines, which can be read by a laser scanner, linked to an identification number for a particular inventory item. Radio Frequency Identification tags provide the ability to program a 'smart' tag with multiple pieces of information, not just one identification number. A smart tag can be attached to any object that is large enough to hold it. The tag contains a tiny programmable chip with a small antenna capable of sending information when energized by radio waves. Currently, the downside to application is the expense, which can run between $0.20 to $5.00 a tag depending on its type and size." Placing such a tag on a pallet of goods is one thing, but putting a dollar tag on a tube of toothpaste destroys the item's profitability.

"Companies do not want to utilize RFID tags for low-value items," she continues, "because of the high cost percentage. For a large retailer like Wal-Mart, there are efficiencies to be gained by having suppliers use RFID tags. They can track the product movement from their distribution centers to their stores by having the RFID readers at strategic locations. No need for manual keying or manual manipulation of hand-held bar-code scanners. Inventory is tracked as the pallets are driven past the readers when entering the back stock room. The readers track the flow of inventory in both directions, that is, stock returned to the back in preparation for return to the manufacturer."

"Many companies are currently conducting trials to test the practical application of this new technology," Lewandowski informs. "Currently, radio frequency identification is an expensive electronic means of transferring data into a computer. Many different tag and software companies are coming out with various RFID versions to sell to distributors. Part of the challenge will be to standardize the technology so that one kind of tag, reader, and software can be purchased and used by both manufacturers and retailers. In order to be a viable option in the future, it's necessary for the value of the data captured to exceed the overall cost of the RFID tags, hardware, and software," she concludes.

IN CLOSING

But what about RFID capabilities for the future? Where is RFID taking us? Where is the future continued evolution of the global procurement process leading to? In Chapter 12, we will provide additional information and bring answers to those and other questions.

THE FUTURE

What do we see for the future in the world of importing and exporting? Our view includes freer trade, an increased focus on cargo security, and more automation than ever before. Those are the three areas that will shape the future of a global supply chain. This closing chapter will briefly discuss how each of these trends is expected to transform importing.

The U.S. has stretched far out to its neighbors abroad to conduct business. You have learned how the U.S. government presides over international trade activities, the hidden pros and cons to global procurement, exposure to additional costs embedded in the cracks, best practices for reducing costs and improving delivery turnaround for the industry, and where technology can lead you. Learning what is in store for quicker, freer, and more secure trade continues to be a challenge. The future for global transactions will offer the potential for completely paperless trade transactions, fully secured with global standards throughout entire route of each shipment.

FREE TRADE, OR IS IT?

The average duty during the early 1900s stood at 58.2 percent. Today, the U.S. is one of the world's lowest tariff nations. As you learned in Chapter 8, bilateral and regional trade agreements have catalyzed the U.S. trend toward lower tariffs and freer trade, a trend that continues today. As a result, the future of global procurement will continue to grow, expand, and evolve. The trend towards lower tariffs is not isolated to the U.S.

While the progress of the World Trade Organization (WTO) is slow, deliberate, and often marred by controversy, the general trend of WTO member nations is to lower tariff barriers. It is not inconceivable to forecast that during our lifetime, most WTO nations will have either zero or nominal import tariffs. Due to the slow progress of the WTO, zero-for-zero tariffs can be expected to proliferate through a global spider web of bilateral and regional trade agreements. Perhaps an intermediate step will be region-to-region free trade agreements, such as an EU-NAFTA regional trade alliance or an EU-APEC (Asia-Pacific Economic Cooperation) free trade agreement.

What can you expect when tariffs go away? There will always be trade disputes, even in a totally free-trade world. As a result, as tariffs approach zero, we anticipate the number of antidumping cases and retaliatory tariffs to increase rapidly. When the countries of the world, the U.S. included, can no longer use normal tariffs to protect their domestic industries from foreign competition, they will be forced to utilize alternative dumping or other retaliation duties. These types of duties are designed to keep foreign competition out of the country and are typically much higher than the normal import tariffs that currently exist.

For example, a typical trade retaliation duty can be 100 percent of the value of the imported merchandise. In this scenario, the savvy procurer must monitor actions taken by the U.S. government to institute dumping or retaliation duties on the commodities you are importing. Typically, any such penalizing tariffs will be targeted towards specific commodities from specific countries; for example, a 100 percent tariff on Gouda cheese from France, or even towards specific companies, such as a 28 percent dumping tariff on German ball bearings produced by XYZ Bearings, GmbH.

CARGO SECURITY: A GROWING AND EVOLVING CHALLENGE

As discussed in Chapter 9, Customs began a major transformation following the terrorist attacks of 9/11 and acted quickly to initiate the Customs-Trade Partnership Against Terrorism (C-TPAT), Container Security Initiative (CSI) and the Free and Secure Trade (FAST) programs. The future of import procurement will contain a necessary component of cargo security (see Figure 12.1).

Customs will seek to establish harmonized global supply chain security standards and to build partnerships with the Customs services of all U.S. trading partners in an attempt to prevent a terrorist attack resulting from the cross-border movement of cargo or people. The future may be now. To illustrate Customs' commitment to these objectives, we have included their December 10, 2004 press release in its entirety below.

The World Customs Organization (WCO) for the first time ever endorsed a Framework of Standards to secure and facilitate global

Figure 12.1. Customs can use a mobile laboratory when needed at port of entries around the U.S. (From the www.cbp.gov photo gallery.)

trade that is based upon principles designed and implemented by the U.S. Customs and Border Protection (CBP). CBP Commissioner Robert C. Bonner, joined by WCO Secretary General Michel Danet, WCO Policy Chairman and South African's Revenue Service Commissioner Pravin Gordhan, and the Director General of Jordanian Customs Mahmoud Qteishat announced the approval at a joint press conference in Amman, Jordan.

The WCO represents 164 Customs administrations from around the world and accounts for 99 percent of all global trade.

"The action taken today by the WCO will, not only build a system that enhances the flow of legitimate trade, but it builds a global security system — growing all economies, strengthening international partnerships, and securing the world against terrorism. I applaud the leadership demonstrated by the WCO," Commissioner Bonner stated.

The WCO Framework is designed to encourage cooperation between worldwide customs administrations to secure international supply chains and facilitate the movement of goods. The use of advanced electronic information and smarter, more secure containers are vital components.

Additionally, the framework will create an international, consistent system for identifying businesses that offer a high degree of security. In return they receive tangible benefits including the speedy clearance of low risk cargo through customs.

While also in Jordan, Commissioner Bonner signed a Customs Mutual Assistance Agreement (CMAA) with Director General Qteishat of Jordan's Customs Department to improve trade and secure it against terrorism. The CMAA will allow CBP to exchange information, intelligence, and other assistance with Jordan.

"International trade is increasing rapidly and terrorism is a global threat. It is now critical that Customs agencies around the world share information, not only to improve the flow of trade, but also to secure trade routes," Commissioner Bonner said. "Everyone wins when we establish consistent standards to promote international trade, thwart criminal activity, and defeat terrorism."

Additionally, the agreement provides a basis for cooperation and investigation in the areas of commercial fraud, smuggling, export controls, and related security. The CMAA will be mutually beneficial to the U.S. and Jordan by enhancing their abilities to enforce customs laws. Currently, U.S. domestic laws, and most foreign national laws, do not permit disclosure of much information in the absence of a formal agreement or treaty.

"The signing of this mutual agreement recognizes an excellent existing working relationship and further acknowledges Jordan as a strong, strategic partner," Commissioner Bonner stated.

CBP has signed agreements with a number of other customs administrations worldwide. As of today, 54 agreements have been signed.

It is clear from this press release that the U.S. government is seeking to have a global impact on terrorism by creating harmonized standards for cross-border cargo security. Customs has already begun to work with the international community and the WCO to make that happen. We foresee that Customs will increase the number of partnerships it creates with other countries' Customs organizations as it has with Jordan, in an effort to secure all cargo coming into or out of the U.S. Also, once a partnership is established with the Customs agency of a foreign country, it paves the way for expansion of the CSI (see Chapter 9) and more Customs inspectors on foreign soil inspecting cargo before it ever leaves the exporting country.

Bureaucrats can be frightfully truthful on their way out the door. In late 2004, Robert Perez, Customs' C-TPAT director since the program's inception, announced that he was leaving his C-TPAT post at Customs to move on to an internal reassignment. On leaving his C-TPAT position, Perez brushed aside criticism from participants that they are not getting better treatment from Customs as they were promised when joining the program by stating the following. *"If firms are in C-TPAT just for faster handling, we don't want them in the program. The focus should be the benefit firms get from securing their own facilities and assets,"* he asserted. This exiting quote may provide us with some insight into the future of cargo security and C-TPAT.

While Customs created C-TPAT as a totally voluntary program, in late 2004, Customs quietly began to consider basing participation on industry minimum-required security standards and to propose minimum mandatory standards for C-TPAT members. Customs' initial proposal was released to a select and small group of companies. It was clear from the first draft that Customs took what only the largest retail importers had in place for their security programs and proposed it as a one-size-fits-all standard for security. Shown below are some highlights of Customs' initial draft security standards.

- Initial draft business partner requirements include verifiable processes to select manufacturers, product suppliers, and/or vendors, carriers, terminal operators, brokers, and consolidators. The importer would be required to ensure that the pertinent security measures are in place and adhered to by the business partners, and are documented in a security profile or report in the C-TPAT profile submission for these suppliers. Business partners must provide a report that describes their current securing procedures to identify potential weaknesses and to verify that the standards are being met. Also, service providers, such as brokers and carriers, would be required to indicate their participation in C-TPAT for the Carrier Initiative Program (CIP), Super Carrier Initiative Program (SCIP), and the Business Anti-Smuggling Coalition (Basic) and the importer would be required to document all of this.

- Regarding container security, Customs proposed that importers require that procedures be in place at the time of container stuffing and sealing to maintain the integrity of the cargo, including a high-security mechanical seal affixed to the loaded container. Customs' proposal included as minimum seal requirement that container seals must meet or exceed current PAS ISO 17712 standards for high-security mechanical seals. Procedures must also be in place to verify the physical integrity of the container prior to sealing. Seal changes must be recorded, reported, and updated in a timely manner, in addition to the container being checked at each delivery point. Containers must be stored in secure areas.

- Customs' proposal requires physical access controls to prevent unauthorized entry and access to facilities, and to require positive identification of all employees, visitors, and vendors at points of entry for employees, visitors, and deliveries; challenging and removing unauthorized persons; and securing physical access. Draft personnel security requirements include screening of perspective employees to verify pre-employment, background investigations, and personnel termination procedures. The proposed standards explain that procedural security includes the preparation of documents that are complete, legible, accurate, and protected against the change, loss, or introduction of erroneous information.

- The shipping and receiving of cargo should be reconciled against advanced information on the cargo manifest and departing cargo should be verified against purchase or delivery orders. All cargo discrepancies must be resolved or investigated. Mail and package deliveries should be screened before dissemination. Physical security includes the fencing, gates and gatehouses, parking, building structure locking devices and key controls, lighting and alarm systems.

Later drafts removed the previous language that characterized the Customs' measures as "minimum standards" or "minimum criteria." Instead, importers would be required to implement documented and verifiable processes for determining risk in their supply chain. Such processes would need to take into account factors from the company business model, such as volume, country of origin, routing, potential terrorist threat via open source information, etc. In response to such a threat assessment, "appropriate" security responses will be required. On March 25, 2005, CBP officially released "minimum criteria" for importer C-TPAT participation (see Chapter 9). CBP has promised similar criteria for other groups eligible for C-TPAT — brokers, carriers, foreign manufacturers, etc.

At the time of publication, C-TPAT remained a voluntary and unregulated program. In 2005, the Government Accounting Office (GAO) released a critical report on C-TPAT that in part spawned the March 25 minimum criteria for importers. Whether or not C-TPAT will become mandatory and/or regulated is yet to be seen. What we can say with certainty is that the future of a global supply chain must be integrated with security measures from start to finish if you want your import supply chain efficiency to remain as it is today. Customs has increased costly and timely cargo examinations more than threefold since 9/11. While it is likely that C-TPAT partners are not seeing any fewer examinations than before 9/11, they are most likely still enjoying pre 9/11 exam rates. A future terrorist attack on U.S. soil would surely increase the overall number of exams and further expand the exam rate differences between those importers in C-TPAT and those who are not.

International Trade Data System

Customs has also been working on extending and accelerating implementation of the International Trade Data System (ITDS). The ITDS is an interagency initiative designed to standardize and streamline international trade data processes within the U.S. government. Its purpose is to provide a single electronic window into the multiple government agencies integrating the collection, use, and dissemination of international commercial information processing. Although only eight U.S. government agencies employ it today, ITDS promises significant efficiencies in the interaction between the government and international business community.

Nevertheless, in the post 9/11 world, the increasing need for security, both for government and business, demands that confidential business information remains *confidential*. The AAEI (as discussed in Chapter 6) and others in the business community have been working hard, particularly with the top officials in the White House, to push the ITDS to fulfill its promise, without allowing secure business data to find their way to places they do not belong.

CUSTOMS AUTOMATION

The third area where we foresee the most changes in importing is in automation. As Customs services in countries throughout the world begin to mirror the Advance Manifest requirements that the U.S. instituted post 9/11, it is foreseeable that the exporting country's export declaration (the Shipper's Export Declaration [SED] or Electronic Export Information [EEI]) in the U.S. may serve as the importing country's import declaration (the entry summary or CF-7501 in the U.S.).

The groundwork for this phenomenon has already begun in Europe. To simplify and standardize Customs procedures, the European Union implemented an electronic system called the New Computerized Transit System (NCTS). This system facilitates transit procedures through electronic communication with customs authorities. In Germany, NCTS forms part of Germany's new Automated Tariff and Local Customs Handling System (ATL@S). Under this system, the German Customs Administration plans to automate a major proportion of the handling procedure for commercial commodity trade with other countries with the aid of information technology.

The ATL@S system electronically shares the import and export declarations and confirmations between the importing and exporting countries within the European Community. A goal of this system is to advance the standardization and simplification of Customs procedures throughout Europe. This is also a goal of the WCO. The quotes below taken from WCO's website will help to illustrate this fact.

> Trade facilitation is one of the key factors for economic development of nations and links into national agenda on social well being, poverty reduction and economic development of countries and their citizens.
>
> In the context of the international trade environment Customs plays a critical role not only in meeting the goals of the governments but also in ensuring effective controls that secure revenue, compliance with national laws, ensuring security and protection of society. The efficiency and effectiveness of Customs procedures has a significant influence on the economic competitiveness of nations and in the growth of international trade and the development of the global marketplace.
>
> In a highly competitive world environment, international trade and investment will flow toward efficient, supportive and facilitative locations. At the same time it will rapidly ebb away from locations which are perceived by business as bureaucratic and synonymous with high costs. Customs systems and processes must not be allowed to serve or be perceived as a barrier to international trade and growth.
>
> *Customs Role in Trade Facilitation*
> Customs is a mandatory element in the movement of goods across borders and the procedures applied to these goods significantly influence the role of national industry in international trade and their contribution to national economy. Effective and efficient clearance of goods increases the participation of national industry in the global marketplace and contributes significantly to the economic competitiveness of nations, encourages investment and development of industry and increases the participation of small and medium enterprises in international trade. Modern trading practices make it essential for administrations to provide simple, predictable and efficient Customs procedures for the clearance of goods and movement of people while simultaneously tackling increasingly complicated national and international requirements to ensure compli-

ance with national laws, international agreements and meeting security challenges.

In the current international business environment simple, predictable and cost-effective formalities for cross border movement of goods has been gaining increased focus since this has become central to increasing economic growth through national participation in international trade. The volumes of goods that move across borders have increased exponentially due to changes in the international trading environment stemming from the global integration of modern production and delivery systems as well as from new forms of electronic commerce. Global efforts in the last decade to enhance transparency in international trade and reduction of tariff barriers have had significant results. Attention of governments and other agencies is now focused on non-tariff barriers and their impact on national economies and trade.

As countries throughout the world work towards this goal of improving Customs procedures and systems, more and more data pertaining to one country's import will be electronically available before the merchandise is ever loaded in the exporting country.

Taken at face value, Customs' automation seems like an excellent enhancement for importers, but it will be necessary for industry to ensure that the introduction of entirely new Customs systems does not impose an unjustified extra cost burden. Particularly in view of worldwide efforts to reduce Customs tariffs, new administrative expenditures on Customs handling could have relatively inefficient results. If any such Customs automation in the U.S. will cost companies more than it will save, it will be important for industry to speak out loudly to the government through trade groups such as the AAEI to ensure that our tax dollars and duties are spent wisely.

COULD RFID BE THE WAVE OF THE FUTURE FOR U.S. CLEARANCE?

The new technology of RFID as discussed in Chapter 11 has opened the automation doors for inventory control. Can this concept be taken further to other untapped transactions required for global procurement? Is there a way that one single memory chip can hold all required information needed for procurement, clearance, delivery, and receipt of a foreign purchase? Will bar coding become a thing of the past?

What may become "old technique" are bar codes that are printed labels with black bars and human-readable numbers at the bottom that are scanned with a hand-held wand to read the SKU number on the bar-code label. A bar-code label cannot be placed on the side of a vessel container, but an RFID "smart" tag can, capturing every movement of that container. What more can RFID do for imports/exports someday? Could Customs pick up what is in the load and read that it does have 10,000 pieces of a commodity in the load? Could RFID in the future ideally offer this as clearance? Are costs just too high right now to purchase RFID technology?

Robert Hurley, Sr. Project Manager, RFID, for a major health-care company, has had in-depth involvement with the latest technology rate of RFID. Hurley leads us into the pros and cons of RFID by weighing factors regarding where RFID will lead the global procurement industry. He begins by explaining, "The bar code and RFID will coexist for another twenty to twenty-five years. There are some identification advantages to bar codes and some to RFID. RFID, for example, has a big advantage over a bar code when you don't have line of sight. Bar codes need a line of sight to shoot out the red light, capture, and read that bar code."

"Another big differentiating advantage is that RFID can read multiple items at once, whereas bar codes must be scanned one at a time. To consider a real advantage of RFID, think of a mixed pallet of product not having to be touched as it is driven through a portal and every case is automatically identified to the receiving software." According to Hurley, "This is where you are seeing multiple containers being received instead of one at a time and multiple containers inside another container all at once." He explains that all of the chips that are on the tags are programmable, per developing industry standards. "You have preprogrammed tags, WORM tags (Write Once-Read Many), and so forth. The information you encode for specific products, cases, or pallet is a standard Electronic Product Code (EPC). Think of an EPC as an electronic UPC code that also has a unique serial number for every case. It's like every case with an EPC has its own unique identifying license plate. A UPC might identify a box as merely a case of, say, aspirin. But the serialized EPC, in conjunction with information services, can identify which PARTICULAR case of aspirin it is."

"Global standards are a crucial element of the transition to avoid some of the problems we've faced with all the different global bar-code standards that have evolved over the past twenty-five years," Hurley explains. "For example, consider a product made in Europe that is being shipped to the U.S. In Europe, there is a thirteen-digit EAN Code and in the U.S., the product would need to carry a twelve-digit UPC from the Uniform Code Council (UCC). Industry and the standards bodies have, over the years, tried to harmonize differing identification standards, but the lessons of bar-code migration reinforce the crucial need to START with global standards. And so, there has been a joint venture of UCC and EAN international, creating a subsidiary called 'EPCglobal' (EPCG). This organization is being charged with making sure 'global standards' win the day. Without such a cross-industry, global body, every industry and every country would evolve its own standards. Industries such as transportation, retail, military, automotive, and medical will want to do things differently. The U.S. Department of Defense, for example, operates its supply chain with a code called the Universal Identifier (UID). Since the UID is established and used to control billions of dollars and millions of transactions, it will not go away, even amid global standardization efforts like EPC, UPC, and Global Trade Identification (GTIN)."

Hurley continues, "For people who are thinking about various tags, there will evolve many options with regard to memory and space to write data into the chip. For supply chains such as Retail, you may be able to use a tag with 96 bits of information. The Department of Defense will need 128 to 256 bits of memory to hold not only EPC numbers but also UID numbers. Chips used for pharmaceutical tags may also demand more than the current 64-bit and 96-bit EPC standards. There will begin to evolve quite a laundry list of tags that have different form factors and form memories to meet the needs of supply chains."

"Another very interesting element of how RFID can provide new value to supply chains involves linking RFID with a new breed of miniature sensor technology. For products sensitive to temperature or moisture, tiny sensors can be added to packaging. If sensors record temperature or moisture out of tolerance, the sensor can signal information to be written to the RFID tags on those products to alert someone later in the supply chain to test these items and ensure they are OK. An example is with the world of produce or other elements of fresh food supply," Hurley offers, "or ensuring the cold chain is not broken in temperature-sensitive pharmaceutical distribution."

"All of this is still in the labs, but it's coming. How fast and how deep will be a factor very much dependent on the value of the items. You'll find a faster business case for high-technology gear than for a box of crackers and other low-value commodities." As mentioned in Chapter 11, bar coding costs $0.05 to $0.20 compared to $0.20 to $5.00 for "passive" RFID tags that lack an on-board power source. Hurley informs, "Durable, active, or powered tags can cost anywhere from a few dollars to more than $100. You are dealing only with the ink and costs of application with bar coding. A lot of people in manufacturing will consider this difference, and until it becomes essentially free at the margin level, you are going to see sporadic adoption. Very influential trading partners such as Wal-Mart and the Department of Defense are asking their top vendors to begin putting RFID tags on product. That impetus will drive the effort for a while, but eventually won't create scale unless there is a legitimate business case for all supply chain participants. There needs to be more in the way of technology breakthroughs and the costs need to come down. During the next two to three years, we expect to see pilot experiences validate the real costs and benefits," Hurley predicts.

"Since RFID involves radio waves, weaknesses with RFID include problems with reading and writing in proximity to metal and water. And as is so often the case, a technology's biggest strengths are also its biggest weaknesses. Without needing line of sight, RFID sometimes causes struggles to determine what you are reading. Any product in the antenna field could be read. And when you are trying to do things one at a time, such as writing EPC numbers or serial numbers on tags, you have to be sure you are NOT reading or writing multiple tags at once. If you are an operator of a bar-code wand, you point directly at what you want to read and you know you see the red light and hear the beep. With RFID, you've got embedded radio tag transponders so you'll probably need to set up a system to have a light go on when an antenna picks up a read on a product. But, unless you're careful, you may have no idea what you just read and where it came from. You can be trying to read a case in front of you, yet the antenna may be picking up information thirty or forty feet away on top of a pallet as a result of the radio signal bouncing off metal," Hurley concludes.

Those in the global procurement industry will need to remain abreast of the evolving RFID technology that may hold the key to transforming the way a company runs its supply chain operations — automating processes for the future to improve shelf availability, reduced shipping, receiving and clearance turn-around, improved productivity, and better asset visibility. Breakthrough improvements are anticipated in the future.

SUMMARY FOR THE FUTURE OF GLOBAL PROCUREMENT

The future for an importer will be filled with fewer duties and less paper, but more standards, rules, regulations, and bureaucracy. If you and your organization intend to stay ahead of the crowd in the competitive import arena, you will need strong security and compliance programs, duty optimization programs, and automated systems and processes. This capability necessitates effective communication and trust among individuals and departments. Connect with your customers, colleagues, management, departments, and external service providers. Treat each connection you make as if it is the most important one you have ever made. Because it just may be.

Harold A. Poling, former Chairman and CEO of Ford Motor Company, made the acclaimed comment, "Not all heroes are engaged in events that make headlines, not all are enshrined in halls of fame. Many heroes in our business are the people who do their best ever day, and succeed more often than not." Identify your "unsung heroes and missing links" that can provide more dexterity for your global supply chain operation. Let your in-house international counterparts (primarily the Import, Compliance, RA, and Transportation Departments) speak the international jargon directly with your foreign supplier on your behalf. A clear understanding will then be achieved between both buyer and seller for final terms and conditions of a purchase order to protect your company, future import privileges, and satisfying the ultimate end customer.

As the dynamics for importing have changed as a result of 9/11, global manufacturers and procurement agents have been faced with new challenges, impacting the domestic industry's decision on whether or not to take the plunge into worldwide purchasing and where and how to set up shop. Technology will help with moving towards the future through better coordination and performance measurement challenges. Technology alone, however, is not enough to deal with the problems associated with greatly expanded spans of control and fluid organizational structures. The future challenges are unknown and must be identified by good people and not computers. People are the logicians and have the power to make change.

The intent of our book is to provide readers a clear path through the unknown post 9/11 requirements. Expand your thought process to select the best methodology and best practices for your company. Raise your awareness to existing Customs rules and regulations, purvey street-smart clearance and delivery knowledge, and offer guidance to establish or enhance successful inhouse import operations, where the company controls what information is presented to Customs.

New requirements have stimulated the way every company must manage their global supply chain processes. Observe your importing costs and do analyses before and throughout the purchase order commitment. Meet the new security requirements to reap the awards of reduced exams, unnecessary expenses, and improve delivery turnaround. Research and remain abreast of current duty reduction avenues such as tariff and trade bill opportunities that could reduce or eliminate duties. Benefit from creating partnerships with the brokers, freight forwarder, foreign suppliers, truckers, steamship lines, etc.

Tap into the new market for incorporating an automated compliance system to existing company programs or develop new ones. Identify the most common roadblocks with an entry cycle and what can be done to be proactive and prevent delays, unnecessary costs, and avoid noncompliance issues. Adapt your corporate philosophy to "plan accordingly." Decision makers need to extract and comprehend key information, leading to an integrated understanding of processes, earnings, and costs. This enables management to determine and allocate the proper resources needed for maximum profitability, productivity, and effectiveness under truly logistic conditions. The latter will severely reduce (close to eliminate) rework levels, which is the sound way to improve profitability.

We endeavored to offer this type of guidance through mistake and achievement examples, best practice ideas to creating or reorganizing your company's import activities to ensure compliance, generate teamwork with all players, provide an avenue for cost-control programs, and assist in cost establishments for your supply needs; as well, secure the best delivery turnaround time possible to the ultimate purchaser through seamless transactions. We are hopeful this text will successfully assist your journey into the future of global sourcing and procurement. We thank you for taking the time to learn and perhaps adapt some of these principles and techniques into your own processes.

INDEX